BEING A DETECTIVE

*An A–Z Readers' and Writers' Guide
to detective work past and present*

Stephen Wade and Stuart Gibbon

Straightforward Publishing
www.straightforwardbooks.co.uk

Straightforward Guides

ISBN 978-1-80236-147-6

Typesetting by Frabjous Books
Printed by 4edge www.4edge.co.uk

Reviews for Being a Detective

Want the pertinent facts about facial recognition? Insight into the life of a detective? If you are writing crime thriller, psychological thriller – anything with a crime element – BEING A DETECTIVE is an accurate guide to all things police procedural. Providing easily indexed, expert information about everything from the ABC principle through to Z-cars and zombie knives, this book really is as essential as your laptop. Having completed a forensics course myself, I can honestly say that you will learn everything you need to include in your manuscript from this book. As a crime writer, you will need to get your facts right. I cannot recommend this excellent guide enough **Sheryl Browne – psychological thriller author**

This book has been a great source of interest and inspiration, and is a fantastic tool for dipping in and out of to check facts and ideas **Alex Stone – psychological thriller author**

The authors of this book once again bring their wide knowledge and expertise to cover many aspects of police detective work. As a writer, I really enjoyed the way I could dip in and out, reading the bite-sized vignettes and features. I think this will be a great resource for generating unique, niche ideas to write original plots and twists for an original crime novel. Great stuff! **Philippa East – psychological thriller author**

Being a Detective: An A–Z Readers' and Writers' Guide to Detective Work is exactly what it says. From fascinating insight into interview techniques, to footwear evidence; from the Big Red Key, to the ABC principle, there really is an answer to every question you may have when writing crime fiction. It's not simply a list of dry facts, either – the authors write in an easy-to digest style and shore up their information with case studies. This really is a must-have for writers. It will definitely be sitting beside my own writing desk for the foreseeable! **Barbara Copperthwaite – psychological thriller author**

A fascinating insight into detective work, both in the past and right now. So useful for crime writers but also really interesting for anyone interested in police work generally. Simple clear language and great use of real-life case studies to illustrate various points. A great companion to the authors' previous work, Crime Writers' Casebook **Jackie Kabler – TV presenter and psychological thriller author**

There are no words to describe the marvellousness of this book. It's a must asset for the crime writer. It gives a wonderful insight into the world of detectives and the difficult job they do. I felt having both authors in my living room as if they were present narrating me their special skills. A wonderful work full of technicalities which are a must-know for the writer who wishes to give a plausible brushing on their work. It's the second cooperation between the authors, after their book "the crime writer's casebook" and I was amazed by the different perspectives and new information I got. I highly recommend it **Flo Bell – aspiring crime writer**

Contents

Introduction 1
The Authors 15

THE A–Z OF DETECTIVE WORK PAST AND PRESENT
(COMPLETE WITH CASE STUDIES)

A
ABC PRINCIPLE 23
ABE (Achieving Best Evidence) (Updated to 2023) 24
ALIBI 28

B
BIG HOUSE 30
BIG RED KEY 30
BODY LANGUAGE FORENSICS 31
BOGUS CALLERS 32
BOW STREET RUNNERS 36
BRIEF 39
BRIEFINGS 39

C
CAMINADA (JEROME) 40
CASHPOINT ROBBERY CRIMES 43
CRIMES CLUB 47

CRIMINAL INVESTIGATIONS 50
CYBER CRIME 54

D
DETENTION WITHOUT CHARGE 62
DICKENS AND THE FIRST DETECTIVES 64
DISCLOSURE 67
DNA TAGGING 72
DOGS (Updated to 2023) 75
DRONES 79
DRUGS 81

E
EARLY MORNING BLUES 87
ETHNICITY CODES 87
EXPERIENCE 89

F
FACIAL RECOGNITION (Updated to 2023) 93
FAMILIAL DNA SEARCHING 97
FINGERPRINTS 100
FLYING SQUAD 106
FOOTWEAR EVIDENCE 108
FOXTROT 11 (One-One) 110

G
GENEALOGY 113
GENE HUNT 115
GHOST SQUAD 117
GIVING EVIDENCE 118
GOLDEN HOUR 120

GUN CRIME (Updated to 2023)... 122
GRAPHOLOGY.. 126

H
HISTORY OF DETECTIVES IN BRITAIN 128
HOLMES (Not Sherlock).. 132
HOMICIDE 134
HUMAN RIGHTS 134
HYPOTHESIS 138

I
ICIDP (Initial Crime Investigators Development Programme) 141
INFORMANT (Updated to 2023)..................................... 143
INTERVIEWS.. 147
INSPECTOR.. 150
INTERPOL 150
IOPC (Independent Office for Police Conduct)............... 151

J
JOINT ENTERPRISE.. 152
JOURNALISTS.. 155

K
KEY, OR SIGNIFICANT WITNESS...................................... 157
KEYLESS CAR CRIME 159
KING'S AND QUEEN'S MESSENGERS................................ 162

L
LIFE ON MARS... 165
LIFE SENTENCE... 167
LOCARD'S EXCHANGE PRINCIPLE 170

M

MG FORMS (file for prosecution standard set of forms)......174
MODERN SLAVERY (Updated to 2023).....................................175
MOTIVE 179
MURDER BAG 181
MURDER INVESTIGATION MANUAL......................................182

N

NEWTON COURT HEARING..183
NOVICHOK..185
NUMBER SPOOFING..187

O

ODONTOLOGY 190
OLD BAILEY...193
OPERATIONAL NAMES..197

P

PASSIVE DATA GENERATORS 198
PHONETIC ALPHABET 200
PHONETICS (AND LANGUAGE TEXTS) 202
PHONETIC SCIENCE 204
PINKERTON, ALLAN 209
PLOD..210
PRIVATE DETECTIVES...211
PROCEEDS OF CRIME ACT..214
POLICY FILE 217
PROFILING..219
PROMOTION...222
PSYCHICS IN CRIME DETECTION 224

Q

QUALITIES OF A DETECTIVE 226

Q-CAR.. 232

QUEEN'S COUNSEL (QC) now KING'S COUNSEL (KC)
(Updated to 2023).. 233

R

RANK STRUCTURE.. 235

RECRUITMENT AND TRAINING (Historical)........................ 336

REGIONAL DETECTIVES: PRE-1900................................. 238

RETIREMENT... 242

RIPA (Regulation of Investigatory Powers Act)................. 243

ROGUE TRADERS.. 247

S

SCAMS.. 250

SCOTCH 254

SCOTLAND YARD... 255

SHOULDER SURFING.. 256

SIO (Senior Investigating Officer)................................... 258

SPECIAL BRANCH.. 260

SPECIALIST ROLES... 263

SUPER RECOGNISER 264

T

TACTICAL CONTACT 267

TELEPHONE SCAMS 268

TOOLS OF THE TRADE... 275

TRAINING TO BECOME A DETECTIVE............................... 276

TWENTY-FIRST CENTURY CRIME..................................... 277

U
UNSOLVED MURDERS...284
UNUSED MATERIAL...286

V
VICTIMOLOGY...287
VIDOCQ (EUGENE)..289

W
WARRANT CARD..291
WILD WEST BRITAIN...292
WOMEN IN DETECTIVE WORK...............................293
WOODENTOP...296

X
XAVIER...296
X-RAYS..299

Y
YOU'RE NICKED...300

Z
Z-CARS...301
ZOMBIE KNIVES (Updated to 2023)......................301

A Timeline of Detective History...........................306
Bibliography and Sources.......................................307
Index..312

Introduction

Updates to 2023

Being a Detective was first published in March 2019 and has since received much positive feedback from the crime writing and reading community. Four years on, an awful lot has happened in our society, and we felt it was time to bring the *'Detective'* up to date and to include some of the key pieces of legislation and guidance affecting the police and criminal justice system in the last few years.

The Coronavirus pandemic presented huge challenges for everyone and policing was no exception. For a police service which relies on the support and consent of the community, maintaining a social distance and the wearing of face masks, although totally justified and necessary, did little to strengthen those relationships. Guidance was issued to police officers and staff in relation to keeping themselves and others safe, cleaning their personal equipment, vehicles and workspaces. Decisions on whether to arrest, in some cases, also needed to include the consideration of whether it was safe to do so, from a public health perspective. Staff shortages, due to those impacted by and those having the virus, increased the pressure on all emergency services across the UK.

The onset of COVID also presented some people with the opportunity to use the virus or the threat of the virus as a weapon, with regular reports of police and other emergency workers being bitten, spat at, coughed at, or otherwise threatened with deliberate transmission of the virus. Additional measures were required to protect those workers and to ensure that the gravity of such behaviour was highlighted and reflected in appropriate sentencing, wherever possible.

The police custody environment was also assessed during the Covid pandemic and was adapted to cater for detainees and staff. One of the main concerns related to the provision of legal advice, where requested, for those who had been arrested and were detained at a police station. The usual practice of a personal visit by a solicitor was temporarily suspended with consultations taking place remotely, either by telephone or video conferencing facility. This situation was far from ideal but clearly necessary, given the public health emergency during those critical months of the pandemic.

The criminal justice system was also badly affected by COVID, with criminal courts being closed, trials suspended and the introduction of temporary courts (known as Nightingale courts) in response to the fact that about half of all existing courts being unable to provide services in 'lockdown' conditions. In July 2020, it was announced that ten temporary courts were to be opened in venues across England and Wales, including a medieval chamber and the headquarters of the Ministry of Justice, with the aim of reducing delays and delivering speedier justice for victims. Other 'Nightingale' venues followed and were located in buildings such as theatres, town halls, sports arenas and hotels. In March 2022, it was announced that around half of the Nightingale courts were to close, although it was also acknowledged that there was still a significant backlog of cases. This situation had been the case prior to COVID but was exacerbated throughout the pandemic. The remaining 30 Nightingale courts have been extended and will remain open until March 2023 when the position will be reviewed. In the meantime, additional support measures have been put in place including the increase of maximum sentences at magistrate's court from 6 months to 12 months, the creation of two 'super court rooms' which can accommodate up to 12 defendants at one time and the opening of more than 3,000 Cloud Video Platform virtual court rooms capable of holding over 13,000 hearings every week using audio and/or video facilities.

Assaults on emergency service workers have increased throughout the years and it's reassuring to see that legislation has now been put in place to recognise these offences in their own right and hopefully resultant sentences that reflect the serious nature of such actions. Following the tragic killing of PC Andrew Harper in 2019, his wife, Lissie, has campaigned tirelessly to request harsher sentences for those convicted of killing emergency service workers whilst committing a crime. In June 2022, following the introduction of the Police, Crime, Sentencing and Courts Act (PCSCA), those who kill emergency service workers, including prison officers and frontline health workers in the course of their duties, will receive a mandatory life sentence on conviction. This section of the Act is often now referred to as 'Harper's Law'.

The new PCSCA 2022 doubles the maximum penalty for those who assault police or other emergency workers from 12 months to 2 years, recommends whole-life orders as the starting point for the pre-meditated murder of a child and puts an end to the automatic early release of offenders deemed to be a danger to the public. The Act is wide-ranging and covers a number of different areas which impact modern-day policing. It is a lengthy and, at times, complex piece of legislation consisting of over 200 sections which are divided into 14 separate parts. If you would like to view the legislation in more detail at your leisure then you can do so via the following link: https://www.legislation.gov.uk/ukpga/2022/32/contents/enacted

In this revised edition, we want to make you aware of some

of the key pieces of legislation which have become law since the original publication of *'Being a Detective'* including the **Offensive Weapons Act 2019 (see Zombie Knife**). We've also updated some of the alphabetical entries, with revised guidance and information in relation to subjects such as **FACIAL RECOGNITION** and **MODERN SLAVERY**. Website links are included where appropriate. We hope that it provides an interesting and informative read.

A Guide to the Book

We have become accustomed to the charismatic detective, whether he or she is cerebral (Morse, Holmes) or rough and streetwise (Dalziel, Resnick, Vera) and what they all have in common, in the world of storytelling, is an indefinable quality that fuses instinct with dogged insistence on method and procedure. Yet the detective also must have the everyday appeal of the human being – someone like us, the readers and viewers. Hence Frost constantly chews sandwiches and eats on the hoof, and countless detectives worry about their figure, their kids, their bank balance or their aged parent.

This is in the world of make-believe. Novelists and dramatists rely on such qualities, but they also need the actual stuff of life, the material world of the detective as it is now or as it was back in 1850 or in 1950. Our new book is intended to help the writer ascertain the right facts and procedure, and also will enrich the reading experience we have when we engage with crime fiction. Consequently, we had readers and writers in mind when we conceived this companion volume to our successful *The Crime Writer's Casebook* 2017 (now updated to 2023).

The mix of contributions is as it was before: Stuart Gibbon provides material from the actual world of police detective work in the late twentieth and early twenty-first centuries, while

Stephen Wade adds historical explanations of various aspects of the detective's life.

Our aim from the start was to convey the feel of 'being a detective' – that is, to offer interpretations of all the major aspects of the work since it first began. To Arthur Conan Doyle and Agatha Christie, perhaps above all others, we owe the notion of the mythic perspective on the detective: the character who sits somewhere between brainbox and adventurer in our imagination. In its first century or so, crime fiction rested on the idea that there was an illusion of rationality: that the baddie is punished and the status quo is somehow restored, despite the loss or death of a person involved in the tale. Some might argue that this is a bourgeois illusion, and that for the nitty-gritty wage-earning folk who live with a tough edge on life, the good do not always have satisfaction and closure in affairs of transgression. Be that as it may, the point is that, in most cases, readers want their detectives to win over the enemy, and writers want to make the course of the story exciting and thought-provoking, even if the baddie gets away.

The question facing us here is one of how to place the entries. After all, we want to give the reader a way into aspects of the lives of detectives that are strongly present in life as in fiction, and yet are not easily labelled. For instance, an important part of the work – since the very beginning – has been the 'outsider' image. That is, he or she knocks at someone's door and a sequence of circumstances or events have led them to that arrival; they may be on their own patch, or they may have travelled from London to any places in the shires or beyond England. They will be seen as outsiders. Even within the constabulary, the detective may, and often in the past, did exist on the margins, apt to do extempore things when following a tenuous lead.

The Wider World of Crime

Of course, the nature of crime has changed radically with modernity and with technology. The work of a detective today may entail almost exclusively deskwork and the use of computers. Investigating some categories of fraud will necessarily include teamwork and the contributions of experts with a status akin to the 'geek' of common parlance. The gumshoe has perhaps had his day.

Still, Raymond Chandler's sleuth, Philip Marlowe, put a stamp on our image of the detective for all time, long after the first swell of success for the 'hard-boiled' variation in the crime genre. It is not hard now, to locate the kind of detective who still walks the 'mean streets' and has a 'gentlemanly code of conduct despite the moral chaos around him.

Of course, in comparatively recent decades, we have had the arrival of the female detectives, and the success of every version of this, from Lisa Cody's wrestler-hero through to Cagney and Lacey, and through to Vera, have added interesting new twists on the template stories.

This reference book is exactly that: something to refer to. At times the entry is brief, but sometimes a set of related subheadings are needed (for instance, under 'interviewing') as it is more useful to break down specific topics than to try to isolate them under separate headings and perhaps create some confusion in the reader.

Historical research and a new look at how detective professionals came to be as they are today, has led to a fresh understanding of what the work really entails. Stuart Gibbon's part in this book undoubtedly opens up some genuine, accurate insights into that element in police work.

Readers as well as Writers

Readers, as is now acknowledged, invest time and cash, when they acquire a crime book, in a shared story: the crime narrative may be complex, full of plot twists and clues; it might demand close concentration; it may even require a sound basic knowledge of police work or medical terminology, or even prison argot, and sometimes the reader has to struggle to absorb that information. Our book attempts to help in this enhancement of reading pleasure.

There is no doubt that as the publishing of crime fiction and non-fiction expands across all varieties of sub-genres, from thrillers to whodunits and beyond, readers are faced with a dazzling assortment of contextual reference, and much of this is only cursorily explained. There is the problem of jargon – often expressed in abbreviations for instance – or of cultural reference. Some basic terms are used so often that they become familiar, such as SOCO for Scene of Crime Officer, but there are so many more. One example, explained in the text by Stuart Gibbon, is the name of that brutal-looking object used to batter down the door of a drug-dealer in so many television crime dramas. It is not, by any stretch of the imagination, a battering ram, but a 'big red key' to use the popular term. 'Enforcer' being the correct official name.

That little footnote explains exactly why writers and readers want and indeed relish the proper terminology- the words used on the street. That vocabulary gives everyone involved in the narrative the feeling that they are transported into another world, an imagined world. Most of us will never see at first hand the detective at work, but fiction and drama give us that vicarious pleasure of having a sense of *being there* in our imagination, at least.

A Historical Summary

An important point to make about the topic is that there would be profound opposition to the notion of a detective, certainly from the public, until there was more stress put on evidence in both court and in police procedure. This is apparent in the world of literature as well as that of the real world of the law. Dorothy L. Sayers put this very well back in the 1920s: 'It will be noticed that, overall, the tendency in early crime literature is to admire the cunning and astuteness of the criminal. This must be so while the law is arbitrary, oppressive and brutally administered.'

Peel in his Police Act of 1829 was not starting from a complete void: there had been professional administrators who had made some moves towards a streamlined metropolitan police well before Peel's time as Home Secretary. In the middle years of the eighteenth century, the novelist Henry Fielding and his blind brother John, along with other notable military men, had made some notable steps forward in this context. But the leap from a small force patrolling London at night and night watchmen in their booths to armed and disciplined officers organised in a military fashion was an immense leap forward. One handbill of 1830 raises most of the issues emerging at the time through fear and distortion: *'Ask yourselves the following question: Why is an Englishman, if he complains of an outrage or an insult, referred for redress to a Commissioner of Police? Why are the proceedings of this new POLICE COURT unpublished and unknown? And by what law of the land is it recognised?'*

The aims of the social history in the A-Z are manifold: we aim to look again at the men involved in this steady evolution of detective science and to ask questions about how they learned their trade and how the systems needed to protect them eventually evolved. Police work on a beat system is perilous in the extreme, and many police murders in the first decade of the new force show this vulnerability. My discussion of the P C Clark case (1846) (see pp 59–60) highlights this world of danger they lived in day to day. But the real fascination is what Dickens understood, as he expressed in his piece, 'A Detective Police Party', from *Household Words* in 1850:

> *'From these topics, we glide into a review of the most celebrated and horrible of the great crimes that have been committed within the last fifteen or twenty years. The men engaged in the discovery of almost all of them, and in pursuit or apprehension of the murderers, are here, down to the very last instance.'*

In other words, Dickens saw the magnetic fascination of the public with such men: the sensational murders of the first decades of the detective force – both in London and in the provinces – were major media narratives, and yet the men who pursued the villains were not well known. The detective does not want to be a celebrated person. He wants to enjoy the advantages of being anonymous, of course. But many of the men Dickens met and wrote about were also former military men and so very much accustomed to doing their duty and not crowing about it.

In an age when the penny dreadful magazines and street publications made murder narratives immensely popular (and lucrative for the publishers and vendors) the new interest of a professional force of men in pursuit was a high-profile element in the genre. Formerly, the stories, as in the very popular *Newgate Calendar* for instance, focused on the villains and their adventures, from crime to scaffold in many cases. These stories, first issued in 1773, were republished in the 1820s. They told the rip-roaring adventures of such highwaymen and robbers as

Dick Turpin and Jack Shepherd. Now, writers and publishers had a whole new dimension of crime narrative to exploit. The detective was at the core of this new media production.

Much of the following account of the birth and growth of the detective in England is necessarily concerned with a process of learning, and this has different planes of interest. First there is the everyday strategy for coping with crime on a grand scale. This meant a gradual development of arms, teamwork and logistics. Then there is the ongoing struggle for the individual of talent working within a system, an organisation. At first the organisation was like a regiment: men were sacked regularly for the same misdemeanours for which they would have been flogged or court-martialled in the armed forces. Later, individuals could specialise, as forensic science progressed. Certain advances were stunningly revolutionary for the profession, notably fingerprinting at the end of the nineteenth century and of course, in my circumscribed period, the special elements such as the Flying Squad and the Fraud Squad.

Ironically, when the police force was being formed in England, the founding father of crime detection, Eugene Vidocq, was in England. He did visit the prisons of Pentonville, Newgate and Millbank, but he was really in London to organise an exhibition. He wanted to be a showman, not a professional adviser. As James Morton has commented in his biography of Vidocq: 'Not only was he on the premises during opening hours but he also put on a little production in which he appeared in various disguises, to the delight of the audience...' He had arrived in London three years after the detective force was formed and had played no part in the detective policies; he had, however, been in London in 1835 to advise on prison discipline. He was a man who had known the worst prisons in France, as a prisoner as well as in his role as police officer. In 1845 he was thinking of starting up a detective agency, extending the one he had in France, but this was clearly not his real motive for being there.

Finally, there is the question of the whole range of other contexts in which the detective has moved, as his need for greater knowledge has increased. However fantastic and far-fetched we find Sherlock Holmes to be, Conan Doyle did understand the need to have knowledge or esoteric areas of life inherent in detective work. The basic skills of filing, classifying, noting observations and memorising faces and biographies is there in Holmes. The first detectives appear to have kept an immense amount of local information in their heads as they walked the streets, cultivating contacts and 'grasses.'

This process of absorbing a body of knowledge involved amateur science in all kinds of affairs. A detective in the Victorian period had to constantly add to his geographical and trade knowledge. He also had to be familiar with a complex street slang and code of behaviour.

In the twentieth century, after the revision of the detective training curriculum in the 1930s, we have the emergence of the 'star' sleuths. These were the men the newspapers loved. Popular film and fiction had made figures such as Fabian of the Yard and Sexton Blake the epitome of the flash, showy, intelligent gentleman, an officer type who was part Holmes but part slick modern man, an habitué of parties, hotels and high-level meetings with 'top brass.' Of course, there was capital punishment until 1964, and so these new detectives with impressive credentials and equally notable cars were called on to travel into the regions and help the local bobbies. This gave the newspapers yet more fodder for their sensationalism and love of personal trivia when they made a professional into a media star.

Today, detectives as seen and reported in the media are

perhaps more familiar, closer to our own perceived knowledge of what was once an esoteric, guarded profession; now, although the modern international nature of much major crime has created the mystique of the detective once again, in a renewed form perhaps, it remains true that readers and writers of the crime genre want the mystique not only to stay there, but to become more mythic, less easily understandable from the layperson's perspective.

Our book is intended as a contribution to the growing library of literature of detection, and we hope that the combination of our interests and expertise provide the reader with a valuable resource which will enrich the reading of crime fact and fiction.

The A-Z we provide will cover the social contexts of detective work in the past, and have, side by side with these, a close-up account of being a detective, from the life and experiences of a professional who has know the work from the inside.

For the crime writer, our book will offer:
- A sound reference work on all important aspects of the life and work of detectives, today and in the past.
- Insights into the day-to-day work of a detective
- Descriptive accounts of the stages of development of the detectives within our British constabulary.
- Summaries of case studies illustrating aspects of the profession now and then
- Explanations of terms – technical and jargon- used in detective work.

For the keen and confirmed reader of crime fiction or true crime, we offer:
- Information to enrich the reading experience of fiction or non-fiction.

- Explanations of the technical nature of police work in detection
- Historical context, defined and described to help in understanding past reference
- Professional information, past and present, to deepen character interest

The Authors

Stephen Wade

For me, when I settle into writing up a criminal case (usually from the past) the offence and the details of the offence often fade into the background. Why? Because the man who steals the limelight is the enigmatic sleuth, the man who leads the chase. Detecting a crime and tracking a perpetrator is a very special skill, and one we all find intriguing.

I am a crime historian and a crime fiction-writer. In all my true crime books in particular, the figure of the detective is ever-present, even in tales before detectives officially existed. In fiction, of course, there are plenty of options open to the novelist with a criminal tale to tell. Bernard Knight, for instance, makes his 'crowner' (the old word for *coroner*) into his detective, in the novels set way back in early medieval times. In my many regional case-books, ranging from Dublin to Liverpool, the stories from before 1842, when the professional sleuths appeared, are still packed with detectives.

Before 1842 there were amateur gumshoes as well as a number of professionals in police work who took on the temporary role of detectives. Such was the case with the Bow Street Runners and the King's Messengers. Rarely, magistrates acted in the capacity of detectives, but when that happened it was all done by their own initiative and was beyond their official job description.

My involvement in the history of detectives began when I researched two particular books: *Plain Clothes and Sleuths* (2007) and *Square Mile Bobbies* (2008). Since then there has been a marked growth of interest among social and legal historians in the lives and work of the Victorian and Edwardian detectives, perhaps boosted by the ongoing media fascination with Jack the Ripper and all the detectives who were embroiled in that investigation.

More recently, my research has led me to dig deeper into the life of the twentieth century detective, as I researched and wrote a biography, *The Count of Scotland Yard*, (2018) which is a life of Herbert Hannam, the officer perhaps best known for his leading role in the investigation into Dr Bodkin Adams in the 1950s. Working on this forced me to tackle the knotty subject of police corruption, and also go more deeply into the often crucially important topic of medicine in relation to criminality and the criminal justice system.

When I participated in a crime writing panel at the Ilkley Literature festival in 2017 the writers were asked why they wrote on crime. The two novelists answered that they created a detective and that was a lot of the delight in their work; my reply was that I write mostly true crime because I *am* the detective. With a documented crime investigation, the historian is able to, in a sense, be in the place of the detective of that moment in past time.

Crime history, and of course legal history, give us a unique insight into life in the past, because I would argue that it is in our transgressions that we see the complexity of humanity, and it is in our law-making that we see the balance of tolerance and retribution: somewhere on that spectrum there is perhaps the best guide to what is *civilized,* and what we mean by that word.

I have always been intrigued by the figure of the detective, and of course the word itself has always sold books and magazines. Back in 1936, in the middle of what is known as the 'Golden Age of Crime Fiction' the Quaker Oats company published a little paperback called *The Master Book of Detection and Disguise*. This was for children, and so its statements regarding the profession may be regarded as squeaky clean. It was written by ex-Detective Inspector Alfred Grosse, and his book provides an answer to the question of what makes a good detective and surely holds good today. Inspector Grosse wrote:

'A detective's courage is continually put to the test. The slightest weakness in this respect is his undoing. His duty is to protect the life and property of the public. This must be carried out in spite of danger to his own life.'

He adds to this a handy summary of the sleuth's essential qualities, 'A good memory, careful attention to detail, persistence, and courage are required. A detective must be observant, quick, and above all have the health and physique to carry out the arduous duties of the work.'

For me, the whole subject is far more than simply a puzzle, which is what many readers feel is the attraction of a 'whodunit.' When I write a true crime book, I find myself intrigued by the mind-set and temperament of the detective in a case. There may not be any flashes of Sherlockian intuition, and the age of the amateur may have passed, but the mystery of what the work entails and how people do it, is still there. Stuart Gibbon may not have written a forensic study of cigarette ash (as Holmes did) but he has a huge resource of skills and knowledge which show the reader exactly what a sleuth has to know, and to do, to crack a case. I am in my comfortable study; he has been out there, mingling with the villains.

I came to see that *Being a Detective* was a book sorely

needed by anyone involved in the reading and writing of crime narrative. But it has to be said that I never would have been pushed to conceive of this book without having met and worked with Stuart Gibbon, who is gradually but effectively making the public more knowledgably aware of his profession. We are sure that our collaboration will meet a need in the ranks of both readers and writers of crime narratives, past and present.

We hope that we are not too optimistic in wanting the book to be indispensable to the crime *aficionado*, and we know our readers, because we share that profound fascination with them.

Stuart Gibbon

Stuart Gibbon joined the Metropolitan Police as a Constable in 1982 and served in the capital for nearly twenty years, a large part of this period as a Detective. He transferred to Lincolnshire Police in the year 2000 where he served as a Detective at every rank from Constable to Chief Inspector, during which time he qualified to become a Senior Investigating Officer (SIO) leading murder cases. As a DCI he was seconded to the East Midlands Special Operations Unit (EMSOU) as one of a small number of SIO's responsible for murder investigations throughout the five East Midlands police forces.

Stuart retired from the police service in 2012 and is now a writing consultant (GIB Consultancy) advising authors on police actions and procedures. He also appears on TV and radio as a policing expert and has recently featured in a series of true crime documentaries (999: Killer on the line) on Sky TV about UK murder cases.

Stuart

My earliest memory of wanting to be a detective goes way back to when I was a young kid growing up in my hometown of Gateshead in the north-east of England, where I was born and raised. We came home one day to find that our house had been burgled. The place was a real mess with drawers emptied out and items scattered all over the floor. It's the most awful feeling when someone has invaded your personal space in such a way and the whole experience had quite a profound effect on me at such a young age. I could see how upset my mother was and, to be honest, the house never felt the same after that. I knew from that moment that I wanted to try to make a difference and so my story began.

As a teenager I joined the Northumbria Police volunteer cadets and started to look for opportunities locally. Unfortunately they weren't recruiting at that time so I ended up writing to a number of police forces to see if they had vacancies. I literally looked at a map of England and worked my way south from Gateshead. I had always been a 'home bird' and didn't really want to move away at such a young age, little did I know! I got as far as the Midlands on my map and then, for some reason, I also wrote to the Metropolitan Police in London. Yes, you've guessed it, fast forward to September 1980 and, after a pretty rigorous selection process, I'm on my way to the capital to join what is commonly referred to as *The Met* as a police cadet.

The next eighteen months were (mostly) great fun as I became really fit, learnt a lot about the law and worked in the community. The discipline was strict but it certainly didn't do me any harm. Although moving away from home was difficult, in hindsight it was probably the right decision.

In May 1982 I started my training course to become a fully-fledged police constable at the Peel Centre, Hendon. The site was rather imposing with three huge accommodation tower blocks dominating the landscape. It looked (and sometimes felt) a bit like a prison. We used to joke that the guards on the gates and the high fences were to keep us in rather than other people out! Our weekdays consisted of a parade first thing in the morning where we had to stand to attention and were subjected to an inspection of our uniform and appearance. Anyone who was unshaven or whose hair was too long was in for a dressing-down. The rest of the day was spent learning the law and procedures, a mixture of classroom and outdoor role plays. The back of the training school complex featured a mock street complete with a bus, zebra crossing and road signs. There was also a replica custody suite where you took the people under arrest. It was good to have the opportunity to practice in a training environment and we had plenty of laughs.

The course was sixteen weeks long and crammed full of learning. We had an exam at the end of each week and sometimes during the week, which you had to pass to progress further. At weekends a lot of people took the opportunity to 'escape' and visit their families leaving the complex somewhat deserted. Those who lived a long way from London tended to stay and enjoy the culture of the capital city, when we weren't studying of course!

After successfully completing the course I was posted to Wembley police station as a police constable and spent many happy years working shifts as a uniformed officer. The relationship between uniform and CID, in those days, was somewhat strained at times. Some of the experienced detectives used to portray an air of superiority and weren't particularly friendly or helpful. I remember thinking that, if I ever became a detective, I would make sure that I would go out of my way to help colleagues, whatever their role. Those working relationships have improved massively since those early days as a new generation of detectives have emerged.

My path to becoming a detective was long and included postings to various specialist departments as well as a stint investigating relatively low-level crimes. I worked on burglary, robbery and intelligence units to equip me with some of the skills and knowledge required to be a detective. During this time I was known as a Trainee Investigator (TI), serving my apprenticeship and being mentored by an experienced detective.

In 1996 I passed an interview and was posted to Kilburn police station as a DC. Within a matter of days I had been temporarily promoted to Acting Detective Sergeant and was responsible for the supervision of a team of detectives. Talk about a baptism of fire! It was a really steep learning curve but one which I thoroughly enjoyed. During the next four years I carried out other supervisory roles and was able to establish myself as a detective in a really busy part of north-west London.

In the year 2000 I transferred to Lincolnshire Police and was initially posted to Grantham as a uniformed constable. This was a real culture shock as, not only had I not worn a uniform for about ten years, but I was working in a completely new force with different procedures. Within a few weeks I was temporarily promoted to Acting Sergeant in charge of a shift of about twelve officers. There seems to be a pattern developing here, talk about being outside one's comfort zone. I think I did ok as, after a short spell back in CID, I was successful at interview and subsequently promoted to Sergeant. My initial posting was to the busy town of Boston where I worked in uniform as a shift Sergeant with occasional spells as a custody Sergeant.

The next few years saw me remain in CID and achieve promotions. I am proud to say that, during my police career, I was a detective at every rank from Constable to Chief Inspector.

I became one of a small number of Senior Investigating Officer's (SIO) as a DCI on the newly-formed East Midlands Special Operations Unit (EMSOU) where I was the lead detective in charge of murder investigations. There is no greater responsibility than being tasked with finding a killer and bringing them to justice.

In 2012 I retired from the police service and, after a short break, I set up *GIB Consultancy*, a service for authors and scriptwriters to check the accuracy of their police actions and procedures. I also now work in TV and radio as a policing expert. Although my career was often challenging, for many different reasons, I look back on it with great fondness and respect for those who continue to do a job which is becoming increasingly difficult.

I have thoroughly enjoyed writing *Being a Detective* and hope that you enjoy it too. I think that it will appeal to anyone with an interest in crime, whether a reader or writer. There is also an abundance of information about the types of crimes which are committed today and the tactics used by criminals, which is always useful to know and will hopefully enable you and your loved ones to avoid becoming a victim. I have tried to inject some humour where possible as the subject of crime can be rather heavy at times. *Being a Detective* will take you into the world of criminal investigation, warts and all.

Both my parents sadly passed away very young and without the opportunity to see how much I have achieved but I know that they will be extremely proud. Mam and Dad, this one's for you.

THE A–Z OF DETECTIVE WORK

A

ABC PRINCIPLE

What better place to start this A-Z than with a principle which detectives are taught from the early stages of their career.

The **ABC** principle stands for **A**ssume nothing, **B**elieve nobody, **C**heck everything. Sometimes the word 'nobody' is replaced with 'nothing' and the word 'check' with 'challenge' but the meaning remains the same. It doesn't mean that you shouldn't believe what victims or witnesses tell you but it does reinforce that you should always keep an open mind and try to verify that the information you are given is accurate and can be relied upon. In Murder and other serious crime investigations, there are likely to be many police officers and staff involved and it can be easy for information to be misunderstood or for assumptions to be made. By adopting the **ABC** principle, the detective will approach all investigations in a consistent manner.

CASE STUDY – WEARSIDE JACK

John Humble became known as 'Wearside Jack' after he sent a cassette tape, claiming to be the Yorkshire Ripper, to the investigating police team. His actions prompted the officer in charge, George Oldfield, to concentrate on suspects with a Sunderland accent when the real killer, Peter Sutcliffe, spoke with a Yorkshire brogue. The tape, which was sent to the police and Daily Mirror in 1978, began "I'm Jack, I see you are still having no luck catching me. I have the greatest respect for you, George, but Lord! You are no nearer catching me now than four years ago when I started. I reckon your boys are letting you down, George. They can't be much good, can they?" Humble's 257 word, two-minute recording mesmerised the nation. Mr Oldfield was convinced that the voice was that of the serial killer and, as a result, the investigating team ruled out suspects who didn't have a Wearside accent. Peter Sutcliffe, who was questioned nine times throughout the investigation, was able to slip through the net and kill three more women before he was finally caught. The tape-recording haunted Mr Oldfield who suffered ill-health, took early retirement and died at the age of 61.

Humble was eventually identified in 2005 following a cold-case review which included DNA testing. His DNA profile was matched with a sample he had given in 1991 when he was arrested for being drunk and disorderly. Humble was jailed for 8 years for perverting the course of justice and served half of his sentence before release in 2009. It is believed that he was motivated to send the tape by a desire for notoriety, and possibly due to a hatred of the police in relation to an unrelated matter.

Hindsight is a wonderful thing and I can fully appreciate the intense pressure to catch a serial killer who had brought terror to the streets. Having said that, this example shows why the **ABC** principle is designed to make sure that detectives keep an open mind and avoid making assumptions.

ABE (Achieving Best Evidence)
Achieving Best Evidence in criminal proceedings provides the police and prosecutors with guidance on interviewing victims and witnesses, and guidance on using special measures at court. The recommendations should be followed by detectives

investigating cases where the victim or witness is a child or in some other way, vulnerable or intimidated. The purpose of the guidance is to assist those responsible for conducting video-recorded interviews with vulnerable, intimidated and significant witnesses, as well as those tasked with preparing and supporting witnesses during the criminal justice process.

Vulnerable witnesses

Vulnerable witnesses are defined by Section 16 of the Youth Justice and Criminal Evidence Act 1999 (as amended by the Coroners and Justice Act 2009). Children are defined as vulnerable by reason of their age. The Act makes all children under 18 years of age, appearing as defence or prosecution witnesses in criminal proceedings, eligible for Special Measures to assist them to give their evidence in court.

In addition to the witness who is under 18 at the time of the hearing, three other types of vulnerable witness are identified by the Act. Witnesses who have a mental disorder as defined by the Mental Health Act 1983 (as amended by the Mental Health Act 2007), witnesses significantly impaired in relation to intelligence and social functioning (witnesses who have a learning disability) and witnesses who have a physical disability. Witnesses in these three categories are only eligible for Special Measures if the quality of evidence given by them is likely to be diminished by reason of disorder or disability.

Intimidated witnesses

Intimidated witnesses are defined by Section 17 of the Act as those whose quality of evidence is likely to be diminished by reason of fear or distress. In determining whether a witness falls into this category, the court should take account of a number of factors including the nature and circumstances of the offence, the age of the witness and any behaviour towards them by the accused or their family/associates. Complainants in cases of sexual assault are defined as falling into the category of 'intimidated' witnesses.

Special Measures

The Youth Justice and Criminal Evidence Act 1999 introduced a range of Special Measures that can be used to facilitate the gathering and giving of evidence by vulnerable and intimidated witnesses. The Special Measures that are available to vulnerable and intimidated witnesses with the agreement of the court are the use of screens to give evidence, the use of live TV link, giving evidence in private (limited to sexual offences and those involving intimidation), the removal of wigs and gowns and the use of video-recorded interviews as evidence-in-chief. The use of Special Measures is very much a matter for the court to decide taking into account the witness and the circumstances of the case.

Significant Witnesses (not eligible for Special Measures)

Significant witnesses, sometimes referred to as 'key' witnesses, are those who have or claim to have witnessed, visually or otherwise, an indictable offence (triable at Crown Court), part of such an offence or events closely connected with it and/or have a particular relationship to the victim or have a central position in an investigation into an indictable offence. Interviews with significant witnesses should usually be video recorded because they are likely to increase the amount and quality of information gained from the witness and increase the amount of information reported by the witness being recorded. There is no statutory provision for video recordings of interviews with significant witnesses to be played as evidence-in-chief although the defence may ask the court to play some or all of the recording in support of their case. The above approach in relation to significant witnesses is why the police will often video-record critical evidence in Murder and other serious investigations.

Updated 2023

The use of pre-recorded evidence of victims and witnesses to crimes has now been fully introduced at crown courts in England and Wales. From September 2022, it was confirmed by the Ministry of Justice that the technology would be available at a final 20 crown courts in Buckinghamshire, Cambridgeshire, East Anglia, Essex, London and the south-east, marking the completion of a national rollout (Section 28 Youth Justice and Criminal Evidence Act 1999).

The recording of evidence, as close to the time of the offence as possible while memories remain fresh, will help victims avoid the stress of giving evidence under the full glare of a live trial setting, which many understandably find traumatic. This step will allow victims and witnesses of crimes such as rape and modern slavery to have their cross-examination video-recorded in advance and played during trial, subject to a successful application by the prosecution to the court. Any decision to pre-record evidence will be made by a Judge on a case-by-case basis.

Following the completion of the national rollout to crown courts, which began in August 2020, and has seen more than 3,000 witnesses use the technology in trials, the government has announced that the technology will also be piloted for children and vulnerable adult witnesses for all offences at Leeds Youth Court for a trial period. The Lord Chancellor and Justice Secretary commented 'We're overhauling the entire response to rape, boosting support for victims so that more cases come to court and more rapists are put behind bars. We have delivered on our pledge to roll-out pre-recorded evidence to every crown court in England and Wales, sparing victims of this awful crime the additional trauma of testifying under the full glare of a courtroom.'

ALIBI

The word 'alibi' is derived from Latin meaning 'elsewhere'. The dictionary describes an alibi as 'a claim or piece of evidence that one was elsewhere when an act, typically a criminal one, is alleged to have taken place'. These days the word is commonly used and there is even a British television digital channel with the same name.

Identifying whether a suspect has an alibi is crucial when a detective is trying to prove or disprove whether they have committed a criminal offence. The process is part of what is known as elimination criteria which includes forensic evidence and description, in other words do their fingerprints/DNA match forensic evidence found at the scene or do they fit the description given by a witness and/or CCTV.

A suspect's movements at the time that a crime has been committed are likely to assist in establishing guilt or innocence. As such, this will form part of the questioning during their police interview. They may have been recorded on CCTV several miles away from the scene during the material times or they may have been in the company of others who are prepared to corroborate this. On the other hand, they may be in possession of a shop receipt or some other piece of evidence which suggests that they may have been elsewhere at the time but requires further investigation to confirm. The suspect must be given the opportunity, if they so wish, to provide 'alibi' information which should be subjected to further investigation. Any person who is discovered to have provided a false alibi to the police is likely to be charged with a criminal offence and could end up in prison.

CASE STUDY – MAXINE CARR

One of the most infamous cases of recent decades where a false alibi was provided in an attempt to protect the killer was that of Maxine Carr. She was the girlfriend of Ian Huntley who murdered two 10 year old girls, Holly Wells and Jessica Chapman, in Soham on or around 4th August 2002. Carr told police that she was in the house she shared with Huntley at the time the girls went missing when, in fact, she was more than a hundred miles away at her mother's house in Grimsby at the time. In a police interview after her arrest, she said that she had decided to lie about her whereabouts to "protect him (Huntley) from the past" as she didn't want a false allegation of rape made against Huntley in 1998 to be dragged up again. It was established that Huntley had written out a 'crib card' for Carr, detailing key times for the alibi so that she wouldn't forget.

Carr's failure to expose Huntley's lies during the early stages of the investigation, before either were arrested, initially meant that he was eliminated as a potential suspect as he had an alibi for the relevant times which had been provided by Carr. This undoubtedly meant that Huntley wasn't arrested as early as he may have been had it not been for the account given by Carr.

Carr was charged with perverting the course of justice and assisting an offender. She pleaded guilty to the former and not guilty to the latter. The Court accepted her account that she had only lied to the police to protect Huntley because she believed his claims of innocence. As a result, she was found not guilty of assisting an offender on the basis that she had been unaware that Huntley had committed the murders. Carr was sentenced to three and a half years in prison and was released on probation in 2004 with lifetime anonymity and a new identity to protect her following threats made against her.

B

BIG HOUSE

The 'big house' is a slang term used by detectives when referring to the Crown court. They tend to use this term because the Crown court deals with the most serious cases which are usually investigated by detectives. Many times I've overheard comments in the CID office such as "that burglar has been sent to the big house" or "I can't deal with that as I've got a trial starting at the big house".

BIG RED KEY

I was asked recently what the name was for the object used by the police to force entry to doors so here goes ....

It's also called the 'enforcer' but is affectionately known, particularly by detectives, as the 'big red key'. It's made of steel, tubular in shape, with a steel pad at the end to absorb impact. It has a handle at the opposite end which is angled to help the person using it to swing it accurately. It also has a handle situated towards the middle of the tube to make it easier to carry as it weighs in at a whopping 16kgs. For those who want to know more, it's 58cms long and can apply more than three tons of impact force to door locks.

Officers need to be authorised to use the big red key and must attend training which is known as a Method of Entry (MOE) course. It's not unheard of for an officer to pick up an injury whilst using the key, normally to their back, due to the weight and actions required. Sometimes the door needs to be hit on a number of occasions to effect entry and occasionally the police need to turn to alternative methods if the door is reinforced.

CID will normally have some of their own staff who are MOE trained as they will quite often need to force entry to a property, most of the time when they are in possession of a search warrant. Police are only entitled to force entry if they believe that entry will be refused or that the purpose of the search will be frustrated if they knocked on the door. An example of when forced entry would be justified is for a drugs search warrant as the occupants are likely to flush evidence down the toilet or dispose of it in some other way given the opportunity.

BODY LANGUAGE FORENSICS

One aspect of television reporting of contemporary murder cases that always has a profound impact on the general public is the filmed appeal or interview, either with relatives of the deceased (or the missing person). The detectives on the case are most interested in this film because of course, here is an opportunity to judge, at first hand, the expression- and language – of individuals who may not have been ruled out of the suspects list.

But the question arises about how dependable is the body language exhibited in front of the cameras or merely in the process of an official police interview? Opinions differ, because our body language, taken across the whole range of human variations, is not open to scientific analysis with the same exactitude and reliability as, for instance, language use or phone records might be.

However, there are strong arguments in favour of the use of body language analysis being a very useful tool for the detective. One of the most well-known organisations involved in providing training in the skills of such study is the Emotional Intelligence Academy, and its director, Cliff Lansley, has done excellent work on television in demonstrating to the public how applications in forensic study tend to work. The EIA, on its web site, states that they work with 'leading social scientists to bring the best research in human behaviour to the forefront of academic and professional development.' They give courses on the subject in 26 countries and in eleven languages. Cliff has been seen on television in such features as *Faking It: Tears of a Crime* and *The Lying Game: Crimes that fooled Britain.*

One case that highlights the success in body language analysis as material that *supports*, if not comprehensively defines an offence, is the Mick Philpott prosecution in 2013, whose appeal for information, with his partner, regarding the deaths of some of their children in a house-fire, was filmed, and subsequently analysed by Cliff and others. The list of behavioural traits that were itemized supported police suspicions.

In the end, anything used in support of a line of thought used in an investigation will play a part and will perhaps confirm or support a promising theory.

BOGUS CALLERS

During the last few decades, the problem of people calling at your door claiming to be someone they're not or trying to trick you into letting them into your home has been fairly consistent. These types of criminals are known as 'bogus callers' and are guilty of an offence called distraction burglary. Around 12,000 incidents of distraction burglary take place every year. This offence is often committed against older, vulnerable people who are deliberately targeted because they are less likely to be good witnesses and may not even notice that they have become victims of crime. Due to the serious nature of these offences and the impact they often have on those affected, the subsequent criminal investigation is normally carried out by detectives.

One of the most common methods used involves the suspects (as there are normally more than one) pretending to be from the Water Board, advising the occupier that there has been a problem with the water elsewhere in the street and that they need to come into the house to check the water supply. One criminal will distract the occupier by turning on the taps while the other will take a look around other parts of the house and steal any valuables found. The suspects will often look the part, wearing a high-visibility jacket, perhaps carrying a clipboard and in possession of a false ID card. They tend to be forensically aware and may wear gloves or make sure their clothing covers their hands when touching items. The water board tactic was common when I joined the police in the early 1980's and still is now. A less common method, although one which still happens occasionally, is for the suspects to pretend they are from another utility service (gas, electricity) or the local authority. I know of one particular case where a man knocked on the door of an elderly couple claiming to be from the local council and offering to carry out a free security survey of the interior, suggesting that he may be able to supply free alarms for the property. The man was a bogus caller and once allowed into the house he was able to steal some cash.

From time to time criminals may pretend to be police officers (usually CID) and will call at an address requesting entry. They may be in possession of a false warrant card which they briefly show to the occupier. They may say that they are conducting enquiries in the area and need to come in to speak or that they are looking for someone who may have managed to sneak into the occupier's house. If they are not expected and the occupier has any concerns, they are advised to ask the person(s) to wait outside while they contact the local police on 101 to check identity.

Another less sophisticated but equally effective way that criminals may try to gain entry is to claim that they are unwell and need a glass of water or to use the toilet. Once left unattended they look for items to steal. Of course, not everyone who unexpectedly calls at your door is a criminal, but the police do ask people to be cautious and their message is – IF YOU'RE NOT SURE, DON'T OPEN THE DOOR.

Distraction burglary is a very difficult offence to investigate as the people responsible are usually 'travelling criminals' who live out of the area. They travel by vehicle and normally commit several offences in one day, only staying briefly in any one place. When I was a detective responsible for the investigation of these types of crimes, it was possible to plot on a map the route taken as offences would be committed in towns/villages throughout the county from north to south or east to west over a 30–40 mile radius in the same day.

Unfortunately, it's rare to catch these criminals at the time and, as such, the subsequent forensic examination of the scene is one of the key lines of enquiry. Offenders tend to be forensically aware but sometimes make mistakes. In one of my bogus caller cases, for some inexplicable reason, the offender had asked for a drink and was given a cup of water. You've guessed it, we were able to identify him through DNA from the saliva left on the rim of the cup! In another case, fingerprints were found on the top edge of an inner door where the offender had handled it to open and close the door. The criminals thought that forensics would only fingerprint the handle of the door so they would often move it by touching the top edge. If they weren't wearing gloves this could well leave a nice fingerprint or two. Forensics would tend to dust the whole of the doors for this very reason and sometimes it paid off. We also once obtained the suspect's DNA (presumably from sweat) from the doorbell outside the victim's house. As you can see, these cases are a real challenge for the investigators.

CASE STUDY – BOGUS WATER BOARD

A career burglar who tricked his way into the homes of two elderly women by posing as a water board official has been locked up for four years. A court heard how Steven Wright deliberately preyed upon the vulnerable victims to fund his addiction to the drug 'spice'. Wright targeted an 83 year old woman in the Leeds area in June 2018. He told her that she had a leaking pipe which needed to be fixed. Once inside her home he told her to turn on the tap in her kitchen then go upstairs and flush the toilet. When she returned, she discovered that cash and bank cards had been taken from her purse. Wright used the bank card to buy items at two shops.

Wright committed a second burglary in July 2018 at the home of an 80 year old woman. He told the woman to go to her kitchen and turn on the tap but when she returned, she found him in her bedroom. He picked up a jar of money and left. The woman later discovered that her mobile phone and Kindle were missing.

Wright was arrested after being recognised on CCTV and through his fingerprints being found in the property. He pleaded guilty to two offences of burglary and two offences of fraud. Following his sixth conviction for house burglary the Judge commented "One doesn't need victim impact statements to recognise the trauma that these offences will cause to those that are vulnerable".

CASE STUDIES – BOGUS POLICE

1) A man in his 70's was at home in Cleveland when two men wearing dark blue fleeces and black baseball caps with the word 'POLICE' on the front entered his property. One of the men showed him a card, stating that it was his police identification. The men left the property a short time later having stolen the man's wallet.

2) In January 2018 two men called at an address in Sussex claiming to be police officers. They presented an A4 sheet of paper which they said was a court order authorising them to search the house for drugs and money. The victim was suspicious and threatened to dial 999 but was warned that they would be handcuffed and arrested if they did. While the occupiers sat in the lounge, the suspects went upstairs and conducted an untidy search before leaving with over £1,000 in cash.

BOW STREET RUNNERS

In Henry Fielding's London, (mid 1700s) the idea was that in policing there would be a shift work process, in which the good people of the city would take turns as constables. Of course, as they were unpaid and it was dangerous work, this did not happen. The small number of paid officers extended only to the 'Runners'. These existed in places other than Bow Street, but that location has claimed the name. At Bow Street the magistrates looked after the Runners and also the patrols. These were a small force of road patrol officers who policed the outskirts of the city. In central London the 'Charlies', the watchmen, were supposed to watch the streets in some areas, but they were subject to corruption and were not exactly fit men.

It is easy to see why there was a need for an outfit like The Runners: when a crime was committed, there would be a mixed bunch of various officials around to conduct some kind of investigation. These would involve the watchmen, the local constable and sometimes the militia. The magistrate could also, on rare occasions, participate, but this was usually in dishing out orders rather than being an active investigator. In this context, the need for someone to take a role we would now see as that of a detective, was extreme. The Runners would send their best men into such a situation.

David J. Cox, author of the definitive account of the Runners and their work, called his book *A Certain Share of Low Cunning*, suggesting that to fight transgression effectively required the defenders of society to work on the same level as the perpetrators. Even after the landmark 1829 Police Act, the best men of the Runners – the Principal Officers – were kept on. David Cox quotes the report of a Home Office Committee:

'...the officers attached to the police offices would be more expert in the Detection of crime than the common Metropolitan Police officers; they are more practised in that particular business, more experienced in looking for and searching out proofs, and therefore more expert in tracing and detecting crime than the common Metropolitan Police officer.'

Dickens, writing in 1850, had another viewpoint on the Runners:

'We are not by any means devout believers in the old Bow Street Police. To say the truth, we think there was a vast amount of humbug about These worthies. Apart from many of them being men of a very Indifferent character, and far too much in the habit of consorting with thieves... they never lost a public

occasion of jobbing and Trading in mystery and making the most of themselves...'

Henry Fielding has to take the credit for the 'thief takers'; however, he added this small select group of men to the Bow Street staff after he became Chief Magistrate at Bow Street in 1748. John Fielding, following him in 1754, was really responsible for the larger force that became the Bow Street Runners. Like Lister, however, Henry Fielding saw the importance of communication. He started the Covent Garden Journal in 1752. This only lasted for a year, but it was far-sighted and was a beginning in this important branch of detective work. A report in the issue for 10 March 1752, for instance, is the first instance of the manoeuvre of 'putting a person up for identification.' With details such as ' Saturday night last one Sarah Matthews, a woman of near fourscore brought a woman of about twenty-four before Mr Fielding' and 'It appeared that her former marriage was a falsehood ad that the old lady was the lawful wife...'

Of course, when there were severe riots, this force could not cope. When there were major problems of social disorder, the army were called out; the militias were accustomed to a tough repression in these cases. A common solution to the problems of disorder was simply to intensify the military actions, treating rioters as an enemy army. By the end of the eighteenth century, when the country was quite used to large bodies of military and naval men around the land, the militia regiments were often keen to practise using swords and guns against the 'rabble.'

The Bow Street Runners would be the professionals called in to lead in the detection of crime, and they would go out of London at times to investigate regional cases when serious crimes were committed.

BRIEF

A 'brief' is the term used by detectives when referring to the solicitor who is representing a client in police custody. The custody officer will phone the CID to let them know that the 'brief' has arrived.

BRIEFINGS

Briefings are a vital part of daily business for Detectives as so much can happen in a few hours let alone days. It may be that you have returned to duty after a day or two off and have to self-brief by looking at the crimes/incidents that have occurred while you've been away or looking through the intelligence items to see who is wanted by the police or has been recently arrested.

At most police stations there is a daily briefing, often conducted using video conference, to discuss notable issues from the previous 24 hours. This is normally chaired by a senior officer and attended by supervisors from the neighbourhood policing areas along with intelligence staff and sometimes a CID supervisor. The briefing will normally be scheduled for around 8.00am and will also include discussion on the next 24 hours and resource implications. The briefings are minuted and kept for future reference as the chair and attendees may not always be the same on each occasion. CID may also hold their own daily briefings so that the supervisors can allocate work and appraise themselves of who is available. It may be that additional CID staff from elsewhere in the area have to be called in to assist if it is going to be a particularly busy day and support is required.

During a Murder investigation there are likely to be several briefings per day, particularly during the first few days as there is so much information to share and events tend to happen very quickly. When I was Senior Investigating Officer (SIO) for a Murder I would try, where possible, to chair the briefing myself so that I could hear, first-hand, the updates given by those present. In my absence, I would ask my deputy and then have a separate meeting with them to appraise myself as soon as practicable afterwards. Even when the investigation moves into week two and beyond, there is likely to be a briefing each day.

In addition to a regular briefing for all staff involved in a Murder investigation, it's common practice to also have a number of smaller briefings to cover specific areas of the investigation. These may include the forensic management team, the intelligence team, the family liaison team and the telephone investigation team amongst others. The contents of each briefing are noted and retained. An effective briefing is a two-way process where everyone has the opportunity to contribute. Briefings are often the place where critical information is shared and valuable conversations take place. De-briefings are also very important during criminal investigations whether they take place immediately after a Murder to establish exactly what the first attending officers did, or at the end of a working day to check what has been done and what is still outstanding.

C

CAMINADA (JEROME)

Caminada is arguably the most charismatic and impressive detective of the Victorian years (if we except the fictional Sherlock Holmes of course). He was born in 1844 in Manchester; his mother was Irish and his father Italian. In 1868 he joined the Manchester Police and was to have a career with them stretching out over thirty years. He often worked by using disguises and was adept and using and exploiting local knowledge and unorthodox sources. Even when he retired in 1899, he still carried on doing the work, being a private sleuth. He died in 1914.

By the time he joined the detective office, the modus operandi of adopting plain clothes and disguise was accepted. Caminada was apparently adept at this activity, being something of a 'quick change artist' and gathering a fearsome reputation for being able to slide into the criminal fraternity unobserved. He was also good with his fists and was a hard, honest officer, respected across the city by everyone who knew him. Most of his cases in the memoirs he published in his retirement concern violent robbery and domestic argument that escalated into murder or manslaughter. But there are plenty of examples of the 'new crime' as well. His account of Elizabeth Burch represents this increasing occurrence of fraud and deception in the period which has, after all, been seen by historians as an economic depression.

Elizabeth Burch began as a Court dressmaker, based in Sussex Place, Kensington, working with her two sisters. But they had financial problems are were destined for bankruptcy when Elizabeth in desperation hit on the idea of writing begging letters. Astoundingly, she was successful and Caminada ascribed her future career as a con merchant to this early success. Before her arrival in Manchester, she also worked a cunning swindle in Ashford, Kent, where she profited from her ruse of pretending to be an heiress expecting £150,000 from a rich man whom she had helped one day when he collapsed in public. Burch had quickly developed the skills needed to extract cash from the gullible. When she came to Manchester the scam was linked to the Liberator Building Society as a bogus collector.

This was in 1894 and by that time Caminada was a very experienced detective. Burch had assumed a succession of false names, mostly aristocratic, after hitting on the idea of filching letterheaded paper from the rich and well-connected. When Caminada finally tracked her down she was 'Lady Russell' and was indeed acting that part to perfection. He wrote in his memoirs: 'Looking at us from over the top of her gold-rimmed spectacles, she said she was connected to a titled family, was a lady of private means, and was collecting subscriptions for the people who were suffering from the recent colliery explosions in South Wales.' Caminada had to rely on tough questioning to get anything on her, and he finally arrested her, charging her with obtaining contributions by fraud. On remand, and still writing letters in the role of her assumed identity, Burch provided Caminada with a case study in deception and fraud, in terms of how the scams worked.

He learned that she would obtain documents having lists of subscribers; she would then write to them asking for money, but all done in patently legitimate and very worthy terms. Most of the names selected were women and she would write in heavily emotional style, saying such things as ' *I enclose a letter from a friend who has asked me to help the poor things. It will tell you more of their sufferings and needs than I can.*' That particular letter was signed *'(Lady) Marion Clarke.'* Burch also had notebooks with lists of prominent Manchester people in specific areas of the city. These were people whom she called to see and gull face to face.

But now comes the most significant part of this case. An organisation called the Charity Organisation Society had been set up in 1892, four years before Burch was arrested in

Manchester. In that time she had been active in all kinds of contexts in her fraudulent activities. The COS, set up by C S Loch, existed to monitor charitable functions and locate those who were honest and those who were not. Amazingly, Loch had known for four years that Burch was not a legitimate correspondent. Loch wrote to Caminada: 'So far as can be learned there is nothing against the character of either Miss Burch or her sisters.' The detective was astounded that the COS had not started an investigation into Burch's scams years before she arrived in Manchester.

But the Folkestone charity people thought very differently and sent Caminada plenty of information about her nefarious transactions. When Burch was in the police court for the second time, there were four witnesses collected by Caminada, including ladies from Kensington and Harrow. There was a fairly confident line of thought given by her defence – passing the buck to the aristocratic contacts who had supposedly allowed Burch to collect money for them for no profit. Poor Burch, they reasoned, duped by the powerful and lazy, and now a victim of her own good heart. However, Caminada's hard work had paid off. Burch was sentenced to six months' hard labour in Strangeways.

CASHPOINT ROBBERY CRIMES

Crimes linked to cashpoint machines or ATM's (Automated Teller Machine), if reported to the police, will usually be investigated by detectives. The tactic may be as simple as standing close behind the user and trying to see their PIN number, then stealing their bank card or slightly more sophisticated methods. Criminals are even using heavy agricultural machinery to target retailers. In a 12 month period during 2016–17 there were 137 ATM-related crimes reported to Leicestershire Police alone.

The criminal may try to interfere with the machine itself, perhaps by placing a piece of plastic, known as a 'Lebanese loop', into the bank card slot. This will allow the card to be inserted into the machine but won't return the card at the end of the transaction. The customer will then leave the machine, understandably thinking that the card has been confiscated, allowing the criminal to return, remove the loop and take possession of the bank card. This tactic will often be used with another criminal standing close behind the customer in an effort to see the PIN number or perhaps in company with a miniature camera installed at the top or side of the cash machine cubicle to record PIN numbers. An alternative method for the criminal is to attach a 'skimmer' to the card slot. This is a small device which fits over the top of the slot and is designed to look just like the genuine slot. It's intended to copy the information on the magnetic strip of your card as you insert it. This information can subsequently be used to commit fraud.

This type of crime is challenging to investigate as it is often committed by criminals who are not local to the area and who are very well-organised. The main lines of enquiry for an investigator would usually be any CCTV in the area and potential forensic evidence if any items have been left behind by the criminals. Fraudsters will work in teams and often travel the country to commit this type of crime using the rail network or main arterial roads.

Some Organised Crime Groups (OCG's) use methods which are not quite as subtle but can prove equally effective. The country has seen a steady number of ATM thefts during the past few years with criminals using JCB's, forklifts, teleporters, tractors and even explosives to help them to remove the cash machines completely. They will often target shops, post offices and other premises which have a cash machine on the outside of the building for public use. Inevitably, the use of such heavy machinery and equipment results in a large hole in the building and structural damage which can take months to rectify. The targets are often in remote rural locations where the police response time may be delayed due to the geography of the police area. The most popular times for these offences to be committed is between 2am and 4am and those responsible will have no hesitation in using and threatening violence against anyone who may confront them, including police officers. The suspects can sometimes be seen on CCTV brandishing baseball bats or other weapons outside the premises during commission of the offence. They will also drive dangerously and have been known to 'ram' police and other vehicles who try to stop them. They will use stolen or 'cloned' vehicles (false number plates) and will arrive and leave the scene in convoy. The ATM, if successfully removed, will be taken from the scene in the back of a van or truck.

OCG's have also been known to use oxyacetylene (welding or cutting technique using a very hot flame produced by mixing acetylene and oxygen) to cause an explosion intended to blow a hole to allow access to the cash machine. This is obviously a reckless and extremely dangerous method with no regard for public safety. The type of organised crime discussed in this section will often cross police boundaries and will be most effectively investigated by detectives from specialist regional teams.

CASE STUDY – LEBANESE LOOP

Three men have been jailed after targeting a pensioner in London with the 'lebanese loop' scam at a cash point. The men in their twenties were sentenced to 12 months imprisonment after being caught on CCTV scamming a 79 year old man by distracting him after tampering with the machine. The three fraudsters had interfered with the cash machine in Bethnal Green so that bank cards would get stuck inside the machine before watching the man enter his PIN number. They then reassured the man that the card would not come out resulting in him leaving the scene. The fraudsters then removed the 'lebanese loop' and used his card to withdraw money.

CASE STUDY – JCB

A gang of ram raiders used a JCB to try to steal a cash machine before smashing a police car window and escaping from the scene. CCTV footage showed the stolen industrial vehicle, known as a telescopic handler, being repeatedly driven into the front of a Co-op store as the thieves tried to smash their way inside. Police arrived seconds later and the offenders fled after breaking the windscreen of the police car, causing cuts to the faces of the two officers inside the vehicle. The raiders fled empty-handed from the shop in Derbyshire following the raid which took place at 1.54am in April 2018. The three men involved, who had their faces covered, were able to escape after causing significant damage to the building.

CASE STUDY – OXYACETYLENE

A gang that blew up cash machines across the UK, stealing hundreds of thousands of pounds, has been handed prison sentences ranging from 10 years to life imprisonment. During their year-long crime spree they targeted 13 banks and shops, with some ATM's being blown up using powerful explosives and others being dragged away using stolen vehicles. The thieves made off in stolen high-performance cars which were then hidden in a lorry which doubled as a hangout for the criminals to hide in.

The gang's technique for blowing up the ATM's involved running oxyacetylene canisters directly into the cash machine and igniting the gas with a spark from a car battery. In total, the robbers stole a total of £550,000 during the raids which took place across England and Scotland. They had access to a stolen HGV which they used as a base. The lorry was fitted with hammocks and additional fuel so that they didn't need to risk being caught on CCTV at service stations. The lorry also had gas equipment, power tools and a ramp to enable a stolen Audi to be driven in and out. They had even cut a small section from the outer skin of the HGV covers so that they could get in and out without drawing attention by opening the rear of the lorry. Seven members of the gang received a total of 92 years imprisonment for offences of conspiracy to commit burglary and conspiracy to cause explosions.

CRIMES CLUB

In the last years of the nineteenth century, when the detective forces of Britain had become widely established, and after the advent of Jack the Ripper, the image of a detective and the process of detecting crime became prominent in popular culture and in literature, and of course, there being few professional criminologists around, the ground was open for amateurs to play a part in studies of detection and in the pursuits associated with tracking down dangerous criminals. Amateurs mixed with professionals in all kinds of contexts, but the Crimes Club is arguably the most famous of these, with a very select group of celebrities at its core.

This association, which still exists today, is a society of like-minded writers and lawyers, criminologists and aficionados, of true crime. They were at first named 'Our Society' but later became The Crimes Club.

They first assembled at the Great Central Hotel in London on 17 July, 1904, after being discussed informally at the home of the son of the great actor, Sir Henry Irving, Harry Brodribb Irving, the year before. This was followed by a dinner at the Carlton Club in December 1903, and from that it is certain that the more formal conditions and guidelines for activities were formed. Although members wanted the club to remain easy and chummy, with chats about fascinating criminal memorabilia or talks on infamous cases by professional members who were in the legal profession, word got around, and others wanted to join in.

They were an assortment of mainly university men, many from Oxford, where they had learned the importance of networking, but back then, the word used for that was simply, *society*. They had all acquired the gentlemanly accomplishments expected of men of letters who wanted to stay in favour among their peers in the publishing world of the time. Most of them could hardly be called, in the parlance of the twenty-first century, movers and shakers. No, they had merely a common interest and they saw the benefits of sharing knowledge and experience.

The meetings soon attracted all kinds of members, and in 1909, one of the original members, Ingleby Oddie, resigned; he was miffed at the new identity of the club- something more streamlined and rather academic than at first conceived. The other founding members were, from the more celebrated persons: Sir Arthur Conan Doyle, Churton Collins, James Beresford Atlay, Lord Albert Edward Godolphin Osborne, George R Sims, Max Pemberton, Fletcher Robinson, Harry Irving, C A (Lord) Pearson and A E W Mason, and from the less well-known, there were Arthur Lambton and a medical man from Norwich, Dr Herbert Crosse.

There were many other personalities on the fringe of the club, also with profound interests in matters legal and criminal. There was George Ives, who started a vast collection of press cuttings in 1892, and his archive of such material was destined to run to six thousand pages after sixty years of collecting. Many of his cuttings concerned criminal matters, and as his editor, Jeremy Brooks noted in an anthology taken from the Ives cuttings, the man hated injustice, and he wrote books on penal reform too. Ives never joined the Crimes Club, but he did join Conan Doyle in another club: the Authors' Cricket Team, along with J M Barrie and P G Wodehouse. Here is yet another example of Conan Doyle being gregarious in a world of clubs and societies. He was always, since the time of his first real successes in literature, eager to be seen in society, and to mix with his peers.

In some ways, in its first identity, as Arthur Lambton wanted it, the Club was as much a source of play and relaxation as the charity cricket matches many of them played. Conan Doyle had even bowled out the great W.G.Grace. Conan Doyle and Alf Mason put on their whites alongside stars of the music hall and the theatre. That was the spirit of the Club in 1903. But it was soon to transform itself into yet another exclusive group with an interest in a very topical theme- the nature of the criminal and the challenge of understanding the nature of the most heinous or the most astounding crimes.

The members typified the authors of their generation: creative minds coming into full powers of narrative and commercial know-how in an age of vast expansion in their readership. The 1890s had brought them new possibilities and new markets, as the popular journalism encouraged by George Newnes and Alfred Harmsworth, expanded. One of the Club members, Arthur Pearson, was of that breed, with his magazine *Pearson's Weekly*. Matthew Arnold referred to this popular writing with a strong literary impulse mixed together with informative, didactic work, as 'the new journalism.' With this came the rise of literary agencies (the first had appeared in 1875 with A P Watt) and the arrival of net book agreements for retail. The profession also had the Society of Authors which began to organise advice, legal help and dissemination of information. In short, being a writer was, at the turn of the nineteenth century, becoming more of a career choice, although it was tough on those, such as George Gissing, who insisted on literary standards related to classic literature. For men like Conan Doyle and George Sims, the opportunities widened, such was the demand for popular storytelling. In that literary climate, the notions of brotherhoods of writers were extensions of professional attitudes. The working lives of writers became topics of intense interest, so much so that *The Idler* magazine ran a long series of interview pieces with the title, 'Lions in their Dens.'

CRIMINAL INVESTIGATIONS

With the advances in technology and the onset of social media, a criminal investigation can look very different now to when I first started investigating crime. You were often reliant on witness evidence, forensic evidence (fingerprints) or perhaps CCTV to solve the crime. A criminal investigation starts at the time when the police become aware that a crime may have been committed and carries on until all reasonable lines of enquiry have been exhausted or the case is concluded at court or by some other form of criminal justice disposal. The investigation can last several months, particularly if it's serious and/or complex. These cases are usually investigated by detectives. Criminal investigations will be either pro-active or reactive, depending on whether the crime has just happened or is being reported some time after it took place. The number and type of enquiries conducted will depend on the type of crime and the circumstances. There will be far more lines of enquiry in a murder investigation than a low-value theft but there will be some similarity in the type of enquiries (CCTV, house to house enquiries etc). As a detective you may have numerous lines of enquiry but the following are just a few of the most common.

Forensic evidence

Forensic evidence can often prove vital in a criminal investigation. When I first joined the police, any fingerprints found at the scene of a crime had to be physically taken to the fingerprint bureau to be checked. A set of fingerprints taken from a suspect in custody also had to be taken by vehicle, sometimes many miles. Fingerprints can now be scanned and sent electronically, vastly reducing the time required to obtain results. An arrested person will now have their fingerprints digitally scanned and checked so that if they have given false details upon arrival their true identity will be established very quickly (see Fingerprints).

DNA research was very much in the early stages during the 1980's but we are now in the enviable position where DNA can be obtained from very small samples at a crime scene. There have been some concerns raised in the media about the strength of DNA evidence when there is no other corroborative evidence in a case. My view is that it really depends on the circumstances. If a cigarette butt has been recovered at a crime scene and there is no other evidence to incriminate the suspect then I can fully understand the need to exercise a great deal of caution as the butt could be present due to some other reason than having been dropped by the suspect during commission of the crime. If, on the other hand, the DNA is on the clothing of the victim and indicates clearly that it was deposited by the suspect during commission of the crime, then that is pretty damning evidence. With a full DNA profile, the odds of it being someone other than the person identified is normally 1:1Billion.

Other types of forensic evidence which may form part of a criminal investigation include footwear marks, fibres and tool marks. It is generally the case that fingerprints and DNA normally provide the strongest evidence. Having said that, other types of forensic evidence could provide supporting evidence which may strengthen the case.

Passive data

Passive data is a term used to describe automated systems that gather information for purposes unconnected to criminal investigations but which can be accessed by investigators. Modern-day detectives are able to utilise passive data more than ever before as technology advances and new systems are created. Examples of passive data include CCTV, ANPR (Automatic Number Plate Recognition) and telephone billing data. More and more vehicles are now fitted with cameras which record events. The increase in dashcam footage can also provide compelling evidence for the investigator.

CCTV is probably one of the first, and potentially most important, lines of enquiry that a detective will be trying to find in any criminal investigation. Sometimes this will include a walk around the area where the crime was committed to physically look for security cameras or other indication that CCTV may be present. Most towns and cities have local authority CCTV cameras positioned which are often monitored live by trained operators. The footage from each camera is recorded and retained for a period of time in accordance with local policy. This provides the investigator with the opportunity to view the footage from the relevant area to see if any evidence has been recorded. Even if the footage contains nothing of value to the investigation, the recording should be retained as it is disclosable in any future prosecution. Private householder CCTV is quite common these days and it's not unusual for people to have their own cameras and recording systems. During one of my murder investigations a physical search of the surrounding streets near the scene identified a house which had a camera on the front pointing towards the street. With the consent of the property owner, we viewed the footage which showed three people walking in the direction of the scene and running away some time later. The footage also showed the headlights of a vehicle arriving further down the street a short time before the people came into view. Although the footage wasn't of sufficient quality for identification purposes, it did confirm the times during which the offence was committed, the number of suspects and the fact that they had arrived at the scene in a vehicle. All this information helped to build up a picture of what had happened and assisted in identifying those responsible. During the same investigation CCTV in other locations showed the route taken by the suspect vehicle. The most compelling piece of CCTV evidence was of superb quality and in colour. It showed the three occupants of the suspect vehicle stopping at a service station a number of miles from the scene shortly after the offence. All three got out and spent a few minutes inside the shop buying cigarettes and refreshments. The footage enabled us to link the suspects to the vehicle and identify all three occupants. This evidence was part of the case which resulted in convictions for Murder and sentencing of those responsible to a minimum of 54 years in total.

Social media

The world of social media is now huge and is only going to get bigger. In every criminal investigation the detective needs to bear this in mind as there will often be evidence of some description captured in the social media lives of those involved. It's not uncommon these days for events to be recorded on a mobile phone or some other device and then circulated on social media, possibly even before the police are aware. This is a real challenge for investigators to manage and control. It's also not unusual for suspects to incriminate themselves by posting comments or images in the belief that they won't be shared or come to the attention of the police. The social media life of a victim of crime may also hold the key to a motive for the crime or the identity of those responsible. There have also been a number of serious crime cases where the suspect has incriminated themselves by searching the internet in the mistaken belief that, once their search history has been deleted, it can't be retrieved. However, every time a keystroke is made on a computer it leaves a 'digital footprint' which can be recovered. Computers and other electronic devices can often be the source of vital evidence as was the case in one of my murder investigations, when internet searches on how to 'incapacitate a person' and 'avoid detection at a postmortem' were recovered from a computer accessed by the suspect. The beast which is social media will continue to present challenges for the detective.

CYBER CRIME

Talking of challenges, I have no doubt that cyber crime will present one of the toughest for investigators as the fraudsters and online criminals continue to develop their tactics. The City of London police, the national lead force in relation to fraud which runs Action Fraud (the national fraud and cyber crime reporting centre), has revealed that cyber crime victims lost £28 million between October 2017 and March 2018 alone. The primary type of cyber crime reported to Action Fraud was in relation to the 'hacking' of social media and e-mail accounts. Unlike most other crimes, cyber crime is often committed by criminals who never come into contact with their victim and are usually based in another country. Put plainly, cyber crime is any criminal act involving computers and networks, including other more traditional crimes conducted through the internet. There are many different types of cyber crime but I'm going to expand on just three of the more common.

Malware and computer viruses

Also known as 'ransomware' and 'trojan horses' this relates to software utilised by a criminal on your device with the result that your computer, laptop, tablet, or mobile phone no longer works as you would like it to. In some cases, it also collects information or data which has been saved on your device and passes it on. There are many different types of malware or viruses which do different things. A lot of them are designed to steal personal information and pass it to the creator of the virus with the intention of stealing your identity. If you've saved online banking information, they could use it to log in themselves and take money from your account. Alternatively, they may trick you into visiting a fake banking website to steal your details. In some cases, ransomware is designed to deny you access to your files unless you pay a fee.

Malware can get onto your computer by adding a file from somewhere like an external hard drive, or more commonly by downloading a file when you're connected to the internet. The virus may not be apparent as it doesn't always show any visible signs on your computer. The virus may use something called 'spyware' which tracks your browsing history to gather information about your online shopping and banking or 'key-logging' which can detect the exact letters or numbers which you type on your keyboard with the intention of stealing your usernames, passwords and bank card details.

One of the most common examples of this type of fraudulent activity is when people receive an e-mail purporting to be from HMRC informing them that they are entitled to a tax refund. In order to claim their refund, they need to visit the HMRC website and provide some personal details. They may also need to pay a fee online. The link provided in the e-mail will take you to a fake copy of the genuine HMRC website which looks very authentic. Any details provided thereafter will be gathered by the fraudster and used to defraud you. HMRC are fully aware of this tactic and advise people that they will never e-mail anyone in this way. They will always contact individuals by post using their full details rather than the 'Dear Customer' or similar generic phrase used by the online criminals. The most sensible advice to try to avoid this type of criminal activity is never to download anything unless you can be sure of its origin and never to click on a link or attachment in an unsolicited communication.

Phishing
Phishing is a form of cyber crime where a criminal poses as a legitimate organisation in order to obtain your personal information such as passwords or bank card details. This type of fraudulent activity is often carried out via e-mail or text message. Phishing is spelt in an unusual way as some of the earliest identified hackers were known as 'phreaks' and the word 'fishing' was altered to recognise this fact. The term relates to the fraudsters fishing for potential victims by sending

fake communications with urgent messages in the hope of persuading the recipient to visit a bogus website. Phishing e-mails are usually accompanied by an urgent request for you to act on the contents such as informing you that your bank details have been compromised or advising you that you are entitled to a reward or discount. The e-mail will tell you to follow a link to enter information such as bank details or other information which can be used to defraud you.

Sexual exploitation

When you think of cyber crime this may not be the first thing which pops into your head but the internet is used daily by criminals looking to take advantage of vulnerable people. Child Sexual Exploitation (CSE) is a form of child sexual abuse which may involve physical abuse, grooming or the use of indecent images of children amongst other unlawful activity. A lot of this behaviour takes place on what is known as the 'dark web' which is part of the worldwide web that requires special software for access. Organised criminal groups use the 'dark web' to share illegal content and discuss their unlawful behaviour. Some of these groups operate on the internet used by millions of other people but tend to use encryption and other security measures in an effort to hide their actions.

Due to the rise in cases of CSE a lot of police forces now have their own specialist teams to deal with internet crime involving children. These teams, often a mix of detectives and officers seconded from uniform, will investigate cases of individuals living in their policing area who are believed to have accessed indecent images of children or have been involved in other activity which suggests that they are intending to commit sexual abuse against a child. This activity is known as 'grooming' and is a process used by people with a sexual interest in children carried out to prepare a child for sexual abuse. It is often very carefully planned and can take place over a period of weeks, months or even years.

During my career as a detective, I was called upon to investigate a number of child grooming cases. One in particular contained all the hallmarks associated with such cases. The victim was 14 years old and lived in a nice town in the south of Lincolnshire. She spent a great deal of time (as a lot of teenagers do) in her bedroom on social media. She began talking online with a person who told her that he was 19 and was just looking for other teenagers to chat online with. Over a period of time the conversations began to get more explicit and the older youth told the girl not to tell her parents about him and to make sure that they didn't know about their chats. This progressed to requests for the girl to take pictures of herself in various states of undress and to share them with him, which she did. He also sent her gifts through the post including some jewellery and a 'pay as you go' mobile phone with credit so that they could talk privately. This contact went on for several months until he suggested that they should meet at a pre-arranged location and the girl travelled several miles to meet him. There was no evidence to prove what happened after they met but it is believed that they went to his house where sexual activity took place. Her parents had realised that something was going on and had reported their concerns to the police. The investigation proved difficult as the girl refused to co-operate and denied that anything untoward had ever taken place. She also stated that she was in love with him and was prepared to wait until she was older to be with him. Once he was identified, traced and arrested it transpired that he was in his mid 30's and of interest to his local police force for similar behaviour. He was charged, convicted and sent to prison. The victim was supported by her parents and local authority but had been convinced by this man that he had done nothing wrong.

As you can see, cyber crime is a huge challenge for investigators for a number of reasons. The criminal(s) will often operate remotely using a computer which means that they could easily be on the other side of the world yet still manage to defraud people. As their criminal activities usually cross national or international borders, it's extremely difficult for law enforcement to locate and prosecute them. The use of the 'dark web' provides a platform for criminals to ply their trade in an environment which is very difficult to infiltrate. Finally, with the advances in technology their tactics will change and they will find new ways to commit cyber crime, enabling them to remain one step ahead of those who are trying to apprehend them.

CASE STUDY – PHISHING

A hacker who carried out attacks on a string of companies before selling customers' data on the 'dark web' has been jailed for more than 10 years. Grant West, 26, carried out cyber attacks on High Street brands including Sainsbury's, Asda, Uber, Ladbrokes and Coral. He obtained the e-mail addresses of more than 160,000 people and sent them phishing scams purporting to be 'Just Eat' in order to secure their personal data. West, who used the online identity 'Courvoisier', sold the information on the dark web, stashing his ill-gotten bitcoin profits in online caches. His scam, which lasted more than two years, came to an end when he was arrested in a first-class train carriage in the process of accessing the dark web. At the time he was living in a caravan park in Kent and was returning from a trip to visit his girlfriend and co-defendant in Wales.

West used the stolen e-mail addresses to send out messages

posing as 'Just Eat' with offers of cash rewards in exchange for customers filling out a survey. Respondents were asked to confirm personal e-mails and supply extra details to claim the reward. The information, which included everything required to make purchases online, was then advertised and sold to customers visiting his dark web 'shop'. West built up huge caches of bitcoin and other crypto currency in online 'wallets'. Police also found £25,000 in cash and a quantity of cannabis when they searched his address. He admitted to a number of criminal offences including conspiracy to defraud, unauthorised modification of computer material and money laundering.

Earlier this year (2018) he was jailed for 10 years and 8 months at Southwark Crown Court. The Judge described him as a "one-man cybercrime wave" who had "secreted away" some of the £1.6 million worth of crypto currency which was still unaccounted for. He further commented "This case should be a wake-up call to customers, companies, and the computer industry to the very real threat of cybercrime. Regrettably, as this case has demonstrated, security of information held electronically is, at best, poor. When such inadequate security is confronted with a criminal of your skills and ambition, it is totally unfit for purpose and worthless. Unfortunately, you saw the potential of using your skills to make a great deal of money, not lawfully but by crime". A number of companies suffered substantial losses as a result of this fraudulent activity.

CASE STUDY – ONLINE GROOMING
The case of 15-year-old Kayleigh Haywood is an example of how interaction with others on the internet can have devastating consequences. Kayleigh was contacted via Facebook by Luke Harlow, aged 28, who asked her how she was. Within ten minutes the pair had swapped mobile phone numbers and

went on to exchange 2,600 messages, mainly by text. On Friday 13th November 2015, about two weeks after their first contact, Kayleigh agreed to visit Harlow and to stay at his flat. Using classic 'grooming' behaviour Harlow had started to refer to Kayleigh as his "princess" and had advised her to keep the impending visit secret. She was dropped off at a local college by her father who believed that his daughter was staying with a friend of hers. During that Friday evening, after Harlow and Kayleigh first met, she was given "substantial amounts of alcohol" and "sexually touched by him" according to later reports. Kayleigh made contact with her parents the following morning but this was the last time she was heard from. A neighbour of Harlow's, Stephen Beadman (29) arrived at the flat during the Saturday evening after being told by Harlow that he had a "bird" there. Beadman would later claim that Kayleigh was drunk and that he "couldn't get any conversation out of her".

In the early hours of the Sunday morning Kayleigh was seen fleeing from the flat. She was naked from the waist down and was grabbed by Beadman who pinned her to the ground. Later that day Kayleigh's parents, unaware of what had happened to their daughter, reported her missing. The following day both Harlow and Beadman were arrested in connection with the disappearance of Kayleigh. On Wednesday 18th November 2015 the body of a young girl, later identified as Kayleigh, was found in a hedgerow on the outskirts of Ibstock, Leicestershire.

Following interviews and enquiries by the police, Beadman and Harlow were charged with a number of criminal offences. At subsequent court appearances they would admit their guilt, Beadman to the rape, murder and false imprisonment of Kayleigh and Harlow to false imprisonment, sexual touching and grooming Kayleigh. He also pleaded guilty to attempting to meet two other 15-year-old girls for sexual purposes and had contact with a 13-year-old, in addition to having indecent images of young girls on his computer. During Harlow's trial the prosecution read out a series of social media messages sent by him to a 15-year-old girl. Among these messages was one saying "I wish I could kidnap you for Christmas but I would probably be arrested and sent to prison". Beadman was sentenced to life imprisonment with a minimum term of 35 years, Harlow was jailed for 12 years.

The case raised issues over internet safety and prompted Kayleigh's family to campaign for a new law to ban under 16's from opening social media accounts. The local MP, who had been helping the family, suggested that education surrounding the dangers of social media should begin at 8 years of age, possibly younger. The senior detective in the case commented "There are people who have sinister reasons for being on social media and are prepared to exploit and target young people in order to gratify themselves". Leicestershire police have produced a short film about Kayleigh's case and the dangers of online grooming which is set to be shown in schools.

D

DETENTION WITHOUT CHARGE

A question I get asked quite a lot by crime writers is "How long can the police keep a person in custody without charging them?" so I thought I'd cover this subject here. There is a 'fly on the wall' TV series called '24 hours in police custody' which follows Bedfordshire police as they investigate crimes. I would recommend this programme to anyone interested in police investigations and procedures. At the start of each episode the narrator explains that the police have 24 hours to deal with a suspect, that's not strictly true. Whilst it's right to say that quite a lot of cases are resolved within that period, a number of investigations, particularly those which are serious/complex and investigated by detectives, will require more time.

The legislation which governs police treatment of detained people is the Police and Criminal Evidence Act 1984 (commonly referred to as PACE). When a person is arrested and taken to a police station they will be 'booked in' by the custody officer, normally a uniformed Sergeant. The period in custody will be measured by the 'detention clock' which begins at this stage. During their detention, periodic reviews will be carried out to make sure that the investigation is being conducted properly and that their detention is still necessary. The first of these reviews will be carried out by a police Inspector who is independent and not connected with the investigation. The review should take place 6 hours after initial detention. If the person remains in detention, then a second review (by an Inspector) should take place 9 hours later and a third review (Inspector) after a further 9 hours. So, if I was arrested and taken to the police station at 0200 hours then my first review should take place at about 0800 hours, my second at 1700 hours, and my third at 0200 hours the next day.

There is scope for the police to keep a person in custody for longer than 24 hours without charge provided that it can be justified and it is authorised. To do so the investigating officer must, sometime after the second review but before the third, (between 15- and 24-hours detention) apply to an independent police Superintendent responsible for that area who will decide whether the request is justified. If satisfied, the Superintendent can grant up to a maximum of 12 hours additional detention time which would make the total detention time of 36 hours.

They can't grant more than 12 hours but may refuse to grant any further time or may grant less, for example 6 hours, depending on the circumstances.

The law provides for additional detention time beyond 36 hours by application to a Magistrates court for a warrant of further detention. If granted, this may provide up to an additional 36 hours making a total detention period of 72 hours. If the police required further time, they would again have to attend the Magistrates court to apply for an extension to a warrant of further detention. The court may grant additional time but this final extension can't be longer than 36 hours nor can it take the total detention time past 96 hours. So, the answer to the question is that a person can be detained without charge (except for terrorism cases where it can be longer) for up to 96 hours providing that the detention is justified and authorised in accordance with the law. During my career I have never been involved in an investigation where a person has been detained for anywhere near 96 hours as they are usually charged or released within the first 24–48 hours. Having said that, it is fairly common practice in serious cases for detectives to apply for a warrant of further detention, often referred to in the media as the police asking for extra time to question someone.

DICKENS AND THE FIRST DETECTIVES

The plain clothes branch was formed at Scotland Yard on 15 August 1842. It was headed by Nicholas Pearce with John Haynes as deputy. The other six men were: Stephen Thornton, William Gerrett, Frederick Shaw, Charles Goff, Jonathan Whicher and Sergeant Braddick. Rowan and Mayne had sent a memo to the Home Secretary on 'the detective powers of the police.' Their first detectives were a mixed bunch but their varied experience was a significant advantage to them in their future work together. Haynes, for instance, was a chemist and Goff had come through the ranks. The new outfit was to be known simply as 'The Detective.' It was only, in one sense, a rationalisation of a pattern that had been slowly emerging: Metropolitan Policemen had been sent out on special missions, to the provinces sometimes, to help with intractable problems of detection, such as the journey to Uxbridge of Sergeant Otway in 1837; Otway and Pearce had become a regular team in such adventures.

There was another reason why a detective force was a needful initiative: the supervision and investigation of the police themselves. This was to be made apparent in the complex case of the murder of P C Clark at Dagenham in 1846. Clark had gone missing on his country beat and a wealth of suspects were assembled after his body was found brutally murdered in a field. But a part of that picture was the possibility that police officers had been working a scam with some Thames smugglers and ship-robbers. During the course of the investigations into Clark's death, it became clear that groups of officers in remote areas could wield a great deal of local power, and that could easily corrupt.

But 'the Detective' had arrived and the phenomenon drew the attention of the public and the media. One man who saw the allure of the detective's life and character was Charles Dickens. Not only did Dickens invent the first substantial characterisation of a detective in English literature when he made Inspector Bucket in Bleak House; he also wrote thousands of words in non-fictional genres to give his public a relish for this new breed of men. In his *Uncommercial Traveller* sketches, he went out for a night with the Liverpool police, but in 'The Modern Science of Thief-Taking', written for the periodical *Household Words* in July, 1850, he begins to use his knowledge of the new men in print.

He met Jonathan Whicher and calls him 'Whichem' in various essays. Dickens understood the spirit of the human nexus in the nature of thief-taking. That is, relationships have to be forged across the line, into the no-man's-land between the established police practice and the risk-taking double-identity of this 'new science':

In order to counteract the plans of the swell mob, two of the sergeants of the detective police make it their business to know every one of them personally. The consequence is, that the appearance of either of these officers upon any scene of operations is a bar to anything or anybody being 'done'. This is an excellent characteristic of the detective, for they thus become as well a Preventive Police.

There is more than this in what Dickens understood, however. As a man who knew the physical materiality of London from his interminable nocturnal rambles, he saw the new crimes and instinctively sensed their subtlety: 'But the tricks and contrivances of those who wheedle money out of your pocket rather than steal it; who cheat you with eyes open; who clear every vestige of plate out of your pantry while your servant is on the stairs...for the detection and punishment of such impostors a superior order of police is requisite.'

When Dickens actually met these intriguing gentlemen who had to provide this new policing, he celebrated it with a piece on 'The Detective Police Party' and here he used his novelist's acuteness and sixth sense about people to give his public an insight, as when he described 'Stalker': 'Stalker is a shrewd, hard-headed Scotchman – in appearance not at all unlike an acute, thoroughly-trained schoolmaster from the Normal Establishment at Glasgow.'

DISCLOSURE

There has been a lot of adverse publicity surrounding the process of disclosure in criminal cases and, although it's a complex subject, I thought I'd try to briefly explain what it is and how it should be managed.

The Criminal Procedure & Investigations Act 1996 (CPIA) came into effect on 1st April 1997 and introduced a statutory framework for the disclosure of material to defendants which the prosecution did not intend to use as evidence in the case. This is known as unused material. Prior to this legislation the issue of disclosure of unused material had been managed using common law rulings which had become unwieldy. It was clear that there was a need to balance the exchange of information between the prosecution and defence parties.

The Act introduced three key words for investigators – **record**, **retain** and **reveal**. Investigators should **record** information at the time it is obtained or as soon as practicable. The information should be recorded in a durable and retrievable format. Investigators should **retain** all material, including information and objects, which are gathered in the course of a criminal investigation and which may be relevant to that investigation. Material may be relevant if it appears to have some bearing on any offence under investigation or any person being investigated unless it appears incapable of having any impact on the case. **Revelation** is the act of notifying the prosecution which is the responsibility of the disclosure officer. Disclosure is the act of providing material to the defence that has not previously been disclosed which might reasonably undermine the case against the accused or assist the defence case.

Perhaps the best way to explain disclosure is to talk through the process of submitting a case file to the Crown Prosecution

Service (CPS) after a person has been charged with a criminal offence. The investigating officer will prepare a case file which will include a number of forms (known as MG forms – see **M**). Most of these forms will outline the case for the prosecution including a case summary, copy of the charge and record of interview. The investigating officer, in most cases, will also assume the role of 'disclosure officer' which means that they must make a written record of all unused material which the prosecution don't intend to rely on but which may impact on the case. There are specific MG forms within the case file which the disclosure officer must complete to confirm that they have listed all unused material not relied upon by the prosecution. The form MG6C is used to list all non-sensitive items of unused material which have to be described in detail. If the item is available and can be easily attached to the case file then the officer should include a copy. Examples of non-sensitive unused material may be CCTV footage which has been viewed and doesn't show anything of evidential value, a witness statement from a person who isn't a key witness and doesn't provide relevant evidence or a printed copy of the police computerised incident report. The form MG6D is used to list all sensitive items of unused material which won't normally be sent to the CPS unless specifically requested. In a relatively straightforward criminal investigation there may be very little material listed on this schedule. Examples of sensitive unused material include police tactics, covert issues and sensitive intelligence reports. The final form relating to unused material is the MG6E which needs to be signed by the disclosure officer to confirm that all unused material in the case has been listed on the schedules and that there are no outstanding items not listed.

The investigating officer has a responsibility to correctly manage and document the unused material from the very start of the criminal investigation until the case is concluded. They should make sure that all relevant items are listed and that the CPS lawyer dealing with the case is aware of and understands the significance of each item. It depends entirely on each individual case but there are usually at least ten items of non-sensitive unused material, even in the simplest of investigations. In a murder investigation there will be hundreds, possibly thousands which is why the more serious and/or complex investigations have at least one dedicated disclosure officer. Disclosure is a process which will often present disagreement between prosecution and defence and, if handled incorrectly, can lead to an acquittal and adverse comment from judiciary. I think a lot of the problems originate from a lack of training provided to the police which results in a misunderstanding of their role and responsibilities as a disclosure officer.

In June 2018 the CPS published the outcome of their review of rape and serious sexual offences (RASSO) cases. This followed an announcement earlier in the year that senior prosecutors were assessing all cases in England and Wales where someone had been charged with rape or serious sexual assault. More than 3,600 cases were examined to ensure that disclosure was being managed effectively. This additional scrutiny was undertaken after concerns were raised over how disclosure was handled by the CPS and the police, following decisions to halt several prosecutions late in the process. Specialist RASSO prosecutors assessed each case to be satisfied that the police had pursued all reasonable lines of enquiry, and that there was a clear strategy for disclosure to be carried out effectively and in a timely manner. Of the 3,637 cases which were assessed, some were at an early stage whereas others were close to trial. Prosecutors identified where additional work was required and, in many cases, the police were asked to conduct further investigations. In total 47 prosecutions for rape or serious sexual offences which were halted were found to have issues with the disclosure of unused material. Common themes which were found included communications evidence such as texts, e-mails and social media being examined too late in the process, the failure to identify and obtain material such as medical or social services records and the emergence of new evidence after charge. In response to the review findings the National Police Chiefs' Council Lead for Criminal Justice commented "In recent months, we have seen some prosecutions stopped far too late in the process with very serious impact on the lives of those involved – this is not right or fair. The changes we're implementing will help to prevent this happening to others by ensuring reasonable lines of enquiry are identified early by police, prosecutors and the defence working together with timely review of the material generated. Real progress is already being made with new training to officers rolled out, improved processes and experts/champions identified in police forces and CPS areas. We are also working at pace to consider how technology could help us, and to review our progress so we can be sure the changes are making the difference we expect". The number of prosecutions which have collapsed due to disclosure errors has risen by 70% in the past two years.

CASE STUDY – DISCLOSURE

The trial of a young man accused of rape collapsed after it emerged that police had not examined 30,000 Facebook messages linked to the alleged victim. The man, named only as 'Cameron', had been charged with rape and five counts of sex with a girl under 16 in 2015. He had met the alleged victim, who cannot be identified for legal reasons, through Facebook. The man was found not guilty after the CPS conceded that there was no reasonable prospect of a conviction. The police admitted that the large quantity of messages hadn't been properly investigated and were only discovered after a review of the case by Avon and Somerset police. The Judge described the result as "another example of these non-disclosure cases".

'Cameron' described how he had lost his job as a result of the allegations and spent a tortuous three years on bail waiting to have the opportunity to clear his name. He denied all allegations. His defence solicitor commented "I believe our criminal justice system is in a state of utter collapse. We are running Russian Roulette with defendants going to court and not knowing whether the matter has been robustly investigated or not. That is simply not right. The CPS had only seen four of the total 30,000 messages. They claim that the complainant only handed them over late in the day. I don't think they ever asked for them."

Avon and Somerset police explained "During a review of the case, in January 2018, the victim disclosed additional evidence that involved some 30,000 private messages on a social media account. Following an extensive examination of these messages, new evidence emerged which was disclosed to the CPS who decided that a successful prosecution was no longer viable and offered no evidence at a subsequent court appearance."

The term 'disclosure' also applies to the process prior to the interview of a detained person when the investigating officer supplies the solicitor with some information about the case and a general outline of the subjects to be covered during the interview. This process is designed to enable the solicitor to advise their client appropriately before the interview is conducted. The process will normally take place in an interview room at the police station with the police officer providing information to the solicitor in the absence of the detained person. It used to be a verbal exchange with the solicitor writing down the information but these days most pre-interview disclosure is written and handed to the solicitor. It is then a matter for the officer if they wish to answer any further questions from the solicitor as the police don't have to disclose all evidence prior to interview. In a serious and/or complex case the disclosure is likely to be staged as there will be a number of separate interviews covering different topics or evidential elements. This means that the process will be repeated prior to each interview with different information being disclosed on each occasion. In a murder case the disclosure will usually be prepared and sometimes delivered by the Interview Advisor who will be a Detective Sergeant or Detective Constable.

DNA TAGGING

DNA tagging spray is a relatively new tactic used by the police to help them track down suspects who use mopeds or motorbikes to commit crime. There is a huge problem with this type of crime in London and an increase has been noted in other parts of the country where the technology has also now been rolled out. The SelectaDNA tagging spray can be used by police officers to spray bikes involved in robberies, assaults and smash and grab raids. The spray marks the bikes, clothing and skin of any riders and passengers with a uniquely coded, invisible DNA that will provide forensic evidence linking them to a specific crime. The Metropolitan police have deployed SelectaDNA to help them deal with the problem of moped thefts, acid attacks and other bike-related crimes in the capital.

One of the biggest challenges facing the police in their pursuit of these criminals is the lack of identification evidence as the suspects will either be wearing crash helmets or have their faces covered when committing the offences. The deployment of a product which can help to resolve identification issues will hopefully increase the prospect of successful prosecutions. If suspects are arrested or bikes recovered the DNA code will link them to specific crimes. The spray can be projected onto suspects without causing any harm and can be detected on clothing weeks or months later. If the suspect has been sprayed and has managed to evade capture, the police can attend the home addresses of known suspects to check the person, their clothing and footwear. Once used, the spray can be detected under special lighting which is already a standard feature in police custody suites. A representative from Selectamark, the company which produces SelectaDNA Tagging spray commented "This is a great example of how innovative technology is helping police catch criminals. It only takes a tiny drop of DNA spray to tag and identify an offender and this tactic will undoubtedly lead to more seizures and prosecutions". The company also provides search dogs trained to sniff out SelectaDNA forensic markers on offenders. These dogs are the first in the world to be trained for this purpose and have already worked with UK police forces during several operations.

CASE STUDIES – DNA TAGGING SPRAY
1) Two teenagers who stole a scooter and later failed to stop for Metropolitan Police officers have been arrested after they were found to have traces of DNA tagging spray on them linking them to the stolen bike and related offences. The spray is invisible to the naked eye but illuminates when exposed to UV light enabling police to identify offenders.

The scooter was originally stolen whilst the owner was making a delivery in Camden. Two days later the same scooter was seen with two males on board. The scooter failed to stop and was pursued by police. At one stage it mounted the pavement, at which point officers sprayed DNA tagging spray at the males, and used a tyre deflation device which caused the scooter to come to a stop. The males abandoned the scooter and made off on foot. One youth was detained quickly and the other was found hiding in a garden shed. Both youths were found to have traces of DNA tagging spray on them which linked them evidentially to the stolen scooter and related offences.

2) A man who used stolen scooters to steal mobile phones and other valuables has been jailed after he was identified by a new DNA tagging spray used by the Metropolitan police to tackle moped and scooter-enabled crime. Spencer Duarte, 21, from Essex was jailed for 4 years in May 2018 and was disqualified from driving for the same period. He was also given a 3-year Criminal Behaviour Order to prevent him from riding a two-wheeled vehicle and using a mobile phone not registered to him. The court heard how Duarte stole a scooter and used it to rob and steal mobile phones. He had pleaded guilty to the theft of a scooter, seven further counts of theft from a person, using a motor vehicle without insurance and driving whilst disqualified. He was also found to be in breach of a licence and was recalled to prison.

In December 2017 police recovered an abandoned scooter displaying a false number plate in Haringey. The scooter and a helmet, both used by Duarte, were examined under ultra-violet light and found to be covered in DNA tagging spray. In February 2018 Duarte committed a number of theft offences where he snatched items from members of the public whilst riding a scooter registered to his girlfriend. One victim, who had his phone snatched by Duarte, gave chase and tackled him causing him to come off the moped. Duarte abandoned the vehicle, helmet, clothing and stolen property before making off.

novel experiment by the North-eastern Railway Police, dogs are being used as detectives on the docks at Hull. They consist of a number of trained Airedale terriers which patrol throughout the day and night...'

In 1910 the terriers made their arrest, as the railway police magazine reported: 'Early one morning a policeman accompanied by a dog was patrolling St Andrews Dock and, seeing a man loitering in a suspicious manner called upon him to stop. The man took no notice and the man slipped his dog –one of the best. The dog soon had the man trapped.' The window of a refreshment room was found broken and two other men were inside. Three burly fellows were escorted to the police station, and they were soon in Hull prison; in fact, they were notorious burglars of the city.

A new dog training centre was opened at Hedon Hall after the war, run by Inspector John Morrell who started breeding dogs for special uses as well; later, dogs became more important, of course, in PAD work (Passive Alert Detection). Also, as we know from television almost every day, the 'sniffer dog' searching luggage as well as areas around a scene of crime, is a familiar sight.

There is no doubt that there is a very special bond between handler and dog, but also, in the realms of detective work, the police dogs, in their separate categories, play a significant role in leading investigations in fruitful directions.

Updated 2023

Police dogs remain an invaluable companion in the fight against crime and, in addition to general purpose use and firearms support, are now often used to detect things with their sense of smell, calculated as anywhere between 10,000 and 100,000 times more acute than that of a person. Specialist dogs (often, but not exclusively, spaniels and Labradors) are trained to detect the presence of lots of different things including drugs, cash, firearms, explosives, accelerant, mobile phone SIM cards and human bodies. They are a huge asset and a valuable part of the policing family. Dogs are now even being trained to detect the presence of seminal fluid in a move which is likely to be of great benefit to the investigation of sexual offences.

CASE STUDY

Two very special 'sniffer' dogs and their handlers passed their training in early October 2022 and became ready to share their expertise with other police forces across the country. Police dogs (PD) Rosie and April join PD Sybil as the only three dogs in the UK who are trained to detect seminal fluid only, training which it is hoped will help convict more offenders. The training has been part of a highly successful forensic search dog project pioneered by Derbyshire Police. The skills of the dogs and their handlers will be of vital importance during sexual offence investigations, checking crime scenes where traditional methods of examination are unlikely to work. The three dogs are able to detect tiny amounts of seminal fluid without being distracted by other scents. Their noses are so sharp that they can detect as little as 0.016ml, sometimes years after it has been deposited. The two Labradors, both around 15 months old, completed a rigorous training programme developed by Derbyshire Police Dog Section in conjunction with Crime Scene Investigators. Rosie will be based in Derbyshire with April being part of the Cheshire and North Wales alliance. The police officer who led the training commented 'In the last six weeks they've learnt to identify and search for that scent in numerous scenarios that we've set up for them: indoors, outdoors, in vehicles, on grass, tarmac and materials such as bedding and clothing. The dogs can indicate the presence of seminal fluid in places where traditional kits can't, and once they've identified the scent – that piece of material or vegetation can be sent away and any extracted DNA profiled, leading to more prosecutions for serious sexual offences.'

DRONES

An unmanned aerial vehicle (UAV), commonly known as a drone, is an aircraft without a human pilot aboard. UAVs are a component of an unmanned aircraft system which include a UAV, a ground-based controller and a system of communications between the two. Now the technical jargon is out of the way, I'm going to explain how drones are being used effectively by the police but also by the criminal.

Police forces are now using drones to help with investigations, look for missing people and detect crimes. Lincolnshire police are one of a number of forces who now use drones as part of their daily business. In February 2018 they were called to a rural area by a member of the public who had discovered an overturned car. It was in the early hours of the morning and the conditions were freezing. A ground search had failed to locate the driver and a thermal imaging drone was deployed. It found him unresponsive and hypothermic about 500 feet from the car in a deep ditch. The man was taken to hospital for treatment and has made a full recovery. He would not have been found so quickly were it not for the effective use of the drone. The force has also used thermal imaging on a drone to identify a man who was producing cannabis at his house. The location was rural and surrounded by trees and bushes, making it very difficult to gather evidence. In the early hours of the morning the drone was deployed and flown across an open field before hovering some 50 metres from the property. The heat source was identified and provided valuable evidence which led to the successful execution of a search warrant. In June 2018 the man who lived at the address was jailed for 3 years for producing cannabis on a scale estimated at a value of up to £50,000. The filming from the drone took just over one minute and the drone was airborne for only five minutes in total.

For some time now our prisons have struggled to cope with items such as drugs and mobile phones being smuggled inside using various methods. It's recently been revealed that drones are now being used to fly drugs to the windows of inmates in what has been referred to as a 'drone delivery service'. The inmate will order a supply from within the prison using a smuggled mobile phone then simply wait for delivery. The Justice Secretary commented "Spice and other drugs are ordered with a Deliveroo responsiveness on mobile phones from prison cells and delivered by drones direct to cell windows". It is believed that nearly 6,500 prisoners, one in thirteen, have links to this type of organised crime.

CASE STUDY – OPERATION CANVAS

A gang who flew drugs, mobile phones and other items into prisons using high-tech drones have been jailed after being recorded on cameras set up to monitor wildlife. The group, led by serving inmate Craig Hickinbottom, smuggled cocaine, cannabis and technology into seven prisons across England and Scotland. Members of the gang flew remote-controlled drones, equipped with a fishing line and hooks, directly to cell windows inside the prison. Inmates, who were in contact with the drone pilot via mobile phone, then used items such as an extendable broom handle to retrieve the contraband. CCTV from inside the prison provided evidence of drug dealing as it recorded other prisoners visiting the cells and leaving in possession of packages. Unfortunately for the gang, cameras which had been set up to film wildlife outside HMP Hewell in Worcestershire caught the gang by chance while they were launching the drones into the prison grounds. Prisons in Worcestershire, Staffordshire, Birmingham, Yorkshire, Cheshire, Liverpool and Perth were all targeted. Eight members of the gang, all from the West Midlands, were jailed at Birmingham Crown Court after admitting their roles in the conspiracy. Ringleader and former armed robber, Craig Hickinbottom, directed the "large-scale and persistent plot" while serving sentences at two different prisons. He admitted conspiring to bring contraband into prison and conspiracy to supply psychoactive substances. Described as a "leading player" in the smuggling operation, he was jailed for 7 years and 2 months. Hickinbottom's brother John, was jailed for 4 years and 8 months for his "significant" role. Drone pilot Mervyn Foster, who made 49 flights into jails was given a sentence of 6 years and 8 months imprisonment. Other members were either jailed or given suspended prison sentences, depending on their role.

DRUGS

I'm not going to talk about the more common drugs of abuse such as cannabis, cocaine, heroin etc as, although they are still used regularly throughout the country, their existence and effects are fairly well-known. Instead, I'm going to explain a little about some of the drugs which are causing real problems in our towns and cities and have led to a significant rise in drug-related deaths. Firstly though, I'm going to talk about how drug-dealing is managing to take over a number of our communities even though the people selling the drugs are not local.

County lines

You may be familiar with the term 'county lines' as it is featuring more and more in the media. It relates to mobile phone numbers which are used to facilitate the distribution of drugs throughout the country. There are estimated to be about 1,000 county lines in existence at present, each one capable of 'earning' between £3,000 – £5,000 per day. The dealers who control the phone are known as 'workers' and the supplier who provides the drugs is called the 'plug'.

As our large towns and cities become saturated with drugs and the people who sell them, it has become necessary for criminals to move to other areas to ply their trade and avoid competition. Coastal areas such as Bournemouth, Portsmouth and parts of East Anglia have been targeted by county lines due to the mix of local and tourist demand. These areas are known by the dealers as 'cunch' (an area outside large cities) or 'OT' (out of town). There is a very specific method used by the 'workers' when infiltrating an area, which consists of three phases. Firstly, they will identify the location and make sure that they can access it without too much difficulty. They will often travel by train to avoid the road network and the police intelligence systems which may identify them. The second phase is to locate potential customers to buy the drugs. They will spend some time walking around the local area to identify the places where drug users and alcohol-dependent people frequent. They will then engage with them and make it clear that they are prepared to sell drugs to anyone who may be interested. They will pass on the county line mobile phone number and provide any potential customers with a sample of drugs to gain their trust. They may charge for the drugs but, at times, they may provide it free of charge on the first occasion to encourage others to engage with them. They will very quickly build up a client-base which they will maintain using the county line. The final phase is a process known as 'cuckooing' where the dealer will identify a property occupied by a vulnerable person, move in with them, and use the property as a base to sell drugs from. They will use the threat of violence to ensure that the occupier doesn't inform the police and complies with their requests. Some of the dealers involved in county lines are as young as 11–12 and have been 'recruited' by older youths as they are considered to be expendable.

Fentanyl

Fentanyl is a powerful synthetic opioid analgesic used to treat those experiencing severe pain or to manage pain after surgery. It is believed to be 100 times more potent than morphine and 50 times more potent than heroin. This drug has been responsible for the deaths of many people in America, including the singer, Prince, who is thought to have died from a fatal mix of fentanyl and benzodiazepine pills, a particularly dangerous combination. It's entirely possible that he didn't even know that he was taking fentanyl. Investigators found pills labelled as prescription hydrocodone, but made of fentanyl, in his home suggesting he may have bought them on the black market.

The ingredients required for fentanyl are easily available in China and then imported ready for manufacture. The drug was originally developed as an anaesthetic in Belgium in the 1960's and, because it is so much more powerful than heroin, only small quantities are required to achieve the same 'high'. As little as 0.25mg (the size of the head of a pin) could prove fatal. Initially, the Mexican drug cartels laced the fentanyl into heroin to increase the potency of low-quality supplies. They then moved into producing counterfeit tablets with a devastating effect. The pills are now sold on the streets with the buyer having no idea of the contents or strength. Fentanyl has a number of street names including Apache, China Girl, Murder 8 and TNT. It is used as a substance of abuse in the UK and can be purchased via the 'dark web'. The number of deaths in England and Wales due to fentanyl rose by 29% in 2017.

Monkey dust

Monkey dust, also known as MDPV, is an off-white powder which can be swallowed, injected, or snorted. It comes from a family of drugs known as 'cathinones' and includes the stimulant 'khat', popular among some sections of the Somali and other West African communities. Before 2010 cathinones could be bought in 'head shops' (a retail outlet specialising in paraphernalia used for the consumption of cannabis) but they were re-classified as a Class B drug in legislation rushed through Parliament to tackle the rise of the drug mephedrone.

Monkey dust dampens perceptions of pain and causes powerful hallucinations which lead to severe paranoia. In the UK, police officers have reported that users often feel they are being chased and can lash out or climb buildings to escape resulting in serious injuries. One user was seen to jump from a two-storey building onto the bonnet of a car before getting straight up and fighting with police. The effects of the drug can last for several days and can rapidly lead to addiction.

The county of Staffordshire has seen a noticeable increase in the use of monkey dust which can be bought for as little as £2. Staffordshire police report attendance at an average of 10 calls per day related to monkey dust whilst the West Midlands Ambulance Service have attended many incidents across their region. The drug has been linked to several deaths during this year (2018).

Spice

Spice is the blanket-term used on the streets to describe products which are mimics of cannabis. Spice is made from dried and chopped up plants which have been sprayed with the drug. It can be up to 700 times more potent than cannabis and can be more addictive than heroin. It used to be what was known as a 'legal high' where it was sold online and in 'head shops' until the Psychoactive Substances Act 2016 made it illegal to produce, supply or import it. It is now recognised as a Class B drug along with cannabis, amphetamines and codeine. Some of the side-effects of taking spice are tremors, seizures and psychotic episodes. It's sometimes called the 'zombie' drug as users can be seen slumped in an apparent state of semi-consciousness. This is due to a significant reduction in the respiratory system which causes the body to shut down due to low oxygen levels.

A number of Police and Crime Commissioners have written to the Home Office requesting that spice is re-classified to a Class A drug alongside the likes of heroin and cocaine. Lincolnshire PCC commented "At present, the current justifications for the classification of B are rooted in the chemical similarities which spice shares with cannabis. However, such parallels are purely chemical, as the physical and psychological effects these substances have on their users are on a much more extreme scale to those of cannabis. In practice they are more comparable with Class A drugs such as heroin and it is therefore imperative that it and the dealers who peddle this misery are treated with the same severity and concern. The wide scale abuse of these debilitating drugs within towns, cities and even villages across the UK is one of the most severe public health issues we have faced in decades and presently the response to tackle the issue is woefully inadequate." Emergency services continue to respond to spice-related incidents, with synthetic drugs being increasingly linked to deaths throughout the country.

CASE STUDY – NITROUS OXIDE

A young mother has been left unable to walk after her regular use of party high 'hippy crack' caused spinal cord damage. The 24-year-old lost feeling in her body from the chest down after contracting a disease from inhaling nitrous oxide, also known as 'laughing gas', through balloons. She had been using up to 15 balloons at weekends while her son visited his father. But recently she woke up to find that she was unable to move. She is now having to relearn how to walk and use her hands after doctors established that the nitrous oxide (NOS) had caused Lichtheim's disease, also known as subacute combined degeneration of the spinal cord. The disease is thought to start when nitrous oxide starves the body of the vitamin B12, the lack of which damages the fatty sheath protecting nerve fibres in the spinal cord which control movement and sensation. The condition is treated with vitamin B12 injections with most people recovering completely, if treated, within a few weeks of the onset of symptoms. If treatment is delayed, the person may not recover from movement problems caused by the irreversible damage to the nervous system. The woman has managed to take a few steps with the help of physiotherapists but is expected to be in hospital for a significant time. It's illegal to supply or import NOS for human consumption, but the small silver canisters are still available in shops as they are legally used for whipping cream and as an anaesthetic.

E

EARLY MORNING BLUES

Someone once asked me what it was like to be 'on-call' as a detective and whether I was able to sleep, knowing that the phone could start ringing at any time. Now I'm no poet but I put the following together to describe my thoughts at that time and, as you may have guessed, I called it the 'Early Morning Blues'.

The tune seems so very familiar to me, as I open one eye I struggle to see.

The music gets louder, the silence no more, a glance at the clock shows a quarter to four.

That old friend 'Nokia' is calling my name, during on-call week it's always the same.

"Morning Guv'nor", bellows the chirpy chap, "Murder in Boston", he starts to yap.

"The scene is secure, the body insitu, SOCO's on way, it's over to you".

Going on to give me lots of gen, I just wish I'd picked up a decent pen.

Being a senior detective isn't all 'lights and action' but it certainly provides job satisfaction.

As I struggle to put on my socks and shoes, I need to shake off these early morning blues.

ETHNICITY CODES

The police use codes (sometimes referred to as Identification Codes) to describe the physical appearance of a person when transmitting descriptions over the radio. There are generally seven different codes, known as **IC** codes, which you may be familiar with if you watched police dramas such as 'The Bill'. An example of such a transmission from the police control room may be along the lines of "There has been a burglary at 10, High Street where the person responsible is described as an IC1 male, 5'10", wearing a dark hooded top and blue jeans". The recognised codes are

IC1 – White (Northern European)
IC2 – Hispanic (Southern European)
IC3 – Black
IC4 – Asian (Indian subcontinent)
IC5 – Chinese, Japanese or other Southeast Asian
IC6 – Arab or North African
IC9 – Unknown

In addition to circulations from the control room, officers may use the codes to relay their perception of a person's ethnicity, based on a visual assessment, following a stop in the street or some other contact with a member of the public. If I had stopped a person in the street and wanted to carry out a Police National Computer (PNC) check on that person I would do so using what is referred to as the NASCH factor (name, age, sex, colour, height). My transmission would be along the lines of "Could I please have a PNC name check on the following person who I have stopped in Camborne Place, NW10. Surname – Burglar, First name – Billy, date of birth 01/04/1973, Male, IC1, 5'10". The name would be spelt out using the phonetic alphabet (see **P**).

Self defined ethnicity codes (SDE) are a set of codes used by the Home Office to classify an individual's ethnicity according to that person's self-definition. The codes are also called '18 + 1' codes, as there are 18 of them plus one code **NS** for 'not stated'. This code system originated from the 2001 United Kingdom census. British police forces are required to use the SDE 18 + 1 codes (as opposed to the commonly used radio shorthand IC codes) when spoken contact has taken place and an individual has been given the opportunity to state their self-perceived ethnicity. Other examples where a person may be asked how they would describe their ethnicity would be during the post-arrest procedure or when completing the personal details on the rear of a witness statement form.

The SDE 18 + 1 codes are

A1– Indian	**M3** – White and Asian
A2 – Pakistani	**M9** – Other Mixed
A3 – Bangladeshi	**NS** – Not stated
A4 – Chinese	**O2** – Arab
A9 – Other Asian background	**O9** – Any other
B1 – Caribbean	**W1** – White British
B2 – African	**W2** – White Irish
B9 – Other black background	**W3** – White Gypsy or Irish Traveller
M1 – White and Black Caribbean	**W9** – Other White background
M2 – White and Black African	

The above codes are self-defined so a person could define themselves as, for example, a black African when their visual appearance may suggest otherwise. The person recording their self-defined ethnicity must record the answer they are given as opposed to their own opinion.

EXPERIENCE

When most people think of a stereotypical British detective, they probably think of middle-aged white men who like a drink and can be prone to the odd temper tantrum. The likes of Morse,

Taggart and Gene Hunt may reinforce those perceptions. When I joined the police in the early 1980's a high percentage of the CID office was made up of older men who had 'been there, done that and worn the tee-shirt' so to speak. There were one or two female detectives, referred to as WDC's at that time, but they were very much in the minority. Some of those experienced detectives were set in their ways, resistant to change and somewhat lazy. The relationship between CID and uniformed officers wasn't very good and there was certainly a drinking culture amongst a lot of the detectives.

One of my first encounters with CID took place after I had managed to arrest two burglars who had broken into a house. At the time I was a young, inexperienced PC who was 'wet behind the ears' and rather naive. Back at the police station I saw this colossus of a man walking towards me with a huge grin on his face. He was black and built like a brick out-house. He introduced himself as a Detective Sergeant and shook my hand so firmly that I thought I may need medical attention. During the next couple of days he took me under his wing, even giving me a lift to and from court in his 3.0 litre Ford Granada. That was the start of a very positive working relationship and a friendship with a detective who worked hard, played hard and was one hell of a squash player. I was later to discover that Detective Sergeant Norwell 'Noz' Roberts had been London's first black police officer and had a very successful career as a detective in spite of vile insults and racist abuse during the early years of his service. He was to receive the Queen's Police Medal (QPM) for Distinguished Service, one of the highest honours given to a police officer, in 1996, before retiring from the police service the following year. Thankfully, there are a lot more female and ethnic minority detectives these days, a number in the more senior ranks, and the service benefits greatly from this.

Do you need to have experience to be a good detective? The answer is, not necessarily, but it certainly helps. I spent a number of years learning how to become a good detective and experienced the role in every rank from Constable to Chief Inspector. Unfortunately, the current climate affords neither the time nor the resources to do the same. There is now a chronic shortage of detectives in many forces and police officers are expected to investigate serious crimes without the relevant training or experience. This isn't fair on those officers or the victims of those crimes. Detectives are leaving their forces through resignation or retirement and not being replaced. The role of the detective is no longer an attractive option for most officers. The shortage of detectives across England and Wales has been described as a "national crisis" with at least 5,000 more required, 800 more in London alone.

In response to this shortage, the Metropolitan Police is offering new recruits the chance to join the service as 'trainee detective constables' as soon as they complete a two-year course. For the first time, aspiring sleuths can apply directly to become detectives without having to work as uniformed beat officers. Those applying must have a degree and have lived in London for three of the last six years. After a series of assessments and interviews, trainees, each mentored by a former detective, will complete an 18-week course to learn the basics of investigative policing, before spending 12 weeks working in London's boroughs and completing a further 7 week course. A senior officer leading the detective recruitment programme commented "This programme aims to provide a dedicated career pathway for people who are interested in becoming a Detective Constable to help them move swiftly into this area of policing. The MPS detective pathway will bring new recruits in at constable level who have demonstrated a potential towards investigation. They will be fully trained as a Police Constable but the training will have a focus on investigations."

Not everyone supports this approach of recruiting people with no previous experience of being a detective. A former senior detective commented "I have very serious doubts about this direct entry detectives' scheme especially right now when, frankly, the Met's CID is at the point of collapse. To be a detective you need three things: knowledge, skills and experience. Someone coming into the CID direct will have none. They can only develop the practical skills, such as identifying and retrieving evidence, carrying out interviews and putting together a good case file for the CPS by actually doing the job. By the traditional route, uniformed officers start building up their knowledge on patrol, not just in their formal training but informally by watching and working with experienced colleagues. They assist with more serious crimes, perhaps on a crime scene cordon, conducting house to house enquiries or assisting with operations run by senior detectives investigating murders, rapes and armed robberies. Direct entry detectives will have none of this so we must expect them to take some years building up full effectiveness. Senior management seem to think having a degree will mean none of this will matter. Sadly, they are wrong. The best degree in the world won't help at all with skills and experience, though it may mean knowledge is acquired more quickly. Most concerning of all is the fact direct entry detectives will be thrown into this chaos. There will be little time for them to learn their trade. There will be few experienced detectives with the time to guide them. It is not so much being thrown into the deep end as being thrown into the mid-Atlantic in hurricane season. I really hope they do well and that this is the answer to the Met CID's problems. I fear it isn't." Other police forces across the country are looking to follow a similar route with direct entry to CID.

My personal view is that experience is something which can take many years to build up and which can often only be gained by actually doing the job with the appropriate guidance and supervision. Criminal investigation is a specialist area of policing and deserves the level of funding and resources to maintain its effectiveness. I too hope that the current situation can be resolved so that the history and reputation of the British detective isn't lost forever.

F

FACIAL RECOGNITION
During the past few years, a number of police forces have been trialing Automatic Facial Recognition (AFR) at various public events and festivals. AFR uses CCTV or surveillance cameras to record and compare facial characteristics with images on police databases. The system is being piloted in London, Humberside, South Wales and Leicestershire. Manufacturers of the systems say they can monitor multiple cameras in real time, 'matching' thousands of faces a minute with images already held by the police, often images taken of people in police custody. The Metropolitan police piloted the system at Notting Hill carnival in 2016 and 2017, at the cenotaph on Memorial Sunday and at Westfield shopping centre in Stratford with further trails planned. The force claims that the technology is an "extremely valuable tool."

However, lawyers for Big Brother Watch argue that the use of AFR breaches the rights of individuals under the Human Rights Act, including the right to privacy and freedom of expression. The director of the civil liberties group commented "When the police use facial recognition surveillance, they subject thousands of people in the area to highly sensitive identity checks without consent. We're hoping the court will intervene, so the lawless use of facial recognition can be stopped. It is crucial our public freedoms are protected." It's likely that the Metropolitan police and other police forces will welcome the opportunity to argue the case for AFR and try to put it on a solid legal footing alongside other unique characteristics stored on databases, such as fingerprints and DNA. The body which advises London Mayor Sadiq Khan on policing and ethics has called on the Met to be more open about the use of AFR, setting out where and when it will be used before undertaking any further pilots.

In addition to the Human Rights issues, the technology has faced a lot of criticism for a lack of accuracy. The Metropolitan police accepted that its system had incorrectly 'flagged' some 102 people as potential suspects and South Wales police said its technology had made 2.685 'matches' between May 2017 and March 2018, of which 2,451 were 'false alarms'. Both forces state that they do not consider these to be 'false positive matches' as additional checks and balances are in place to confirm identification following system alerts. Whatever your view on facial recognition and its use by police there is clearly more work to be done in relation to if, how and when it's used in the future.

Updated 2023

Cheshire Police have begun rolling out facial recognition technology to assist in identifying offenders and supporting victims of crime. The process began in June 2022, in a first for Cheshire, and will use two forms of facial recognition – Retrospective Facial Recognition (RFR) and Operator Initiated Facial Recognition (OIFR).

RFR is a useful intelligence tool that assists in establishing the identity of a person and whether their image matches against other images stored on the Police National Database. As the name suggests, it is used retrospectively after an incident has taken place and works by comparing still images of unknown faces, for example CCTV footage, against a reference image database, such as custody photographs, in order to identify the person. Officers will then be able to use this intelligence to further their investigations and hopefully bring more offenders to justice.

OIFR is a similar tool which is currently available to officers patrolling the streets. Officers carry an electronic mobile device containing a phone application, which can be used to take an image of a person's facial features and then compare it in real-time to a reference image database. This process can be used in an attempt to confirm the identity of the person they are dealing with, in cases where that person may have refused to give their details or was believed to have provided false particulars and was unable to provide identification. This smart tool can also be used if a person is unable to provide their details because they may be unconscious, seriously injured, or incapable due to the influence of drink or drugs. During a trial of OIFR, some officers from the force Roads and Crime Unit have been given access to the phone application with the hope that this will eventually be rolled out to other areas of the force. The technology will only be used when appropriate and will only search images of those who appear on the police database.

Assistant Chief Constable Welsted, Cheshire Police commented 'Facial recognition will not replace traditional means of identifying those who have committed a crime. It's important to remember that officers have always been able to spot a person who is wanted for a crime and stop them in the street but with this technology, we will be able to increase the speed and accuracy in the way in which this can be done'.

CASE STUDY

A registered sex offender who was tracked down by facial recognition technology after filming a teenage girl in public toilets, has been jailed. Dorniel Nica from Chester was sentenced to 36 weeks imprisonment at Warrington Magistrates' Court in November 2022. He was also handed restraining orders against two separate girls and ordered to pay costs. The court heard how on 2nd October a teenage girl had been in a cubicle at the public toilets in a shopping centre when she saw a hand holding a black mobile phone coming from underneath the adjacent cubicle. She believed the phone to be recording and used by a man in the cubicle next to hers. The victim joined up with her friend and they both approached police officers at Warrington bus station to tell them what had happened. A search was carried out of the area to no avail. After making enquiries, the officers checked CCTV at the shopping centre which showed a man entering the female toilets at 5.12 pm and leaving some 43 minutes later. The man could also be seen on the CCTV footage wandering around the shopping centre before leaving the area. Officers took an image of the man from the CCTV footage and submitted it through Retrospective Facial Recognition (RFR) software. The search returned a match for Nica and he was located and arrested the following day at an address in Warrington, on suspicion of voyeurism. His mobile phone was seized by police and he was subsequently charged with voyeurism and attempting to observe a person doing a private act. The police officer in the case commented 'Thanks to the new technology available to us, we were able to identify Nica quickly and effectively, allowing us to make further enquiries and ascertain his whereabouts. This led us to get justice for Nica's victims and put a prolific offender behind bars and off the streets of Cheshire.'

FAMILIAL DNA SEARCHING (see also Genealogy)

Since 2002, the UK has been the pioneer in the use of familial DNA searches, routinely performing them on serious and violent crimes when appropriate. The use of familial searching may become an investigative option for detectives if they have an unsolved case with a DNA profile for the suspect which doesn't match anyone already stored on the National DNA Database (NDNADB). They can request a list of DNA profiles which are similar to the unidentified profile as this may provide them with the identity of a family member of the suspect. A number of historical 'cold case' murders and other crimes have been solved, many years later, as a result of the use of familial DNA searching.

The killer of 16-year-old Colette Aram, who was raped and murdered in 1983, had evaded capture for 25 years until his son was arrested for a motoring offence in 2008. A routine swab was taken from the driver which proved to be nearly identical to that of the killer. Paul Hutchinson was jailed for life with a recommendation to serve a minimum of 25 years for this brutal and senseless crime.

The killer of 17-year-old Melanie Road, who was sexually assaulted and stabbed 26 times in 1984, was eventually identified over 30 years later after his daughter was arrested for an unrelated domestic incident. Her DNA was found to be similar to that of the unidentified killer. Christopher Hampton eventually pleaded guilty to murder and was sentenced to life imprisonment with a minimum term of 22 years. Familial DNA searching solved this case.

CASE STUDIES – FAMILIAL DNA

1) In the early hours of March 21st, 2003, Michael Little was driving his lorry on the M3 in Surrey when his windscreen was broken by a brick which had been thrown from an overpass. He was able to bring the lorry safely to a stop but subsequently died as a result of a heart attack. The recovered brick was seized by police and later found to contain two DNA profiles, Mr. Little and another unknown person. Enquiries conducted in the area at the time established that a car had been broken into and the suspect, in trying to get the car started, had cut themselves and left some blood at the scene. A full DNA profile was obtained from the blood which matched the unknown DNA profile from the brick which had killed Mr. Little. The profile was searched on the National DNA database with no success. Analysis of the profile established that the person was a white male and the advice of a behavioural advisor suggested that he was under 35 years of age. Police believed that he may live locally and carried out voluntary DNA sampling of some 350 men from the surrounding area. Unfortunately, this also proved fruitless.

A decision was made to carry out a familial search in relation to white men under 35 living in Surrey or Hampshire. As a result, 25 people with similar DNA were identified, including a relative of the suspect, whose DNA matched 16 of 20 DNA markers. Police interviewed this person and discovered that he had a 19-year-old brother, Craig Harman, who lived near to the crime scene location. The analysis of his DNA proved that he was the unknown offender and he subsequently confessed. In April 2004 Harman pleaded guilty to manslaughter and was sentenced to 6 years imprisonment. This case was the first time that familial DNA had been used to identify and convict someone in the UK.

2) Familial DNA searching was first used to identify and convict someone for murder in the Nottinghamshire area. In April 2001, 87-year-old Gladys Godfrey was attacked in her home and pushed to the floor by a man who then exposed himself. Despite being 4ft 11ins tall and weighing just six stone, Gladys was able to defend herself against the attacker, hitting him with a lemonade bottle before he made off with her handbag.

In September 2002, the same man returned and subjected Gladys to the most appalling physical and sexual assault. She died as a result of her injuries and a murder investigation was launched. Detectives had a sample of the killer's DNA from the murder scene which matched DNA samples from the previous attack, confirming that the same man was responsible for both crimes. Unfortunately, efforts to trace the killer proved fruitless as his profile wasn't on the National DNA database, indicating that he had never been previously arrested. Despite police taking over 1,000 voluntary DNA samples from men living in the area, they were no closer to finding the man responsible. The investigating team sought help from the Forensic Intelligence Bureau, formed in 2003 and part of the Forensic Science Service which, at the time, provided support to police forces across England and Wales. Familial DNA searching was still being developed but was able to provide a list of DNA profiles which could belong to a relative of the killer. Using parameters, such as geography, the list was refined to create a top 20 of potential matches. The second person on this list was a close relative of a man called Jason Ward who was able to assist them. When police located Ward, they were able to confirm that it was his DNA which had been left at the crime scene, together with his fingerprints.

Jason Ward lived within two miles of the crime scene and was a 'loner' who lived with his parents. He spent much of his time playing computer games and had alcohol and solvent abuse issues. He initially denied killing Gladys but, due to the strength of the prosecution evidence, he eventually pleaded guilty to rape and murder. In May 2004 at Nottingham Crown court Ward was sentenced to life imprisonment with a minimum term of 22 years. This case, along with many others, may not have been solved were it not for the use of DNA familial searching.

FINGERPRINTS

For more than a century police have detected crimes based on fingerprints left at the scene. 'Locard's exchange principle' (see **L**) informs us that evidence will often be left at the scene of a crime, sometimes this evidence is in the form of fingerprints. The challenge for investigators is to find and interpret that evidence.

For many years fingerprints were taken from people who had been arrested for a criminal offence and from witnesses for elimination purposes, using paper, ink, a roller and a block. The ink would be spread onto the block evenly using the roller before each finger would be rolled over the block then rolled onto the paper fingerprint form. Once both sets of fingers and the thumbs had been rolled, a set of plain impressions would be taken of the four fingers of each hand together and the two thumbs. The four fingers on each hand would be inked then held together and placed down onto the form in the appropriate space. The two inked thumbs would then be held next to each other and placed into the appropriate boxes on the form. The final part of the fingerprinting process would involve the taking of palm prints. This would involve the rolling of ink onto the whole of the palm and fingers then either placing the palm onto the designated spaces, normally the rear of the fingerprint form, or rolling the palm onto the paper form using a rolling tube. The process was messy and the general standard of fingerprints was often poor. Sometimes this was due to the amount of ink used, often too much, so that you couldn't see any of the fingerprint ridge detail, only splodges of ink. It may sound strange but there is a skill to taking a good set of fingerprints which give the Fingerprint department the best opportunity to work their magic and compare with outstanding crime scene marks. During my police career the ink and roller method was the norm until the police service began to use advanced methods.

These days the majority of main custody suites are equipped with Live Scan machines which enable fingerprints and palmprints to be taken electronically simply by scanning them. The prints are instantly compared with a national database providing results in a matter of minutes. Live scan is a massive step in the right direction for investigators and will help to confirm the identity of people who are arrested quickly and accurately. The process is also a lot easier and not messy as there is no ink required.

Earlier this year (2018) police began using mobile fingerprint scanners out on the streets. The system being used by West Yorkshire Police searches the 12 million fingerprint records kept in the UK's criminal and immigration databases. The system will allow police to check the identity of an unknown person in less than a minute, returning personal details if there is a match. The scanners are likely to be used if a person cannot be identified by other means or is suspected of giving false details. The system was in development for 12 months and was on trial for three weeks before 250 scanners were issued. As the fingerprint scanners on smart phones aren't large enough to capture the detail required to check against the databases, the Home Office had to opt for handheld scanners which connect to the smart phones already carried by police officers. Rather than all fingers, the officers will scan the tips of two fingers to compare with more detailed scans which are taken from suspects in police custody. The system is mainly going to be used to identify suspected criminals but could also be used to try to identify a person who is unconscious and needing medical treatment or perhaps even dead.

Prints were first conceived in the Argentine police many years before their adoption in Britain, and in the Empire, the notion of fingerprints as identification markers was used partially by the governmental administration in India to stop the process of labourers being paid twice, after making their mark on wages sheets on more than one occasion. It was in a case from 1910 that they were first used to convict killers, but first, we need to glance towards one of the most famous experts on prints in the history of detection.

One of the most celebrated detectives of the twentieth century, Fred Cherrill ('Cherrill of the Yard') explained his early fascination with fingerprints by telling the tale of his going to an old mill with his father in a storm. The miller was ill and someone was needed to grind the corn to meet demand. In the mill, flour was sprayed everywhere, putting a white film over every surface, and young Fred found himself grabbing an eel his father threw across the room at him, with orders to put it in a sack. His hands were caked in eel slime and then he writes, 'Startled, I put out a hand to steady myself. For just a moment my slime-covered fingers rested on the wooden chute, which had become highly polished by all the flour and meal which had passed over its surface...I was gazing at the chute in awed fascination... There, by the agency of nature alone, were my fingerprints!'

Cherrill's story accounts for the long history of the knowledge of fingerprints, long before they were used in forensics. There had been various academics who had done work on prints but nothing had come of it: a professor at the University of Breslau in 1823 had read a Latin thesis on fingerprints in a lecture, and the artist Thomas Bewick had done wood engravings of fingerprints, using them as identifying signatures on his works. In China, for many centuries, thumb-prints had been used in documents for identity purposes in ratification. Similarly, these impressions had been used in India with illiterate members of the population; when the scientist Francis Galton got to work on the subject, he wrote a book-length study, simply called *Fingerprints*, published in 1892. In some ways, the introduction of fingerprinting into police work is similar to the rivalry to reach the South Pole: while Sir Edward Henry was using fingerprints in India for crime investigation, the same work was being done in Argentina by Francesca Rojas. But after Henry had introduced fingerprinting into the repertoire of detection methods at the Yard, it was to effect a revolution in detective procedure.

The prototype scenario and first conviction by the use of prints came in 1902, when the Yard had around one hundred fingerprints in their first small volume of records. It was a murder case, and it took place at Chapman's Oil and Colour Stores in Deptford. An old couple, Thomas and Ann Farrow, ran the shop and they had an assistant, young William Jones, who, along with Louis Kidman, found Thomas's corpse and later the still breathing Ann Farrow.

The old man had been brutally beaten, with a broken cheekbone and a fractured skull; the doctor said that the man had died around ninety minutes earlier. When Ann Farrow had been taken to hospital and the scene was ready for some inspection, Chief Inspector Fred Fox arrived to do his work, with two photographers. Crime scene investigation, in something close to the modern sense, was being born that day. No less a figure than Melville Macnaghten came to assist and then took charge. The killer had not forced an entry: that was the first important detail established. There had been a frenzied search of the whole shop and house, but after going upstairs and hitting Mrs Farrow, the scene suggested that they had come downstairs and then fought the old man again, as he had recovered from their first blow.

There were no witnesses; three masks were found abandoned in the shop so now Macnaghten knew he was looking for three killers, and that made the murder all the more savage and reprehensible. There was no indication as to what weapon had been used in the murderous attacks either. The question now on the detective's mind was whether Ann Farrow would recover and give descriptions. What was particularly unhelpful in the course of following the usual tracing procedure in pawn shops and similar outlets, was that the killers had only taken money. That created a dead end in the normal line of enquiry. It was looking desperate for the Chief; another shopkeeper had been killed in London the same day. Then, the final blow: Mrs Farrow died.

Macnaghten went back to the bloodbath that was the sitting room of the Farrow household. Casting his eye across the room and the pools of blood, he thought of the surface prints that had just been used in smaller scale arrests. Would the Farrow murder be the first opportunity to try this new device? He established that none of the police personnel at the shop had touched the cashbox, then he covered his fingers with a handkerchief and showed his team the print on the box. Collins, of the new Fingerprint Branch, was a sleuth with a scientific bent; he had been working on other types of basic forensics and was excited about this new technique. It was a matter of magnifying glasses and intense study at that time; he had a small collection of filed prints from known criminals and that was that. There had been a long-established method of filing basic records of habitual offenders, so there was some hope of a 'result.' But the print on the cash box had no match in Collins's shelves.

Basic police work, however, provided the lead that would eventually take the investigation back to the cash box. A milkman at work on the day of the killing had seen two men leaving the shop and he gave a description of them. The milkman saw that they had left the door open and told them so but they took no notice as they said there was someone behind them. To tally with this, three men had been seen in a local pub very early that day – and they answered the descriptions. It was when a certain Ellen Stanton came forward that things accelerated; she had seen two men running at the right time , and they had the same appearance as two suspects, and Ellen knew one of them. Macnaghten was now searching for one Alfred Stratton. The man was taken in Deptford. The identification parade failed, but Collins took the prints of Stratton and his brother. One print matched that of Alfred.

What happened then is a pattern for almost all succeeding scientific forensic advances when it came to actually implementing the knowledge and seeing it take part in a process of law in the courts. In other words, this new detective force, with its fingerprints and other types of records, was going to find it hard to convince judge and jury about the new methods of detection. But the Stratton brothers went to the gallows; hangman John Billington officiated at Wandsworth. The judge, Mr Justice Channell, had said in court that the men should not be convicted on fingerprint evidence alone and that was the case. Bt the first trial involving fingerprint evidence had happened;

from that point on the concept would be a little more familiar, and the newspapers played their part in ensuring that.

What was happening in the closing years of the nineteenth century and the first years of the new century was that Scotland Yard was acquiring a much more sophisticated records department than ever before and fingerprints were beginning to play a major part in that. Edward Henry initiated the Central Fingerprint Bureau and together with the Register of Habitual Criminals, the Criminal Records Office was created. Three CID men, Stedman, Collins and Hunt, were to run the new section.

FLYING SQUAD

A book about detectives wouldn't be complete without reference to the iconic Flying Squad which has recently celebrated its 100th anniversary. During that time the squad has been striving and often succeeding in getting the better of Britain's most notorious villains. The London-based branch was formed towards the end of the First World War by veteran detective Frederick Wensley. Initially it comprised of two horse-drawn wagons patrolling the streets of London with officers hiding inside ready to pounce. It was named as the 'flying squad' because it operated across the capital city without adhering to policing boroughs.

The unit was immortalised when it was portrayed in the 1970's TV series 'The Sweeney' starring John Thaw and Dennis Waterman. The nickname is an abbreviation of 'Sweeney Todd' which is Cockney-rhyming slang for 'Flying Squad'. The series featured rugged detectives DI Jack Regan and DS George Carter fighting violent crime in London as part of the Metropolitan Police Flying Squad in their unmarked Ford Granada. The show often featured that immortal phrase "you're nicked".

Many of the most dramatic raids of recent times were foiled

by the flying squad. Their officers arrested 17 of the 19 thieves responsible for the 1963 Great Train Robbery and investigated the infamous raid at the Brinks-Mat security depot in 1983. The biggest operation in flying squad history involved an attempt to steal jewels from a diamond exhibition at the Millennium Dome in the year 2000. Five robbers, armed with smoke bombs, ammonia and a nail gun crashed into the Dome using a stolen JCB excavator. Their plan was to escape on the River Thames in a speedboat. Flying squad officers were lying in wait, some dressed as staff and cleaners with their firearms hidden in rubbish bins. The raid was foiled and the offenders apprehended, eventually being sentenced to lengthy custodial sentences. The squad also investigated the £14 million Hatton Garden safety deposit burglary in 2015 involving those ageing criminals who were referred to by the media as the 'diamond geezers'.

The changing face of crime means that the flying squad will no longer always be able to apprehend suspects on the pavement as in years gone by. The increase in cyber crime means that they will now have to rely on undercover work and the use of informants to help identify those using technology to commit crime. The reduction in armed robberies, particularly at banks and other commercial locations, means that the work of the flying squad will inevitably diversify in an attempt to keep up with cyber criminals who are using crypto currencies (virtual finance allowing users anonymity online) to sell drugs and weapons via the internet.

From an original team of 12 officers, the flying squad will be increasing from 120 to 141 detectives as their remit will be expanded to include offences of kidnap. Although it will still investigate armed robberies, moped smash-and-grab raids and deliberate gas explosions of cash machines (see **C**) will also form part of their work.

I have fond memories of working with the flying squad during my time in the Metropolitan police. On one particular occasion they had received intelligence that there was going to be an armed robbery at a bank or building society somewhere in north-west London. A list of potential targets had been identified and I was part of an arrest team in one of the unmarked flying squad vehicles (known as 'gunships') containing armed detectives. Our days would comprise of an early start, detailed briefing, fried breakfast then 'on the plot' in the vicinity of one of the potential targets. The robbery never took place in our area but I can honestly say that those days were full of adrenaline and tension coupled with admiration for those detectives. They had a reputation for being prepared to run through brick walls to get the job done and having played football with a couple of ex- flying squad detectives, I think that's a pretty accurate description. The image of detectives back in the 1950s, when they became almost media darlings, was linked to the fast car and the suave yet mysterious appearance of the lead officer. The Flying Squad had a profound impact on that image.

FOOTWEAR EVIDENCE

Unless you are dealing with a particularly acrobatic criminal the chances are that they may leave footwear marks at the scene. If the scene is secured and protected at an early stage any evidence left behind may be capable of being retrieved. The recovery and interpretation of footwear marks has improved immeasurably as the police have developed their procedures and systems. It may surprise you that footwear evidence, in one form or another, has played its part in criminal investigations for centuries.

The murder of Elizabeth Pullen, in London, on 29th June 1697 was the first recorded case of footwear evidence forming part of the prosecution case in the UK. The victim was killed in the larder of her own home, having had her throat slit. An impression of a slipper was left in blood at the scene. The suspect, a French woman named Margaret Martell, was traced and found in possession of property belonging to the victim as well as a bloody slipper. Martell claimed her innocence but the overwhelming evidence led to her finding of guilt. She was sentenced to death and finally admitted responsibility for the death when standing at the gallows.

In September 1786, in Kurkcudbright, Scotland a young pregnant woman was murdered in her cottage. Footwear marks observed in the mud outside indicated the assailants escape route. The Stewart Depute made tracings of the footwear at the scene logging observations and crime scene notes not dissimilar to methods employed hundreds of years later. The Depute attended the victim's funeral and screened the footwear of every male present, identifying the suspect through unique characteristics from the sole of the shoe. William Richardson was duly arrested and was subsequently charged with the murder. He was found guilty and sentenced to be hanged. Prior to his execution, he confessed to the murder and directed Gordon to the location of the murder weapon.

These cases demonstrate the power and history of footwear evidence as a means to identify and convict offenders. In the many years since these cases, scientific development introducing biometric samples such as fingerprints and DNA have overtaken footwear as preferred options as they can offer stronger scientific certainty of guilt. Having said that, footwear evidence can still prove to be a valuable contributor to prosecution cases and its value should not be underestimated.

Investigators have been copying the footwear sole patterns of suspects in police custody for many years. In the early stages it was simply a case of rolling the fingerprint ink onto the soles then placing the footwear onto plain paper to leave the impression. This was rather messy and did result in the odd suspect leaving a trail of ink around the police station if the officer had forgotten to clean the soles. As systems developed, they became ink-free allowing the suspect to step onto a pad. The latest technology involves Tread Finder which has been deployed in the Metropolitan police area. Tread Finder incorporates the use of a 300-dpi scanner and newly developed software enabling capture, assisted coding and automated geographical crime scene searching. The suspect simply steps onto a low platform and walks across it before stepping off again. Once scanned the footwear impressions can be viewed by other police forces in a matter of seconds and the system also searches outstanding crime scene marks instantaneously. There are currently around 45,000 sole patterns stored on the national footwear database. This technology is another step forward (pardon the pun) in the fight against crime.

FOXTROT 11 (One-One)

On the afternoon of Friday 12th August 1966, less than two weeks after the euphoria of England winning the World Cup at Wembley Stadium, the capital city was shocked when six shots rang out across Wormwood Scrubs Park leaving three police officers dead. The press reported on "the worst crime London has known this century" with the public outraged and many calls for the recently suspended death penalty to be reintroduced.

At 8 o'clock that morning, Detective Sergeant Chris Head, Temporary Detective Constable David Wombwell and Police Constable Geoff Fox reported for duty at Shepherds Bush police station. They were covering the 9am to 5pm shift that day, assigned to patrol the streets of 'F' Division in an unmarked Triumph 2000, radio call-sign Foxtrot One-One. All three officers were in plain clothes and had been working together for a month or so. Their brief was to look for suspicious behaviour and intervene accordingly as they patrolled in what was then known as the 'Q' car (**see Q**).

That same morning, Harry Roberts, John Duddy and Jack Witney set off from Duddy's flat near Ladbroke Grove intending to steal a car. They scoured the streets in Whitney's scruffy blue 1954 Vanguard estate car, the exhaust pipe held on by a loop of wire. Between Whitney and Roberts in the front of the car was a brown canvas bag containing overalls, a set of cloned registration plates and three loaded guns. After one unsuccessful attempt to steal a car, they went for a pub lunch. Afterwards, suitably refreshed with pints of bitter, they set off again looking for a Ford Corsair to steal. In the balmy heat of the afternoon and having been drinking, the gang's wits were less sharp than before lunch. They didn't notice that they were being followed by a blue Triumph 2000.

As both vehicles entered Braybrook Street, near Wormwood Scrubs prison, PC Fox accelerated alongside the Vanguard and DS Head signalled for Whitney to pull over. The Vanguard stopped near the kerb and PC Fox positioned the Q-car a short distance in front with the engine running. T/DC Wombwell got out of the back and approached the Vanguard. As he did so, he noticed that the vehicle wasn't displaying a tax disc. Following a brief conversation with Witney it was also established that the vehicle had no current MOT certificate and that the insurance had expired three hours earlier. Wombwell walked back to the Q-car to discuss the position with DS Head. Roberts was concerned that the contents of the bag may be discovered and decided to conceal one of the guns in his jacket. Wombwell and Head approached the Vanguard, one either side of the vehicle. Wombwell leaned down at the driver's window to speak with

Witney and Head tried to speak with Roberts who was sitting in the passenger seat. The passenger door was locked and Roberts ignored him. Head asked Duddy to open the canvas bag which was still on the floor between the front seats and Duddy produced the overalls from the bag. Head asked to see what else was in the bag then suddenly, and without warning, Roberts produced the gun, shouted an obscenity and shot Wombwell at point-blank range through the open driver's window killing him instantly.

As the shot rang out and echoed across the adjacent parkland, nearby children stopped and watched in disbelief. DS Head began to run back towards the Q-car shouting "no, no, no" as Roberts got out of the vehicle and shot him in the back. Roberts approached Head and tried to shoot him again, but on two occasions the weapon jammed. Head scrambled to his feet and began to stumble back towards the Q-car before collapsing in front of the bonnet onto the road. Realising that Roberts' gun had jammed, Fox started to reverse the police car at him in an attempt to run him down. Duddy took another gun out of the bag and got out, shooting at the police car causing a couple of the windows to explode. The bullet narrowly missed the chin of PC Fox who then hit the brakes. A further shot from Duddy again missed Fox and shattered the car windscreen. Fox began to pull away but, as he did so, Duddy ran forward and fired again, this time through the shattered nearside passenger window. This third shot hit PC Geoffrey Fox in the left temple causing the police car to lurch forward and over DS Head, trapping him with critical injuries underneath the vehicle. Meanwhile, Witney grabbed his vehicle documents from T/DC Wombwell who was lying dead on the road. All three got back into the Vanguard and made off from the scene.

A passer-by, who had become suspicious of a vehicle driving

so fast near to the prison, had noted the registration number and Witney, the owner of the vehicle, was arrested at his home six hours after the incident. The vehicle, containing spent cartridges and equipment for stealing cars, was recovered the next day in a lock-up garage rented by Witney. He initially denied involvement but soon confessed and named his accomplices. Duddy was arrested a few days later in his native Glasgow. Roberts went on the run, hiding out in Hertfordshire and using his military training to evade capture for three months.

Roberts pleaded guilty to the murders of DS Head and T/DC Wombwell (but not that of PC Fox), while the other two defendants denied all charges. On 12th December 1966, after a trial lasting just six days, the three men were convicted of murder and possession of firearms. They were sentenced to life imprisonment with a recommendation to serve a minimum of 30 years. The Judge commented that the murders were "the most heinous crime to have been committed in this country for a generation or more". The murders caused outrage in the UK, calls for the reintroduction of the death penalty, and saw the formation of the Metropolitan Police Firearms Wing.

Duddy died in Parkhurst prison in February 1981 and, although released from prison in 1991, Witney was later to be murdered when he was beaten with a hammer by his flatmate in 1999. On 11th November 2014 Roberts was released from prison following a parole board review.

G

GENEALOGY (see also Familial DNA)
With the expansion in resources related to DNA over the last few decades, a comparatively new player is on the scene: the

database used in genealogy. The importance of this hit the news prominently in 2019 with a flood of material in print and online relating to the man known as the Golden State Killer. The topic in focus here is the public ancestry database. On a database of over a million people, a search of basic individual details linked with a DNA sample could narrow the search to around twenty people.

That is potentially a staggeringly effective detection tool. One academic has commented, 'In a few years it's really going to be everyone' when he referred to who might be identifiable from such a resource. As for the Golden State killer: in efforts to find this multiple offender, detectives used a database called Gedmatch and fed in material forming a random sample from material collected at crime scenes, then waited for the system to throw up genetic links.

Research on this has been done by many now, but the work of Yaniv Erlich at Columbia University has been well documented. Erlich looked at a database called MyHeritage, which has 1.28 million DNA profiles from family history searches; anyone with a European ancestry who lives in the USA will have a 60% chance of finding a relative in the resource. We could add to the family history resources the other material which is steadily building: individuals who have paid for DNA searches for all kinds of family and legal reasons. The database is growing fast. Jocelyn Kaiser, in an online feature, noted, 'Although these studies are encouraging news for solving crimes, they raise privacy concerns for law-abiding citizens.' But there could be a way to encrypt personal data and then do some gatekeeping and restrict the uploading to these encrypted items.

Of course, this is big business. One case study in this area of detection using such materials is that of CeCe Moore, featured in an article in The Guardian by Zoe Corbyn in 2019. Moore recalled her search for the killer of a Canadian couple in 1987. Usually, Moore's work concerned people looking for their parents, such as adoptees: a subject featured in Britain in the hit TV series, *Long Lost Families*. But as Moore noted when the search for the killer led to a suspect, 'It was a very surreal feeling.'

She led a specialist unit in forensic genealogy at a firm called Parabon, and they work with police. Corbyn provides a neat summary of the process in her *Guardian* feature: 'Moore looks for partial DNA matches between the crime scene DNA profile and other Gedmatch profiles to find relatives, with typically second or third cousins – of which we have an average of about 30 and nearly 200 respectively – needed for a good chance of success.' So the process raises the ethical issues, but will surely be an increasingly useful tool in detective work.

The topic runs parallel to the area of DNA known as familial research, and similarly dramatic results may arise. A sensational instance of this is the discovery of mitochondrial DNA in forensic materials relating to the infamous Crippen murder of 1912; results showed that the famous body in the cellar, thought to be Mrs Crippen, was not actually female. That was established through mitochondrial DNA: that is to say, genetic material taken from a female descendant of the victim.

Work in genealogical sources will more than likely show a similar progression. The real obstacle will be the issue of privacy.

GENE HUNT

DCI Gene Hunt is a fictional character in the BBC One police drama *Life on Mars* which was shown in 2006/7 and the sequel *Ashes to Ashes* (2008-10). The drama depicts policing in the 1970's and 1980's with Hunt portrayed as politically incorrect, brutal and corrupt but fundamentally good. His father was an abusive alcoholic and his brother, Stuart, was a drug addict who died despite Hunt's best efforts to reform him. Initially Hunt is in charge of a CID Division which is part of Manchester and Salford police before transferring to the Metropolitan police in 1981. Gene Hunt has been described as an 'old school copper' who likened himself to the sheriff in the film *High Noon*. His dress sense, typical of the period, included a long, beige coloured camel coat and leather slip-on shoes. The top button of his shirt was always open and his tie was often hanging halfway down his chest. His pride and joy was a Ford Cortina Mark III 2000E which could be seen being driven erratically through the streets during episodes. Hunt was once described by a colleague as an "overweight, over-the-hill, nicotine-stained, borderline alcoholic homophobe with a superiority complex and an unhealthy obsession with male bonding" to which he replied "you make that sound like a bad thing".

Despite Hunt's brashness and overt prejudices, he somehow managed to build up a reputation as an unlikely British sex symbol. One female newspaper journalist commented "the combination of power and, shall we say, lack of political correctness can be a potent one – which is why everyone in Britain fell in love with Gene Hunt, the hulking great throwback in the BBC series *Life on Mars*, and that men wanted to be Hunt, women wanted to be with him". Another described him as her guilty secret even though "he wears a vest and his hair looks like it was styled during a power cut" and despite him being "racist, disablist and homophobic". The character was voted the United Kingdom's favourite television hero in 2008 and in the lead up to the 2010 General Election campaign in the UK, the ruling Labour Party produced an advert likening Conservative David Cameron to Hunt, claiming that Cameron would take Britain "back to the 1980's". There's no doubt that Gene Hunt was a bit of a 'Marmite' character in a series which proved incredibly popular.

I suppose the question I need to address, one which I have been asked on more than one occasion, is whether Gene Hunt and his CID colleagues typified your average detective in the 70's and 80's. I joined the Metropolitan police in 1980 and was posted to a Divisional station in 1982 and, as such, I can only really comment on the latter decade. A lot of CID officers at that time were very professional and, although they liked to play hard they also worked extremely hard. There were, however, some "old school" detectives who wouldn't have been out of place on the set of *Life on Mars* and who treated women and uniformed colleagues as though they were something they had picked up on the bottom of their shoes. Thankfully, those days are long behind us and the modern-day detective bears no resemblance to those times.

GHOST SQUAD

In 1998, *The Times* reported that the Yard had been operating what was termed a 'ghost squad' which had been set up in order to root out corrupt detective officers. The paper pointed out that as part of the squad, former military intelligence officers had been employed. In January of that year, the report stated, there had been nineteen raids on current and former detectives.

In the process of this work, a number of Flying Squad outfits were closed down too. The 'Ghost Squad was created in 1994 by Sir Paul Condon, the Commissioner at the Met. Behind the initiative was the case of what was known as the Harrods affair, in which a report issued by the government had been leaked after actions taken by corrupt officers. When it first began work, the Squad was led by Commander Roy Clark, who had been head of the South-East regional Crime Squad, along with John Grieve, who was in charge of the Yard's Criminal Intelligence outfit. The Times report noted that 'the squad was empowered to use telephone taps, bugs and surveillance equipment. It was told to operate as though it were confronting top-level criminals in the underworld.'

GIVING EVIDENCE

During my initial police training at Peel Centre, Hendon we practised giving evidence in a mock courtroom with the trainers playing the roles of the prosecution, defence and Judge/Magistrate. We were cross-examined and subjected to scrutiny in an attempt to mirror real-life. As far as I can remember it was quite realistic but nothing can really prepare you for the experience of giving evidence. In my early days as a uniformed constable, before the Crown Prosecution Service (CPS) became more involved in the prosecution of cases, I remember being given the odd pile of case papers and told to 'pop down' to the local Magistrates Court to present them on behalf of the prosecution. Most of these cases were relatively straightforward, often drunk and disorderly or other minor offences, but the fact that I was given this responsibility so early in my police career gave me valuable experience in the courtroom. This practice ceased many years ago and is now unheard of.

Detectives normally investigate the more serious crimes which nearly always end up at the Crown Court. As a result, it's not inconceivable that any evidence you give will be in front of a Judge and jury. Even though you are not on trial and are there simply to deliver the facts as you know them, the experience is quite nerve-wracking no matter how many times you go through it. I have given evidence and been cross-examined in many courts, including the Central Criminal Court (Old Bailey), but it never got any easier and always managed to get my adrenaline pumping. You need to have a thick skin when under cross-examination because there will be occasions when you will be accused of lying or being incompetent. Even the most simple of questions can sometimes become difficult in the tense atmosphere of a packed courtroom with a Judge and twelve members of the public looking at you.

One of the favourite defence counsel tactics, when cross-examining the arresting officer in a case, would be to begin with one or two very simple questions to confirm that the officer had actually arrested the defendant and for what offence(s). The next question would seek confirmation that the officer had cautioned the defendant on arrest and then – "Can you please tell the court exactly what you said including the words of the caution". Even though most officers would use this caution many times during their career, it can be a bit of a mouthful (particularly the newer version), and even more challenging when everyone is waiting with bated breath. If the officer couldn't remember the wording or got it wrong, it would provide the defence barrister with the ammunition to challenge other parts of the evidence and cast doubt on the credibility of the prosecution case. There were some detectives who carried a written version of the caution inside their warrant card to refresh their memory and just in case that question was asked of them in the witness box.

If you are a writer and want to cover an arrest scene then you may wish to include the caution which should always be given on arrest (unless it is impracticable due to the person's condition or behaviour). The person must be told that they are being arrested and why, for example "I'm arresting you for criminal damage as I've just watched you kick that window causing the glass to crack". The caution should then be given "**YOU DO NOT HAVE TO SAY ANYTHING, BUT IT MAY HARM YOUR DEFENCE IF YOU DO NOT MENTION WHEN QUESTIONED SOMETHING WHICH YOU LATER RELY ON IN COURT. ANYTHING YOU DO SAY MAY BE GIVEN IN EVIDENCE.** The arresting officer will then explain why the arrest is necessary and, in the majority of cases, this will be in the following words "Your arrest is necessary for the prompt and effective investigation of the offence", in other words so that evidence can be gathered and interviews conducted.

GOLDEN HOUR

The 'golden hour' principle is something which you are told about during your initial police training and which is periodically reinforced throughout your career. As a detective, the outcome of your criminal investigations will quite often be dictated by the actions taken, or not taken, during those critical early stages. The term 'golden hour' is also used in medicine, referring to a period of time, up to an hour or less, following traumatic injury or medical emergency, during which there is the highest likelihood that prompt medical treatment will prevent death. In policing terms, it relates to a period of time, which could be a few minutes or longer, when effective action by those responding to an incident could help to achieve a successful outcome. This could be anything from saving a life to preserving important evidence.

It's not unusual for an offender to remain at the scene of a crime or to return there a short time later. They may claim to be a witness or provide misleading information to those present in order to frustrate the investigation. In cases of arson, where a fire has been deliberately started, the person responsible could well hide nearby or mingle with a crowd of onlookers to watch the firefighters tackle the blaze. Arsonists have also been known to record their actions on a mobile phone so that they have a record which can be viewed again. The behaviour of an offender at the scene of a crime will often be linked to their desire to have 'power' and 'control' over others, particularly investigators. There have been a number of murder cases where the killer has been 'hiding in plain sight', involving themselves in the organisation of searches for the victim and providing media interviews.

During the afternoon of Sunday 4th August 2002, two 10-year-old girls, Holly Wells and Jessica Chapman, left a family barbeque to get some sweets from a local shop. They never returned home and their bodies were found in a ditch several miles away nearly two weeks later. The person who killed the girls was Ian Huntley who worked as a caretaker at a local college. During the police investigation Huntley was certainly high-profile. He was involved in the co-ordination of searches for the missing girls and could be seen in the background during television footage. On 15th August Sky News decided to re-construct the last known movements of the girls in an attempt to trace witnesses and to keep the investigation in the public interest. The reporter, Jeremy Bowen, approached a man "who may have been the last person to see the girls before they disappeared". He was standing outside his house and gave an interview during which he claimed that he didn't really know the girls but had spoken briefly with them before they walked off away from his house. The man appeared genuine and calm throughout the interview. In the background was his red Ford Fiesta car. The man was Ian Huntley and he had already killed the two girls in his house, put their bodies into the boot of his car, driven them away and left them in a ditch. He had also thoroughly cleaned the inside of the house and his car in an effort to remove any forensic evidence which may incriminate him. This is just one example of how suspects may behave in the days and sometimes weeks after committing a crime.

The 'golden hour' may also provide an opportunity to identify witnesses, particularly those who are not local. One of the most important tasks for the first officers attending the scene, as well as securing and preserving evidence, is to trace witnesses who may leave the area, possibly unaware that they have seen or heard something significant.

Forensic evidence is likely to be left at most crime scenes, the challenge is to find and recover it. This is why, particularly in more serious cases, early preservation is vital. The evidence could be fingerprints, DNA, footwear marks, fibres or perhaps even hair. If the scene is secured and protected from an early stage, the chances of a successful forensic examination are greatly increased. Forensic evidence can easily be destroyed, damaged, or removed from the scene, deliberately or otherwise, if the 'golden hour' principle isn't applied.

In addition to suspects, witnesses and forensic evidence, there may be other 'golden hour' actions (known as 'fast-track' actions) which could assist the investigation. The identification and recovery of CCTV, Automatic Number Plate Recognition (ANPR) enquiries and mobile phone data recovery are just some examples.

GUN CRIME

The number of shootings has increased across the UK during 2018 as part of the worrying trend showing an increase in violent crime. Gun crime is prevalent in London but is also happening in a number of other areas including the West Midlands, Manchester and Liverpool. Police firearms operations rose by 19% in the past year or so, as the number of armed officers has been increased amid a growing threat from terrorism and violent crime. The two main drivers of gun crime, in the capital and elsewhere, are said to be drug and gang activity. The gun has become a tool of the drug dealer to enforce their territory and their 'business'. When it comes to the highest harm gun crime, lethal guns being fired, there is a strong link to gang activity with just under half of all offences where a lethal gun was fired being gang related. The total number of murder victims in London alone this year (2018) has soared past 100, with a fair proportion of these resulting from the discharge of a firearm.

So where are these guns coming from? A high percentage of them are being 'smuggled into the country through our ports from places such as eastern and south-east Europe or through the international postal system mixed with legitimate parcels. There is also a loophole in our current gun laws, allowing handguns to be brought into the UK from the USA.

Any gun which was made before 1899 is presently classified as an 'antique' and can be legally owned as, due to its age, the ammunition required to fire it is no longer made. An example of this type of gun is the .44 Smith & Wesson Russian revolver which was developed in 1870 and is now considered to be an obsolete calibre. These types of guns are readily available to buy at gun shows in the USA and can then be brought back to the UK, providing that they are securely packaged. The buyer doesn't need to have a firearms certificate nor do they need to prove who they are when purchasing the gun. Once back in the UK, suitable ammunition can be made to enable the lethal weapon to be fired and used unlawfully. At the time of writing (October 2018) the Home Office are considering proposals for a new definition of 'antique firearms' so that old weapons also have to be licensed.

Any crime involving the possession or discharge of a firearm is a serious offence which should be investigated by detectives. The legislation which deals with these crimes is mostly contained within the Firearms Act 1968. The Act is a particularly complex piece of law which goes into great detail about everything connected with firearms and air weapons. When studying for police exams it is always one of the least popular subjects due to the content and various definitions included.

Updated 2023

From July 2022 a new digital marker is being rolled out across GP surgeries in England that will 'flag up' those who are considered medically unfit to own a firearm. Once applied to the records of a patient who has a firearms licence, it will automatically alert doctors if there has been a relevant change in their medical situation. This could include a change in their mental health, diagnosis of a neurological condition or evidence of substance abuse.

The new system will mean that GP's will be able to alert the relevant police force, who can then take steps to ensure that licensed gun holders who may no longer be fit to own a firearm are swiftly identified, their licence reviewed and, if deemed appropriate, their firearm(s) seized. The new digital marker approach is part of strengthened controls for licensed gun owners being introduced by the Home Office to provide better protection for the public from those who are medically unfit to own a firearm. The system bolsters recent statutory guidance, brought into force in November 2021, which sets out that the police cannot grant a firearms licence until they have reviewed information from a suitable qualified doctor regarding the applicant's medical history. The marker has been designed by NHS Digital to streamline the way doctors can keep track of patients who have applied for, or been granted, a firearms certificate – a process which was previously carried out manually.

The Minister for Crime, Policing and Probation commented 'We have some of the strictest gun control laws in the world and we will not hesitate to bring in even stronger processes where we see the need for them. The imminent inquest into the tragic shootings in Sussex and impending first anniversary of the horrific shootings in Plymouth are a stark reminder of how much we owe it to the public to take these matters seriously. This move is yet another example of us giving the police the tools they require to protect the public.'

CASE STUDIES – GUN CRIME
1) Two men who smuggled guns into the UK on a tourist coach have been jailed. Police stopped Nicholas Barbary and Mark Maynard on the M23 in Sussex, after following them from Coventry, where the pair had retrieved the arms cache. Both men admitted importing a pistol and two automatic sub-machine guns. Barbary was jailed for 12 years and Maynard received 16 years and two months when they appeared at Lewes Crown court. Armed officers found the haul of weapons and ammunition attached by magnets to the underside of a hire van which they stopped near Crawley in January 2017. The package had originally been attached by similar means to the bottom of a coach which had just returned from a tourist trip to Belgium. Neither the coach operator nor passengers were aware that the vehicle had been carrying the weapons. The package was found to contain a loaded Walther P38 Luger pistol, two re-activated Czechoslovakian Skorpion loaded sub-machine guns, an additional magazine and 150 rounds of ammunition.

2) Three people have been jailed for importing blank-firing guns and converting them into deadly weapons. They bought 43 replica pistols for about £150 each and over 1,000 blank-firing cartridges from an online replica handgun site. Following conversion, each firearm was sold for about £1,500. Carlington Grant, Khianna Lewis and Jermaine Dornan were found guilty of selling prohibited firearms and were sentenced to 26 years, 17 years and 9 years respectively. The court heard how Grant and Lewis funded the purchase of the guns and ammunition from a firm in Calais before converting them. Officers spotted two semi-automatic guns, hidden in a shoe box, being handed over in a West Midlands supermarket car park. Serial numbers on those guns led officers to the firm in France which had legally despatched them to an address in Cornwall. Grant and Lewis made four trips to Cornwall to collect the guns before storing and converting them on an industrial estate in West Bromwich which was later raided by police. In May 2017 another of Grant's converted pistols was dropped during an armed raid on a carpet shop in the Midlands. The proceeds of the illegal trade were used to fund a lavish lifestyle of luxury cars and regular trips abroad.

GRAPHOLOGY

As with every secondary discipline backing up detective work, graphology has a definite place and an undoubted importance. Its long history tells us that the applications of the skills integral to analysing handwriting were not always related to crime, but the subject of working in signatures attached to wills, for instance, shows its importance through time. As Barry Branston points out in his book introducing graphology (see the bibliography), the whole subject really became prominent in France around 1830.

The subject has always been linked to psychology, for obvious reasons, and a central notion in the thinking behind the analysis was created by Ludwig Klages. This was the 'Form Level' which dictates whether or not the reading will be a critical one in relation to the personality behind the written words. But in terms of its impact on life in Britain, it was not until 1936 that anything significant may be discerned. This was the publication of *Handwriting Analysis: An Introduction to Scientific Graphology* by H J Jacoby.

In more recent times there have been several prominent cases in which graphology played a major role. For instance, in the investigations related to the murder of Rachel Nickell, Kate Strzelczyk gave expert witness in the trial of Robert Napper; he was found to own some hand-written notes which described the offences which were detected alongside the Nickell case. There has also been the forged signature case of the will of a Mr Swanston.

In relation to the really significant crimes in history, arguably the part played by handwriting analysis in the Charles Lindbergh case of 1932 is one of the most outstanding ones. A ransom note by Bruno Hauptmann was central to the investigation, and an analysis by graphologists of the document led to a successful trial for kidnapping and murder, as the abducted son of Lindbergh was found dead. Hauptmann was given the death penalty.

There are always 'fringe' elements in police work, just as there are in medicine, and one feels that this part of the tool-bag of detection will remain on that fringe.

H

HISTORY OF DETECTIVES IN BRITAIN

There have always been amateur detectives. Instances may be found in classical times, and certainly, before professional detectives, certain officers of the crown undertook detective work as part of their general roles in the legal system. Bernard Knight's Crowner John novels, for instance, show what kinds of duties the 'crowner' (later coroner) did when there was a serious crime on his patch.

Ironically, when the police force was being formed in England, in 1829, the founding father of crime detection, Eugene Vidocq, was in England. He did visit the prisons of Pentonville, Newgate and Millbank, but he was really in London to organise an exhibition. He wanted to be a showman, not a professional adviser. As James Morton has commented in his biography of Vidocq: 'Not only was he on the premises during opening hours but he also put on a little production in which he appeared in various disguises, to the delight of the audience...' He had arrived in London three years after the detective force was formed, and had played no part in the detective policies; he had, however, been in London in 1835 to advise on prison discipline. He was a man who had known the worst prisons in France, as a prisoner as well as in his role as police officer. In 1845 he was thinking of starting up a detective agency, extending the one he had in France, but this was clearly not his real motive for being there.

The professional force arrived in 1842, but it took a very long time for every provincial force to have a C.I.D. This is partly because the legislation on police establishment took the greater part of the nineteenth century, and also, of course, part because of financial considerations.

There is the question of the whole range of other contexts in which the detective has moved, as his need for greater knowledge has increased. However fantastic and far-fetched we find Sherlock Holmes to be, Conan Doyle did understand the need to have knowledge or esoteric areas of life inherent in detective work. The basic skills of filing, classifying, noting observations and memorising faces and biographies is there in Holmes. The first detectives appear to have kept an immense amount of local information in their heads as they walked the streets, cultivating contacts and 'grasses.'

This process of absorbing a body of knowledge involved amateur science in all kinds of affairs. A detective in the Victorian period had to constantly add to his geographical and trade knowledge. He also had to be familiar with a complex street slang and codes of behaviour.

In the twentieth century, after the revision of the detective training curriculum in the 1930s, we have the emergence of the 'star' sleuths. These were the men the newspapers loved. Popular film and fiction had made figures such as Fabian of the Yard and Sexton Blake the epitome of the flash, showy, intelligent gentleman, an officer type who was part Holmes but part slick modern man, an habitué of parties, hotels and high-level meetings with 'top brass.' Of course, there was capital punishment until 1964, and so these new detectives with impressive credentials and equally notable cars were called on to travel into the regions and help the local bobbies. This gave the newspapers yet more fodder for their sensationalism and love of personal trivia when they made a professional into a media star.

The overall course of the evolution of the Detective in England has been one of the steady acquisition of a range of professional skills, but at the heart of this dangerous, challenging and unhealthy profession is an armoury of abilities that defy definition, ranging from instinct to incisive logic. The 'nose' of the true sleuth was learned by bumbling, naïve trial and error. The streets and their turbulent, complex network of crime and criminals taught the detective how the business of crime works. In one of the early cases of the murder of a policemen – the second murdered officer after the 1829 Act, P C Long was knifed in Charring Cross Road and a man was arrested and eventually hanged on the slenderest of details, mainly that he wore a brown coat and a witness had said the killer wore a brown coat. Place that by the side of the incredibly complex investigations of a late twentieth century murder case, when the trappings of science and professional procedure dominate every step of the police work, and the historical process is perceived clearly.

When Leonard 'Nipper ' Read, the man who caught the Krays, was finally induced to write his memoirs (with the help of James Morton) he paid tribute to the man who had taught him the detective's trade: Martin Walsh. What Read had to say about Walsh is arguably the clearest definition of standard and successful detective work ever expressed. Read said:

> 'He was, without doubt, the most dedicated man I have ever met. Everyone knew his qualities. He was tenacious and persistent. The words Could almost have been coined to describe him. He would sit, and have me sit with him, for hours on end observing a suspect. He would watch someone leave a building and say 'he'll be back.' When after a few hours I would say, as an impatient 22-year-old, that we had blown it. He would reply, 'Give it a bit longer.' ... Sure enough, the man would *return.'*

The detective needs some kind of challenge and competition to keep improving and to put up with the waiting and the boredom of the job. Martin Walsh had made that tedious element of the work his motivation and his professionalism. In the first two decades of the new detective police, the most likely reason why skills were sharpened and expertise developed was the fact that the Bow Street Patrol the detectives in the Bow Street command, were still there, some alongside the new officers, as rivals.

One of the main barriers to progress at first was the social and political context. Peel had conceived the notion of a professional police force not only because it was long overdue, but because that particular time, the late 1820s and early 1830s, was a perilous time to be alive: it was a time when the first real impact of mass immigration, extreme urban poverty, the crisis of radicalism and the challenges to the criminal justice system were all having a massive presence in both the metropolis and in the provinces. Riot and disorder had been common features across the land for the last eighty years and more were to follow in the 1830s. The previous system of runners and 'Charlies' (watchmen' had clearly been inefficient and prone to corruption.

Crime and the threat to social stability was noticeable everywhere. After all, in 1812 a Britsh Prime Minister, Spencer Perceval, had been assassinated; in 1819 the massacre of Peterloo in Manchester had shown the ordinary people that the establishment was happy to set the army on them if they gathered for a meeting; London itself had 'no-go areas' in the rookeries where criminals could escape pursuit.

Detection was to come much later, long after the ruling mindset of prevention began to be seen as a failure. The law and its personnel in all areas had to learn that if detection could be established, however clumsily and slowly, then there might be a different kind of deterrent- something totally unlike the threat of beatings, imprisonment, or transportation. As 'Plain clothes' was a detestable concept' it also took a long time for something else to be recognised: the possibility that a police officer might be capable of understanding the villains by learning their cultural basis and their sense of social identity. The 'criminal tribe' was no longer to be a separate, inscrutable sub-group in its own circumscribed 'patches.'

HOLMES (Not Sherlock)

I could have gone for Sherlock, but this version of HOLMES has to get a mention. It stands for **H**ome **O**ffice **L**arge **M**ajor **E**nquiry **S**ystem and it is now used by every British police force. The HOLMES database is a crime investigation tool which allows for all documents to be monitored and controlled throughout a major enquiry. It's used for murders, counterterrorism and other serious and/or complex cases. Every document, witness statement and exhibit is registered onto the database together with every person, address and vehicle which comes to light during the investigation. Everything is given a unique reference number, indexed and cross-referenced so that it can be found at any time in the future.

During the 1970's and early 1980's major enquiries were conducted using a paper-based system with index cards which quite often were damaged or mislaid. There was no effective communication between different police forces nor was there a system to share intelligence. Two high-profile cases brought these issues into the spotlight and resulted in action which was to greatly improve the situation. The 'Black Panther' enquiry, which involved post office raids, the murder of post office staff and the abduction and murder of an heiress, highlighted the lack of standard procedures. This concern increased with the case of the 'Yorkshire Ripper' (Peter Sutcliffe) enquiry which ran from 1974–1981. The crimes of murder and serious assault were committed in seven different police force areas. Sutcliffe appeared in several of the enquiries but once again, due to the lack of standard procedures, his name wasn't linked. It is thought that at least one death could have been avoided had those procedures existed at the time. The police forces involved were severely criticised and, during the following years, steps were taken to improve systems. The HOLMES database will allow enquiries to be linked together and to provide a searchable facility. This means that if I was investigating a murder in Nottingham and Sussex police were also investigating a murder in Brighton then, providing we had established a potential link between the two murders and both forces were using HOLMES, I could look at their database and they could look at ours. If necessary, a number of forces or departments can be linked together in the one enquiry.

The HOLMES incident room will normally contain a mixture of police officers and police support staff. There are a number of different roles which may be filled, depending on the size of the enquiry and the resources available. There will always be an office manager who supervises the day-to-day running of the room, one or more indexers who input and cross-reference data and someone who will read every document which comes into the room to identify further work. The roles of exhibits officer and disclosure officer can also be managed using the HOLMES database. In addition to the office staff, there will be at least one enquiry team, made up primarily of detectives, who will be tasked with tracing and interviewing people, checking for CCTV, taking statements and other enquiries connected with the investigation. These enquiries will be allocated to individual officers/staff, having been typed and printed out from HOLMES. They are known as Actions and are all given a unique number which is generated by the system. For example, DC Faulkner may be allocated Action 108 to carry out a visual check of High Street between numbers 1–80 in an attempt to identify any CCTV at this location and to seize any footage or make sure that it is retained. Once the Action has been completed the officer will write the result on the form and submit it back into the incident room where it will be updated. Enquiry team members are likely to have a number of Actions allocated to them at any one time. The HOLMES database enables a large amount of data to be stored securely in a system which is searchable and relatively easy to use.

HOMICIDE

Homicide is the term used to describe the killing of a person by another and includes accidental death as well as manslaughter. The word is becoming commonplace in the UK with a number of police forces adopting it in their major crime unit title. Examples include the Metropolitan Police Homicide & Major Crime Command and West Yorkshire Police Homicide and Major Enquiry Team. The term is used regularly in the USA but, like Crime Scene Investigator (CSI), it's becoming part of our everyday language. Being old-fashioned, I have always preferred to use the word Murder but, with the massive popularity of true crime TV and podcasts, the word Homicide appears to have become the 'sexier' alternative.

HUMAN RIGHTS

Human rights are designed to afford us protection and should apply to any person who is resident in the UK. The Human Rights Act is a law which was passed in 1998 and is based on the Articles of the European Convention on Human Rights (ECHR). There are 16 articles in total including Article 2 (right to life), Article 5 (right to liberty and security), Article 6 (right to a fair trial) and Article 8 (respect for private and family life). Breaches of Human Rights can, and often do, lead to further action in the courts.

Human rights are now very much a part of everyday policing and must be considered when making decisions which are likely to have an impact on other people, such as searching a house, arresting someone or detaining them at a police station. As a detective tasked with the investigation of serious crimes, your decision-making and rationale must be sound and justified. The mnemonic PLAN (Proportionate, Lawful, Accountable, Necessary) is often used to assist when documenting your thought process.

Senior police officers will use a Policy File (see **P**) to record their key decisions and the reasons why they did or didn't follow a particular course of action. As the lead detective in charge of a murder investigation this could be that you have decided to release the name and photograph of the suspect to the media before arrest, why you have decided to put the suspect under surveillance or many other key decisions. The human rights of everyone concerned and the potential impact of breaching those rights should be considered and documented by the decision-maker.

CASE STUDIES – HUMAN RIGHTS ACT

1) Two victims of John Worboys have won their claims for compensation from the Metropolitan Police after the Supreme Court ruled that the force had failed to carry out an effective investigation into the serial sex attacker. The judgement sets a far-reaching precedent for police liability, by allowing victims to argue that they have been subjected to inhuman or degrading treatment under Article 3 of the European Convention on

Human Rights. The claim was brought by two of Worboys' earliest victims, who reported attacks to the police in 2003 and 2007. The court found that, due to significant errors, police failed to charge the London black-cab driver at the time. A later review of sexual assault cases by the police finally identified Worboys' pattern of drugging and assaulting female passengers.

The Metropolitan Police stated that the court decision will result in the force having to move resources from areas such as fraud in order to comply with the judgement. A senior police officer commented "The appeal to the Supreme Court was not based on factual differences between us and the victims, but on the appropriate interpretation of Human Rights law". A solicitor for women's groups who intervened in the case claimed that forces had been paying compensation and apologising for years in cases where there were significant mistakes. The two women in the case were initially awarded compensation totalling £41,250 by the High Court, which the Metropolitan Police failed to overturn in successive appeals.

Delivering judgement in the case, Lord Kerr confirmed that previous decisions by the European Court of Human Rights in Strasbourg "establish that the state is obliged under Article 3 to conduct an effective investigation into crimes which involve serious violence to persons, whether they have been carried out by state agents or individual criminals". He qualified that right by pointing out that "simple errors or isolated omissions will not give rise to a violation of Article 3... only conspicuous or substantial errors in investigation would qualify". He added "The prospect of every complainant of burglary, car theft or fraud becoming the subject of an action under the Human Rights Act has been raised. I do not believe that this is a serious possibility". The five Supreme Court Judges disagreed about whether police liability would arise only when there had been systematic failures. They decided by a majority that failures in the investigation alone, provided they were sufficiently serious, could also give rise to liability.

2) A group of football fans are taking unprecedented legal action against a police force over allegations that they were forcibly prevented from watching a match. Bristol City Supporters Club & Trust claims that West Midlands Police breached human rights by their actions ahead of a match against Birmingham City in 2015. The group claim that the 51 fans, who were drinking at a pub in the city centre before the game, were "rounded up, branded as hooligans and forced into a 90-minute march back to the train station". The force issued a Section 35 Dispersal Order and supporters were put on trains back to Bristol, according to the group. The Trust has confirmed that it is meeting the fans' legal fees, and suing the force for claims of "false imprisonment" and a breach of Article 5 of the European Convention on Human Rights, which states that "everyone has the right to liberty and security of person". The claims for compensation were ongoing at time of writing (2018).

3) During anti-capitalist demonstrations in London on May 1st, 2001, the police cordoned in around three thousand demonstrators at Oxford Circus for up to 7 hours. The House of Lords held that measures of crowd control undertaken in the interests of the community will fall outside Article 5 (right to liberty) as long as they are not arbitrary, are resorted to in good faith, are proportionate and enforced for no longer than necessary. It was held that the use of the cordon, which had resulted in people being kept in one place without food, water or shelter, was not a deprivation of liberty and, as such, there was no breach of Article 5.

4) In 2001 the law in the UK was changed to allow the retention of fingerprints, cellular samples and DNA profiles of individuals who had not been convicted of a crime or even charged with an offence. In January 2001, S was arrested, aged 11, and charged with attempted robbery. His fingerprints and DNA were taken. Later that same year he was acquitted of the crime. M was arrested in March 2001, aged 38, and charged with harassment. His fingerprints and DNA were taken but there was no charge and the case was discontinued.

Both applicants requested that their fingerprints and DNA samples were destroyed but the police refused, indicating that the Chief Constable had a policy of retaining samples in all cases. The applicants contended that retention was incompatible with their right to respect for private life under Article 8. The Grand Chamber of the European Court of Human Rights held that the 'blanket' approach of the UK to the retention of DNA from individuals not convicted of an offence was a disproportionate interference with respect for private life under Article 8.

HYPOTHESIS

A hypothesis is a supposition or proposed explanation made on the basis of limited evidence as a starting point for further investigation. In other words, you have a certain amount of information but not the whole picture so you consider possible theories. Detectives hypothesise, probably without realising it, during their investigations as they try to establish who committed the crime, how and why. As the Senior Investigating Officer (SIO) in a murder case you are encouraged to hypothesise during the initial stages and throughout the investigation. You must keep an open mind but there is no harm in considering alternative explanations as long as you document your thought-process and rationale. The SIO should involve members of the investigative team and experts such as forensic scientists and the pathologist in this process when appropriate.

To give you an example, if the murder victim had been found in a remote, rural ditch alongside a vehicular track then it may be reasonable to hypothesise that the offender may have some local knowledge of the area (due to the remote location) and that they may have used a vehicle to get there and leave (due to the lack of other reasonable alternatives). There is no harm in this type of approach as long as no assumptions are made or other explanations ruled out without supporting evidence.

CASE STUDY – HYPOTHESIS

The totally naked body of a 17-year-old female was found in the rear alleyway of an area frequented by sex workers and their clients. Two known criminals discovered the body and called the police. The victim was known locally as a drug user. There were no visible signs of injury other than what appeared to be needle marks on her arms and some small circular marks on her face. The victim was lying on the ground on her back in some dirt and there were no traces of her clothing. A post-mortem examination revealed that she had been strangled by unknown means and had died of asphyxiation. There was no evidence of a sexual assault. It was not clear how the victim had ended up at the location, what exactly had happened nor why she was naked. Local sex workers confirmed that they never completely undressed for clients as it was too dangerous and limited their means of a quick escape. The pathologist was of the opinion that there were very few or no defensive marks on the body and the crime scene examiners were initially unsure about where the murder had taken place.

The following hypotheses were considered by the investigation team –

1) The two known criminals who found the body committed the murder.
2) The murder had taken place in nearby flats habitually used by drug abusers and sex workers. The offender or someone else who found the body then panicked and deposited it in the adjacent alleyway.
3) The victim was murdered at the location where the body was found.
4) The murder took place elsewhere and this was a deposition site.
5) The victim had been murdered by a client who was having sex with her at the location. He/she removed and took the clothing to destroy trace evidence or retained it as a 'trophy'.
6) A vehicle was involved and the victim was engaging in sexual activity, death occurring after she had voluntarily or forcibly removed her clothing.
7) The victim was murdered by a friend, boyfriend or relative for reasons unknown.
8) The death was unintentional and may have occurred during an act of autoeroticism.
9) There was no vehicle involved and the victim was on foot with a client.

As you can see there are a number of hypotheses, and perhaps more you can think of, to explain the scenario faced by the police at this early stage of the investigation. Any one or a combination of these hypotheses was initially considered feasible by the SIO. As the enquiry progressed and more material and information became available, a number of the theories were ruled out.

Tyre impressions were later discovered at the scene and it transpired that a vehicle had been used by the offender. The victim had been strangled after sexual intercourse with a client in his car. The actual motive for the murder was never clear but the victim had agreed or was coerced into taking all her clothes off. The body had been dragged out of the car and left in the alleyway, and clothing was later deposited in a skip away from the scene. Through a process of interviewing previous clients and associates, a possible offender was eventually traced and arrested. The tyres on his vehicle matched those recovered from the scene and some fibres from the victim's clothing were found in the boot of his car. After a reconstruction the car appeared the same as a grainy image captured on CCTV, showing a person putting what looked like clothing into a waste disposal skip. The offender was convicted and sentenced to life imprisonment. On this occasion the hypotheses at 5 and 6 were correct along with either 3 or 4.

I

ICIDP

The Initial Crime Investigators Development Programme (ICIDP) is a national programme which has been designed to identify, train and improve the skills of those officers who are to become the detectives of the future. I would refer to this programme as an 'apprenticeship' for those who want to work in CID or specialist investigative roles. The programme can last up to 2 years and consists of a number of different stages, all of which have to be successfully navigated before confirmation as a Detective Constable. The vast majority of people who enter the programme are Constables striving to become detectives but occasionally a Sergeant or Inspector, with no previous investigative experience, may be required to complete the ICIDP programme. An example of this may be a person who is transferring from a uniformed post into a specialist role such as child abuse investigation which requires accredited investigators.

The first part of the programme (Phase I) begins with an induction day where the prospective trainee investigator (TI) is issued with ICIDP distance learning manuals and is required to study the material over a minimum period of 12 weeks. They are then required to sit a written examination known as the National Investigators Examination (NIE). The exam consists of 80 multiple-choice questions testing knowledge of law and procedure relevant to the role of a trainee investigator. You have to pass the exam before moving on to the next stage of the programme. Any candidate who failed to pass the exam before November 2010 was given two further attempts but from that date onwards, they are only allowed one further attempt. Failure to pass the exam results in a withdrawal from the programme and a minimum period of 18 months must pass before the officer becomes eligible to attempt the ICIDP programme again.

Phase II involves attendance on a course which aims to build on the distance learning study for the examination. The course is normally around six weeks and often includes an interview training course in relation to witnesses and suspects. Attendance on Phase II should be commenced within 12 months from the date the trainee investigator achieved a pass in their NIE. Depending on the force the course may be residential with candidates staying at a training college during the week. They will also have to complete a project during the course which they will be required to present to senior managers. The ICIDP course is designed to cover everything required by the modern detective and is the equivalent of what used to be called the CID course.

The final phase of the programme (Phase III) involves assessment in the workplace where the trainee investigator has to gather evidence of their performance in their work role against the National Occupational Standards required in order to complete the programme. They will be allocated a tutor (an experienced DC who has received training in the role of tutor) who will mentor and assess them against a number of competencies such as gathering evidence, searching a suspect, interviewing a suspect and preparing a case file. The portfolio of evidence will be overseen by a local CID supervisor, normally a Detective Sergeant, and can only contain evidence gathered following the completion of Phase II. Once all competencies have been satisfactorily evidenced and met, the portfolio will be checked and 'signed off' by a senior manager and the force Head of Crime. At this point the trainee investigator will be eligible to become a Detective Constable.

INFORMANT

The practice of people giving information to the police in return for financial or other gain is well-established. These people, who are mostly referred to in negative terms such as 'grass, snitch or nark', are at risk of serious injury or worse should their identity and actions become known to the criminal world. The most effective informants are often those who are involved in crime themselves or relatives of criminals who disagree with their unlawful activity. There are many reasons why people may want to give information to the police. If their information has a positive outcome, they may receive payment (which will vary according to the seriousness of the crime and the result). They may provide information in an attempt to remove a threat to them, either criminally or physically. If the informant helps to convict others through their co-operation with the police, they may receive a lesser sentence for their part in that crime or others. In some cases, to keep the process confidential, the police may draft a letter to the Judge (known as a 'text') outlining the circumstances and detailing how the informant assisted the investigation. Neither the existence of the 'text' nor the content will be discussed in open court. The information supplied by informants could be in relation to relatively low-level crime, serious and organised crime or even counterterrorism (as depicted in the 2018 drama *Informer*). Whatever your view, informants can play a very important role in the prevention and detection of crime.

When I joined the police in the early 1980's there were very few checks in place to monitor how, and in what circumstances, informants were used. Detectives would often try to avoid discussing the existence of an informant and record-keeping was poor. The system was open to abuse from both sides. A Scotland Yard investigation into the vicious death of private investigator Daniel Morgan (1987) was condemned years later when it was revealed that a detective had 'coached' his informant. During the 1990's it was discovered that Scotland Yard was using Jamaican 'Yardie' gangsters as informants without realising that they were continuing their criminal activities at the same time. This situation led to stringent oversight of the informant system with new rules and a code of practice.

Police now refer to informants as a Covert Human Intelligence Source (CHIS) and there are strict guidelines in place regarding their use and conduct. Their use has been regulated by the Regulation of Investigatory Powers Act 2000 (RIPA – pronounced 'reaper') since its inception into UK law in October 2000. The legal definition of a CHIS is –

'A person who establishes or maintains a relationship with another person for the covert purpose of obtaining information or providing access to information to another person, or covertly disclosing information obtained by the use of such a relationship, or as a consequence of the existence of such a relationship'.

This is a real mouthful but, in a nutshell, it's about covertly gathering information from another person without them knowing why or what you intend doing with that information.

The person who registers a CHIS and meets with them, as and when required, is known as the 'handler'. They will have responsibility for directing the activities of the CHIS on a daily basis, recording the information supplied by the CHIS and looking after their welfare. Guidelines state that the 'handler' should have a 'co-handler' who provides support, may also attend meetings and takes on the role of the 'handler' in their absence. The person who is responsible for the management and supervision of the 'handler' together with general oversight of the use of the CHIS is known as the 'controller'. This person will be of a higher rank than the 'handler'.

The use of a CHIS is very much a part of modern detective work and the gathering of information from these 'sources' is a standard line of enquiry in most major crime investigations. The SIO will record details of any CHIS-related 'tasking' in a sensitive Policy File along with any other covert or intelligence issues. It was revealed that police had paid out a total of £20 million to informants during a five-year period ending 2017.

I'll leave the last word on the subject of informants to DCI Gene Hunt "Every DCI worth his badge needs a few people he can call on who have their ears to the ground and greedy enough pockets to share what they know. This is also where an officer knows to play the long game – don't go nicking everyone with criminal connections, let the little fish keep swimming for a while. They pay for their freedom by making sure they keep you on track with the big boys".

Updated 2023

Recently, in one year alone, Covert Human Intelligence Source (CHIS) operations enabled the National Crime Agency (NCA) to disrupt over 30 threats to life, arrest numerous serious organised criminals, seize over 3000kg of Class A drugs, safeguard over 200 people, and take nearly 60 firearms and 4000 rounds of ammunition off the streets. In the last year, the Metropolitan Police have made 3500 arrests, recovered over 500 weapons and over £2.5 million in cash, as a direct result of CHIS operations. CHIS are also crucial in preventing and safeguarding victims from involvement in many serious crimes including terrorism, drugs and firearms offences and child sexual exploitation.

Participation in criminal conduct is an essential and inescapable feature of CHIS use, enabling them to appear credible and gain the trust of those who are under investigation. This participation allows them to work their way into the heart of groups seeking to cause us harm, gathering information and intelligence which other investigative measures are unlikely to ever detect.

The **Covert Human Intelligence Sources (Criminal Conduct) Act 2021** makes provision to authorise CHIS to participate in conduct which would otherwise constitute a criminal offence. The Act provides a clear legal basis for a longstanding tactic which is vital for national security and crime prevention/detection. The Act includes an insertion into the *Regulation of Investigatory Powers Act (RIPA) 2000* which creates a Criminal Conduct Authorisation (CCA) allowing undercover law enforcement agents or covert sources to break the law if it is considered to be in the interests of national security, to prevent or detect crime or disorder or in the interests of the economic well-being of the UK (*Section 29B RIPA*). Any application for

THE A–Z OF DETECTIVE WORK

such conduct must be proportionate, only used to prevent more serious crimes from being committed, and when there is no other practicable legal path by which the same outcome could be achieved. Further insertions introduce safeguards in circumstances where the covert source is under 18 (*Section 29C*) or a vulnerable adult (*Section 29D*).

Further information about the Covert Human Intelligence Sources (Criminal Conduct) Act 2021 can be found by visiting the following link: https://www.legislation.gov.uk/ukpga/2021/4/contents/enacted.

INTERVIEWS

Interviews with suspects are a vital part of a detective's work although most of those interviews are carried out by DC's, and sometimes DS's, as the higher ranks normally manage the interview process rather than conducting it themselves. Part of the initial training of a detective will include a specialist interview course which will provide the opportunity to conduct interviews in a training environment. Interviewing is a skill and a good interviewer is an asset to any criminal investigation.

Equipment

There was a time, many years ago, when suspect interviews were conducted on paper with the interviewing officer writing down all questions and answers contemporaneously. As you can imagine this was a very slow process and, in some cases, was open to abuse. The tape-recording of interviews greatly improved not only the flow of the interview but also the integrity of the whole process. Two (sometimes three) audio tapes were inserted into the tape machine before the button was pressed and the interview commenced. These tapes had been initially sealed in cellophane before being opened by the interviewing officer in the presence of the suspect. At the end of the interview the tapes would be removed from the machine and one would be sealed up (known as the master tape) with an adhesive label which the suspect would be invited to sign. The suspect (or their solicitor if represented) would be entitled to be provided with a copy of the interview tape. The master tape would be treated as an exhibit and would be stored securely pending any future court case. Forces are now starting to use DVD recording equipment rather than just audio. The process of opening and sealing the discs is the same unless the footage is recorded straight onto a hard drive or secure digital network, in which case local force policy would apply.

The video recording of interviews is becoming more common, particularly in serious crime investigations. In a murder enquiry, it's likely that some members of the victim's family may be interviewed on video as well as anyone who may have witnessed events closely connected to the offence. This approach is considered to be good practice as it provides the greatest opportunity of securing best evidence. The interview of a murder suspect needs to be well-planned and co-ordinated by an officer who is specially trained. They are known as the 'interview advisor' and will often be a Detective Sergeant (sometimes an experienced DC). They won't conduct the interviews but will oversee the process, briefing and de-briefing the interviewing officers at regular intervals. It's common practice for the suspect to be interviewed several times throughout their detention in serious/complex cases.

PEACE interview model

The PEACE model of interviewing is recognised as best practice when interviewing victims, witnesses and suspects. It is implemented nationally amongst all police services, has been used for a number of years and has a proven track record. It provides a structure to the interview process and helps to ensure that all relevant points are covered.

PEACE is an acronym as follows –
P – Planning and preparation (essential for a good interview)
E – Engage and explain (introductions and reason for interview)
A – Account, clarify and challenge (obtaining an account of events)
C – Closure (confirm account and allow clarification)
E – Evaluation (reflect on information given and identify further action)

The planning and preparation phase of an interview involves a review of the available evidence and the offence concerned. This should include the legal points to prove for that offence and any statutory defences. The suspect may provide a full account during interview but they may adopt a different approach. They have the right to have a solicitor present (except in really serious cases where certain conditions apply). These days it's quite common for a suspect to provide a 'no comment' interview. This may involve them actually saying the words "no comment" in answer to every question or not speaking at all during the interview. If this happens, the interviewing officer(s) should still ask the questions they have prepared as they have a duty to investigate the circumstances. If the suspect says nothing during an interview, then provides an explanation at a subsequent court case, then the court may consider why this explanation wasn't given at that time. This is known as drawing an "adverse inference" and forms part of the police caution which should be given at the start of each suspect interview (You do not have to say anything but it may harm your defence if you do not mention when questioned something which you later rely on in court. Anything you do say may be given in evidence). In addition to a 'no comment' interview the suspect may provide a written statement, known as a 'prepared statement' outlining some information but then declining to answer any questions put to them. This often happens when the suspect is legally represented. The interviewing officers should continue with their questions and should take possession of the written statement as this will form part of the evidence in the case.

INSPECTOR

When the term was first coined, in the first logistical operations organising the new police in 1829, the two men who ran the force, Rowan and Mayne, the inspector was second to the superintendent in the station. The latter was conceived as a basic administrative unit in London, with the line of command being Superintendent- Inspector – Sergeant – Constables. This was the basic hierarchy until Sir Richard Mayne died in 1868.

In terms of the detective branch, the inspector was properly known as the Divisional Detective Inspector. In the first phase of policing, up to the early twentieth century, the idea was that the inspector at a station would eventually move along to the CID and then the career aims would be to attain the rank of Chief Inspector and Superintendent. Some remained in one area, and became Local Inspectors.

INTERPOL

This is the abbreviation for the International Criminal Police Organisation, with its central HQ in France. It was first established in Austria, back in 1923, with the name of International Criminal Police Commission. In 1966 it became Interpol. When it was first modernised, after World War 2, the structure was that each nation in its ranks set up its own group, known in Britain as the National Criminal Intelligence Service. Now, it is simply an alliance of organisations; it does not have detectives in its ranks, who swoop on criminals across the globe and drag them in for questioning. But what it does have is a massive information store.

Its constitution gives the clearest definition of what it exists to do: its function is 'To ensure and promote the widest possible mutual assistance between all criminal police authorities within the limits of the laws existing in the different countries and in the spirit of the Universal Declaration of Human Rights.' The second key article is: 'To establish and develop all institutions likely to contribute effectively to the prevention and suppression of ordinary law crimes.'

Recent developments have shown that the general assembly and presidential status are potentially open to illegal influence, and so, as with all international bodies depending on the probity of its upper echelons, the issue is raised of *quis custodiet custodes*? That is, who will supervise and watch the supervisors and watchers?

But certainly, in an age in which mass communications have become so sophisticated, and in which computer technology has developed in leaps and bounds with every passing hour, Interpol has become a highly valued institution. In today's world, speed of global communication is essential in detection, and the concept behind Interpol has been continuously streamlined over the years.

IOPC

The Independent Office for Police Conduct (IOPC) is the new name given to what used to be called the Independent Police Complaints Commission (IPCC) which oversees the police complaints system in England and Wales. They tend to deal with the more serious cases and have doubled in size since 2013 due to a rise in the number of investigations. One of their key areas of work is in relation to the review of deaths during or following contact with police. Examples may include a death in police custody, following a police pursuit or where there has been police contact or attendance prior to a murder. The IOPC are independent of the police, government and interest groups. They will respond to referrals from police forces by assessing the information supplied to decide whether it requires an investigation. There are four different types of investigation. An' independent' investigation will be dealt with by the IOPC using their own investigators. A 'managed' investigation will be carried out by the local force complaints department under the direction of the IOPC. A 'supervised' investigation is carried out by the local force complaints department under the supervision of the IOPC. Finally, a 'local' investigation is carried out by the force complaints department with no involvement from the IOPC.

J

JOINT ENTERPRISE

There are a number of ways that a person can be convicted of a crime in which they did not play the decisive role – or even, perhaps, any role at all. Collectively, they are known as 'joint enterprise', a principle of common law stretching back hundreds of years. In one well-known case, from 1952, Derek Bentley was convicted of murder after his accomplice in a burglary, Christopher Craig, shot a police officer. "Let him have it, Chris," Bentley had said, perhaps telling Craig to hand over his weapon – or perhaps, as the prosecution argued, urging him to fire.

Under joint enterprise, Bentley had provided what is known as "assistance or encouragement" and was therefore just as guilty as Craig, the 'principal' offender. Bentley received a pardon in 1998, although he had been hanged 45 years previously.

A more recent controversial example was the conviction of Laura Mitchell and her boyfriend, Michael Hall. One night in 2007, the couple, and two other people they were with, got into a fight in a car park outside a Bradford pub, with a man named Andrew Ayres, over the booking of a taxi. Mitchell and Hall then left the scene to search a different part of the car park for her lost shoes. In the meantime, the other two defendants went to a nearby house and armed themselves with knuckledusters and other weapons. In a second, more serious fight, which did not involve Mitchell or Hall, Ayres was killed. The two armed men were convicted of murder, but so too were Mitchell and Hall. Their convictions were upheld by an Appeals Court in 2016. There are many more cases which fall into the 'joint enterprise' category.

The law in relation to 'joint enterprise' was challenged in 2016 following the case of Ameen Jogee, who had been convicted of 'joint enterprise' murder in relation to the death of former Leicestershire police officer, Paul Fyfe, in 2011. While the court heard that it had been Jogee's friend who had stabbed the victim, he had 'egged' him on. Both were convicted of murder and given life sentences. During an appeal, Jogee argued that he was not inside the house when the incident took place and could not have foreseen what his friend intended to do. Delivering the judgement at the Supreme Court, Lord Neuberger said that it was wrong to treat "foresight" as a sufficient test to convict someone of murder. The Supreme Court "set aside" Jogee's conviction but he was subsequently convicted of manslaughter and remained in custody. The Supreme Court ruled that the law on 'joint enterprise' had been wrongly interpreted for more than 30 years. The ruling does not mean that those convicted under 'joint enterprise' will automatically be able to appeal their conviction. The change to the law is not retrospective, therefore a person would have to show that they would suffer "substantial injustice" if they were not allowed to appeal. The ruling applies to cases in England, Wales, Northern Ireland and most UK overseas common law territories but not in Scotland, which has its own rules on 'joint enterprise'.

CASE STUDY – JOHN CRILLY

A man has been released from prison after becoming the first person since 2016 to have a joint enterprise murder conviction quashed. John Crilly has been released after serving 13 years in prison, having been given a life sentence for murder and robbery in 2005. Crilly and an associate, David Flynn, broke into the home of a 71-year-old man in Manchester. The victim died after being punched in the face by Flynn. During his time in prison, Crilly started a law degree. When he heard about the overturning of the joint enterprise law in 2016, he believed that it would apply to his case. He launched a second appeal (the first having failed in 2007) which was successful. He then pleaded guilty to manslaughter and was released due to the time already served. Crilly commented "If you take the 'foresight' burden of proof away, and go on intent, which you're supposed to do, it's impossible to convict me of murder". The victim's family commented "These High Court rulings which lean too favourably towards the offenders and virtually casting aside the opinions, consideration and feelings of victims and their families, help to corrode and undermine public confidence in the justice system".

JOURNALISTS

Long gone are the days of clandestine meetings and pub lunches between journalists and detectives but the relationships between the two are equally as important these days. Both have jobs to do and can help each other out without jeopardising an investigation. The corruption of decades ago, when some detectives would tip off journalists in return for a financial or other incentive, are thankfully in the past. The press have a critical role to play today as TV, radio and social media bring news to us instantaneously. Footage of a crime often appears on a public forum before the police may even be aware of it. As a detective it's important that you involve the press when appropriate as they can be the best way to reassure the community, seek witnesses or appeal for information. In a serious investigation, such as a murder, an initial 'holding statement' will normally be released before additional information as and when appropriate. A Journalist 'door-stepping' in the area could have an adverse impact on the investigation so it's important to keep the press updated when possible. A media or press officer, employed by the force, is invaluable in maintaining positive relationships with journalists and ensuring that they are updated when possible. This also takes some of the pressure off the SIO who will have a number of other demands to manage.

Journalists, for their part, should report responsibly or risk the wrath of the courts. The media may discover that someone is being investigated by the police or another agency- for example, that the person is under arrest. If a media report publishes the suspect's name, or other detail identifying him/her in this context, that person could successfully sue the publisher for libel if the investigation does not lead to a prosecution. Publishing a statement that someone is under investigation, even when this is factually correct, is defamatory because it creates an inference that the person may be guilty.

CASE STUDY – CHRIS JEFFERIES

In 2011 Bristol landlord Chris Jefferies won 'very substantial' settlements in libel actions against eight national newspapers for articles published after one of his tenants, Joanna Yeates, was found dead. Mr. Jefferies had been arrested at one stage by the police but was later released without charge. The newspapers published defamatory material about him. Another man, Louis Charalambous, was charged with the murder of Joanna. Mr. Jefferies' solicitor commented "Christopher Jefferies is the latest victim of the regular witch hunts and character assassination conducted by the worst elements of the British tabloid media".

The same case saw contempt of court issues resulting from media reporting. *The Daily Mirror* and *The Sun* were fined £50,000 and £18,000 respectively over coverage of the arrest of Chris Jefferies. The court heard that one Daily Mirror front page carried the headline 'Jo Suspect is Peeping Tom' beneath a photograph of Mr. Jefferies, and another front-page headline read 'Was killer waiting in Jo's flat?', with sub-headings below reading 'Police seize bedding for tests' and 'Landlord held until Tuesday'. The Sun's front-page headline read 'Obsessed by Death' next to a photograph of Mr. Jefferies and below the words 'Jo Suspect "Scared Kids"'.

The Attorney General at the time said that material in the articles gave an 'overall impression' that Mr. Jefferies had a 'propensity' to commit the kind of offences for which he had been arrested. The Lord Chief Justice, Lord Judge, said that section 2(2) of the Contempt of Court Act 1981 provided that the strict liability contempt rule applied only to a publication which created a substantial risk that the course of justice in the proceedings in question 'will be seriously impeded or prejudiced'. Vilification of a suspect under arrest was a potential impediment to the course of justice, he said, adding "At the simplest level, publication of such material may deter or discourage witnesses from coming forward and providing information helpful to the suspect, which may, (depending on the circumstances) help immediately to clear him of suspicion or enable his defence to be fully developed at trial. This may arise, for example, because witnesses may be reluctant to be associated with or perceived to be a supporter of the suspect, or, again, because they may begin to doubt whether information apparently favourable to the suspect could possibly be correct". Both newspapers expressed an intention to appeal to the Supreme Court.

K

KEY, OR SIGNIFICANT WITNESS

There are three categories of witness for whom there is a requirement to video-record witness testimonies, provided they consent. These are vulnerable, intimidated and key or significant witnesses. A key or significant witness (KSW) is the category most likely to be encountered by a detective, particularly in serious crime investigations. It is an important function and responsibility of the SIO to identify and designate those witnesses who should be afforded KSW status. Such a decision should be documented in the policy file and contained within a witness strategy. In some cases, it may also be necessary to explain why a witness has not been granted KSW status in order to pre-empt questions, should they be asked in future court proceedings. Key or significant witnesses are those who

- have or claim to have witnessed, visually or otherwise, an indictable offence, part of such an   offence or events closely connected with it (including any incriminating comments made by the suspected offender either before or after the offence) ; and/or
- have a particular relationship to the victim or have a central position in an investigation into an indictable offence

While significant witnesses are usually defined with reference to indictable-only offences (those triable at Crown Court), investigating officers may consider designating witnesses as significant in any other serious case where it may be helpful. Interviews with significant witnesses should usually be video recorded because they are likely to increase the amount and quality of information gained from the witness and increase the amount of information reported by the witness being recorded. Video-recorded interviews with significant witnesses can also have the additional benefits of safeguarding the integrity of the interview process and increasing the opportunities for the monitoring and development of interview skills.

In a murder investigation there are likely to be several key or significant witnesses. These could include a person who was present when the murder took place, (who is not suspected at that time) a person who has witnessed important events (such as immediately before or after the murder) and a close family member/friend of the victim who is able to supply important background and family history. The use of video-recorded interviews can be resource-intensive and, as such, the SIO will have to prioritise. An alternative option is to audio-record the evidence, which has the same benefits as a video-recording in terms of the amount and quality of information gathered.

Sometimes a person who has been treated as a key or significant witness can become a suspect as the investigation unfolds. In such a case, the account provided by this person during the video-recorded interview can be re-examined in detail and analysed by behavioural experts who may be able to provide an opinion on the content and body language of the interviewee. This expert advice could inform and assist a future suspect interview.

KEYLESS CAR CRIME

Recent years have seen an increase in vehicle theft and keyless car crime is definitely contributing to those statistics. More than 600,000 cars were stolen in the UK in 1992, but thanks to improved vehicle security and a crackdown on thieves, that number began to fall drastically. By 2016 the number of stolen vehicles had reduced to around 56,000. Unfortunately, the numbers have begun to rise and the number for 2017 was confirmed as 89,000. It has been suggested that keyless entry cars seem to be the reason behind this rise. At one time it was just the high-end executive vehicles which had this system but these days a lot of new cars are supplied without a key, opened using the key fob and started by pushing a button inside the vehicle.

The method used by organised criminals to steal a car via keyless theft, also known as relay theft, is relatively simple. The purchase of a relay amplifier and a relay transmitter, both can be obtained from the internet for less than £100, makes this type of crime an effective way to steal a keyless vehicle. One criminal will stand next to the target car holding the transmitter, while a second criminal waves the amplifier adjacent to the walls outside the front of the house. If the car key fob is close enough (estimated to be between 5–20 metres) the amplifier will detect its signal, amplify it and send it to the transmitter held by the accomplice. This transmitter then effectively becomes the key and tricks the car into thinking that the genuine key is nearby, whereupon it opens the vehicle and allows the criminals to simply get in and drive it away. It takes a matter of seconds to commit this type of crime and the car, particularly if it's a top of the range, will often end up being shipped abroad or to a chop-shop (where prestige cars arc broken down for parts). As if having your car stolen isn't bad enough, some insurance companies are refusing to pay out as the theft leaves no trace of a forced entry (broken glass) and they may infer that you may have forgotten to lock your vehicle.

If you do own a keyless car then there are steps that you can take to prevent this from happening to you. Whether you have a keyless car or a car which uses a key, it's never a good idea to leave the key/fob anywhere near the front door or in clear view. If you are unfortunate enough to be the victim of a burglary, and your keys are on display, it's very likely that your car may be taken as well as other items. If you have a keyless car then you should make sure that your fob is well away from any doors or windows so that any attempt to pick up the signal won't be successful. It's also a good idea to put your fob into something which will block the signal. You can buy a Faraday pouch or RFID wallet or use a tin but you need to check that the signal is actually blocked. You can do this simply by placing the fob inside the container and trying to activate your car. If it's a suitable container you won't be able to activate your car while the fob remains inside. Other suggestions include wrapping the fob in tin foil when not in use or putting your fob in the microwave or fridge. You may also wish to use some visual security on your vehicle such as a steering lock or wheel clamp as a preventative measure. Car manufacturers are working on counter-measures to combat the issue of keyless theft, with new radio technology, software and keys among the developments but we should all try to limit the opportunities for criminals to commit this type of crime.

CASE STUDY – KEYLESS CAR THEFT

The victim of a hi-tech keyless car theft has spoken out to warn others about the crime and try to help prevent further offences. Zuffar Haq, from the Derby area, recently had his Range Rover stolen from his driveway following a crime which took less than a minute to carry out. The thieves used a transmitter which sent a signal to the vehicle's key-fob inside the house, triggering access to the vehicle. They then simply opened the door, pressed the ignition button and drove the vehicle away. The use of electronic devices to steal cars was relatively unheard of until about five years ago. Now, criminals are picking up on the technology, which can be bought cheaply online. As the trend increases, motorists are taking steps to block the signals from reaching their fobs, including storing them in microwave ovens or fridges. Mr. Haq, a Neighbourhood Watch member, now wraps his key fob in foil and keeps it in a tin can. He commented "The key fob was inside the house, approximately 20ft away from the front door but it still worked and opened the car. It was all caught on a neighbour's CCTV camera and it shows the men walking onto the drive, getting into the car and driving off. It was all over in less than a minute. I had heard about this method of stealing cars but I didn't realise how easy and quick it is for them. My reason for talking about it publicly is to warn people that there are thieves stealing vehicles with these devices. Luckily, we had a Tracker on the car which has now been found".

KING'S AND QUEEN'S MESSENGERS

Some of the most compelling historical stories come from the footnotes: the intriguing little small-print sentence at the bottom of the page that invites some further enquiry. When that note is combined with something puzzling and entirely new to the writer, then something opens out- an invitation to dig a little more deeply into the archives perhaps. That is exactly what happened when the idea for this book began. I have written widely in criminal history, and in the course of researching material for *Criminal River*, a history of the Thames River Police, I came across a paragraph recording an arrest made by 'two of the King's Messengers.' In 1810 two Messengers had arrested a man suspected of committing treason. They were not police officers.

In the course of dredging the archives of law and order in Regency England, when the River Police were being formed, I tended to encounter glimpses of these puzzling officers, in such snippets as these:

'On Friday, between six and seven o'clock, Mr Staley, a King's Messenger, was stopped by a single highwayman between Butcher's Grove and Granford bridge on the Hounslow Road, but on presenting a blunderbuss the highwayman rode off. As he was going out of the road his horse stumbled and threw him, upon which he post-boy pursued him...

'Mr Ellys, one of the King's oldest Messengers, on his return home from Minto, the seat of Sir Gilbert Elliot, had nearly lost his life by the carelessness of the driver; the chaise overturned and dragged but by the presence of mind of the old gentleman, he received only a few bruises.

'Sunday night Mr Flint, one of the King's Messengers, arrived at the Duke of Leeds's office with dispatches from Mr Whitworth,

His Majesty's Minister at the court of Petersburg. He was also charged with dispatches from Mr Ewart, the British Minister at Berlin...

Who were these men, who in 1810, when there was no national police force, made an arrest in London? They were not Bow Street Runners, that elite force stemming from Henry and John Fielding's mid-eighteenth-century police court and network of thief-catchers. They were not military personnel. In an age in which proper professional police forces were being discussed and theorized, here were some men who were acting as officers with a power of arrest.

The year was important. In 1810, the paranoia created here in Britain by events across the Channel was at its height. In 1799–1800 the Combination Acts had been passed, and these made it clear that fear was in the streets; gatherings of more than a few folk on street corners were seditious; printers, writers and journalists were likely to be prosecuted and tried sometimes without a trail being guilty *in absentia* as the writ of Habeas Corpus was suspended. Only a year after these strange arrests, the Luddite violence was to erupt in Yorkshire, as machine-wreckers set to work on mills; the Bow Street Runners had been sent up to Huddersfield to help investigate workers' militancy. The special constables were called out. The militia were cleaning their guns.

In the midst of this, two King's Messengers made an arrest. I investigated the case a little, and sure enough, they were part of a very well-established corps of special government officials, and among other things, they had powers of arrest. But as their job title implies, they were essentially people who carried messages for the sovereign, and indeed that is what they are today, though much reduced in number.

But the sense of these men being engaged in something highly dangerous was increased when I learned that they are individuals who work alone, trusted with diplomatic baggage, and who travel almost anywhere. Today of course, there will be many technological developments that make the work more manageable and less risky, but I imagined a man in say 1850 travelling by rail from London to Turkey, with a briefcase strapped to his arm, with no military escort. He was the James Bond of Victoria's state.

Inevitably, as a historian, I have gathered many more questions about these people. The popular media would have us believe that the job began with Richard III, but in fact, they were probably around in Saxon times, working for Alfred and Ethelred. In their role as considered today, though, the tale of their real professional existence, in the reign of Charles II, is probably a valid line of thought. The story is that when Charles was living in exile, he arranged for four trustworthy men to work for him, maintaining contact with home. He supposedly took a silver bowl which had four greyhound figures as part of its design, broke them off, and gave one to each man. They were from that moment, 'silver greyhounds.'

One of the most vivid accounts we have of some of these little-known characters comes from Victorian periodicals. In *The Strand Magazine* in 1896, for instance, we have some profiles of the men: Harry Taylor is pictured muffled in a massive fur coat and fez; Conway Seymour is huge, dignified and reflective; Captain Philip Wynter is every inch the officer, with his solid moustache, immaculately cut and combed sideburns and fixed glare of command. One picture in the feature shows 'the late Major H. Byng Hall, Queen's Messenger, surrounded by the fruits of his many travels.' He sits in a splendid study, so full that it rivals a room of Sir John Soane's, with urns, sketches, statuettes and curios cramming the study as Byng Hall himself writes on a map.

They were mostly army men, the types of retired officers who continuously returned to civvy street and took up responsible posts such as prison governors or administrators in the civil service. Their work has always been a mystery it seems. The writer of *The Strand* feature, J.Holt Schooling, expressed this curious situation in just the way we might do so now: 'The silver greyhound has been from time immemorial the badge set apart for the Queen's (or King's) Foreign Service Messengers. Most of us know that such persons exist, but there is only a very hazy notion of who Queen's Messengers are, and beyond the fact that they '"carry the despatches" very little is known about these gentlemen and their duties.'

Their story takes us from obscure beginnings through to the Messengers in diplomatic work, and along the way, there are a few candidates for the James Bond role. In Chaucer's time, as J.J. Jusserand explained, they were more Basildon Bond than James Bond: 'The king kept twelve messengers with a fixed salary; they followed him everywhere, in constant readiness to start; they received three pence a day and eight pence a year to buy shoes.' But by 1890 they were very special officials, men of the highest probity and trust. Fortunately for the modern reader in search of a dramatic narrative, their lives and adventures were not without incident and adventure.

L

LIFE ON MARS
Life on Mars is a British television series broadcast in 2006–7 which tells the fictional story of Sam Tyler, a DCI with Greater

Manchester Police. After being hit by a car in 2006, Tyler awakens in 1973 to find himself working for the Manchester and Salford police, a predecessor of GMP. Although at the same police station he now finds himself a Detective Inspector, working under the command of DCI Gene Hunt. The series tended to depict CID in the 70's as heavy-drinking and about as politically incorrect as you can get with sexism, racism and the odd homophobic comment thrown in. The BBC defended their position, stating that the characters, particularly DCI Hunt, were "extreme and tongue-in-cheek".

I didn't join the regular police until 1982 and, as such, I can't comment on the previous decade. I can, however, confirm that the CID in the 1980's was very much dominated by white men who liked a drink. Of course, not all detectives were the same, but there were a few who would not have been out of place on the set of *Life on Mars*. I recall one particular detective who used to visit the section house (police living accommodation at the rear of the police station) trying to find anyone who had vodka or whisky. You may wonder why this is unusual, but it was quite often at six o'clock in the morning and became something of a routine. CID had their own pub which they tended to use and back in those days, drinking and driving was fairly commonplace.

My first attachment to a murder investigation was a real eye-opener and something I'll never forget. I teamed up with an experienced DC who had been there, done it and got several tee shirts. He was a really lovely bloke and could, I was soon to find out, drink for England, or Wales in his case. I was to become his chauffeur for the next few weeks and we must have visited every pub in that district of London, some on several occasions. He was on first-name terms with every landlord and was clearly well-respected by them all. He was also one of those people who never seemed to get drunk no matter how much he consumed. Although he liked a drink, he was also a consummate professional, worked hard, and was the best exhibits officer I have ever had the pleasure of working with. I learned so much about life in the CID in those few weeks.

When I left London and moved to the rural county of Lincolnshire, a number of the police stations had their own social clubs with bars. It was quite common, and part of the winding-down process, to pop in for a 'debrief' at the end of the shift. It wasn't too long before these bars were closed down and the practice of meeting up straight after work began to diminish. I was actually formally interviewed for the position of DC in one of those bars. I hasten to add that the bar was closed at the time but it was still a rather surreal experience as I entered the room and walked past the 'fruit machine' to take my seat in front of the interview panel. Times have certainly changed, for the better I think, but I still look back fondly at those days and wonder how the *Life on Mars* detective would approach the world of modern policing.

LIFE SENTENCE

When a court passes a life sentence it means that the offender will be subject to that sentence for the rest of their life. When passing a life sentence, a Judge must specify the minimum term (referred to as the 'tariff') an offender must spend in prison before becoming eligible to apply for parole. The only exception to this is when a life sentence is passed with a 'whole life order' meaning that such an offender will spend the rest of their life in prison.

Mandatory life sentence

The sentence for those found guilty of murder is fixed by law and is one of life imprisonment. The Judge will set a minimum term an offender must serve before they can be considered for release by the Parole Board. The minimum term for murder is based on the starting points set out in Schedule 21 of the Criminal Justice Act 2003 (as amended). Depending on the facts of the offence the starting point for the minimum term served in prison for an adult ranges from 15 to 30 years. For an offender under 18 years of age the starting point is 12 years. For the purposes of setting the starting point for the minimum term the law sets out four categories

- In cases such as a carefully planned murder of two or more people, or a murder committed by an offender who had already been convicted of murder, the starting point for an offender aged 21 or over is a 'whole life tariff' (they will never be released), an offender aged 18–20 the starting point would be 30 years and under 18 is set at 12 years
- In cases such as those involving the use of a firearm or explosive the starting point is 30 years for an offender aged 18 or over and 12 years for an offender aged under 18
- In cases where the offender brings a knife to the scene and uses it to commit murder the starting point is 25 years for an offender aged 18 or over and 12 years for an offender aged under 18
- In cases that don't fall into the above categories the starting point is 15 years for an offender aged 18 or over and 12 years for an offender aged under 18

Having set the minimum term, the Judge will then take into account any aggravating or mitigating factors which may increase or decrease this term. The Judge may reduce the minimum term to take account of a guilty plea. Aggravating factors may include premeditation, a vulnerable victim or an abuse of a position of trust. Mitigating factors may include provocation, vulnerability of the offender or self-defence.

The offender will only be released once they have served the minimum term and if the Parole Board is satisfied that detaining the offender is no longer necessary for the protection of the public. If released, an offender serving a life sentence will remain on licence for the rest of their life. They may be recalled to prison at any time if considered a risk to the public. They do not need to have committed another offence in order to be recalled.

Whole life order

For the most serious cases, an offender may be sentenced to a life sentence with a 'whole life order'. This means that their crime was considered so serious that they will never be released from prison. As of 30th June 2018 there were 66 offenders serving a whole life sentence. These include serial killers Peter Sutcliffe ('Yorkshire Ripper') and Rosemary West (wife of Fred West).

Discretionary life sentence

There are a number of crimes, including rape and robbery, for which the maximum sentence is life imprisonment. Having said that, it is fairly unusual for a person to receive a life sentence for this type of offence.

Parliament has made provisions that deal with how offenders, who are considered dangerous or who are convicted of a second very serious offence, may be sentenced to life imprisonment. The key provisions are

1) Life sentence for serious offences
A sentence of imprisonment for life must be imposed, where the following criteria are met (Section 225 Criminal Justice Act 2003):

- the offender is convicted of a specified offence (listed in Schedule 15 Criminal Justice Act 2003); and
- in the court's opinion the offender poses a significant risk to the public of serious harm by the commission of further specified offences; and
- the maximum penalty for the offence is life imprisonment; and
- the court considers that the seriousness of the offence justifies the imposition of imprisonment for life

2) Life sentence for second listed offence

The court must impose a sentence of imprisonment for life, where:

- the offender is convicted of an offence listed in Schedule 15B of the Criminal Justice Act 2003; and
- the court would impose a sentence of imprisonment of 10 years or more for the offence; and
- the offender has a previous conviction for a listed offence for which they received a life sentence with a minimum term of at least 5 years or a sentence of imprisonment of at least 10 years;
- **unless** it would be unjust to do so in all the circumstances.

Both Schedule 15 and 15B of the Criminal Justice Act 2003 include offences such as manslaughter and Section 18 assault (wounding with intent to cause grievous bodily harm) along with many other serious offences.

LOCARD'S EXCHANGE PRINCIPLE

Edmond Locard (1877–1966) was a forensic scientist, popularly regarded as the 'Sherlock Holmes of France'. He studied medicine in Lyon and began his professional career by assisting Alexandre Lacassagne, a criminologist and professor. Locard then went on to partner anthropologist Alphonse Bertillon, who was known for his system of identifying criminals based on their body measurements. During the first World War, Locard worked with the French Secret Service as a medical examiner. He identified the cause and location of soldiers' deaths by analysing their uniforms. In 1910 the Lyon Police Department granted Locard the opportunity to create the first crime investigation laboratory where he could analyse evidence from crime scenes in the attic of the police station.

Locard is considered to be a pioneer of forensic science and criminology who developed methods of forensic analysis which are still relevant today. He contributed considerable research into *dactylography*, the study of fingerprints, believing that twelve points of comparison found between two fingerprints would be enough for a positive identification, a method which was adopted over others.

Locard's most famous contribution to forensic science is known today as 'Locard's exchange principle' which states that 'every contact leaves a trace' as, whenever a crime is committed, the perpetrator will leave evidence at the scene and take evidence away with them. Locard explained that "it is impossible for a criminal to act, especially considering the intensity of a crime, without leaving traces of this presence". American forensic scientist, Paul Leland Kirk, an avid supporter of the principle, provided this detailed description –

"Wherever he steps, whatever he touches, even unconsciously, will serve as a silent witness against him. Not only his fingerprints or his footprints, but his hair, the fibres from his clothes, the glass he breaks, the tool mark he leaves, the paint he scratches, the blood or semen he deposits or collects. All of these and more bear mute witness against him. This is evidence that does not forget. It is not confused by the excitement of the moment. It is not absent because human witnesses are. It is factual evidence. Physical evidence cannot be wrong, it cannot perjure itself, it cannot be wholly absent. Only human failure to find it, study and understand it, can diminish its value".

When two surfaces come into contact with each other, there will be an exchange of material between the two. So, if I shake you by the hand, there will be a transfer of evidence. I will leave something on your hand, perhaps a minute flake of skin, a hair or a fibre and I will take something similar from you away with me. If we had a fight and I killed you, then there is likely to be even more transference on both of us and in the area where the fight took place. This evidence will always be there, the challenge for investigators is to find and interpret it. Locard's exchange principle is as relevant today as it has ever been and is why the forensic examination of a crime scene is so important.

CASE STUDY – IAN HUNTLEY

In August 2002, two ten-year-old girls, Holly Wells and Jessica Chapman, left a family barbeque to get some sweets and never returned. Nearly two weeks later their bodies were found in a ditch several miles away. The person who murdered them was a man called Ian Huntley, who worked as a caretaker at a local college in Soham. The girls were murdered in his house and then driven to a remote location in the boot of his car. Due to the condition of the bodies when found and the actions of Huntley, it was impossible to establish exactly what had happened to the girls prior to their death.

Huntley went to great lengths in an effort to destroy any

forensic evidence. He cleaned the house thoroughly using a bleach or similar substance. Police officers who went inside the house during the investigation noted a very strong 'lemon' type odour. Given that both girls were inside the house and the struggles which no doubt took place, the fact that no DNA or other evidence belonging to the girls was found is an indication of how thoroughly it was cleaned. Huntley also tried to remove any forensic evidence from his car, a red Ford Fiesta. Like the house, he cleaned it thoroughly. He even took it to a garage and had all four tyres changed, despite the fact that the tyres were in good and legal condition. He was obviously aware that he would have left tyre impressions along the track near the 'deposition' site and didn't want his vehicle to implicate him.

Despite significant efforts to hide his tracks, it was to be forensic evidence which helped to convict him. Pollen recovered from Huntley's car and his shoes exactly matched the type found in the ditch at the deposition site. A distinctive mix of chalk, brick dust and concrete was recovered from the foot-well and wheel arches of his car. This was confirmed as the same as that used to cover the road leading to the ditch where the girls were found. Some of the clothing worn by the girls when they disappeared was found, torn and burnt, inside a bin in the grounds of the college where Huntley worked. Head hairs, identified as belonging to Huntley, were recovered amongst the clothing. The prosecution were able to say that, in total, there had been some 154 transfers of evidence (one-way and two-way) between Huntley and the two girls. The strength of the forensic evidence was crucial in helping to secure the conviction of Huntley for the murder of two innocent young girls.

M

MG FORMS

When submitting a file for prosecution or charging advice the police use a standard set of forms known as MG forms. The forms, together with a manual of guidance, were originally produced by the National Policing Improvement Agency (NPIA) which is now known as the College of Policing. Although there are around twenty different MG forms, the police are only required to complete those which are relevant to their case. An initial submission to the Crown Prosecution Service (CPS) may only contain an abbreviated version of the file but if the case proceeds to trial the file will have to be upgraded. The most commonly used MG forms are

MG4 – a copy of the charge sheet which is printed out from the computerised custody system
MG5 – a summary of the case
MG6 series (unused material schedules)
MG9 – witness list
MG11 and MG11A – witness statement form and continuation sheets
MG12 – exhibit list
MG15 – record of interview

The MG forms are available on the police IT system and can be filled in and then printed out. If the police require charging advice from the CPS, they will usually prepare the file and send it to their local CPS branch. If it is a particularly serious case which requires a charging decision at that time then the police will contact CPS by phone to discuss with a lawyer. If a charging decision is required at a time when the local CPS branch is not available, such as after 5pm or at weekends, then the police have to contact an on-call CPS lawyer who is likely to be from another area. They will briefly discuss the circumstances then send the relevant MG forms electronically. The charging decision will be made by that lawyer and their advice will be printed out and attached to the case file.

MODERN SLAVERY

Even though most people think that slavery only exists over-seas, modern slavery in the UK is thriving. The Government estimates that tens of thousands of people are in modern slavery in the UK today. Most people are trafficked in from other countries, but there is also a significant number of British Nationals in slavery. Most commonly, people are trafficked into forced labour in industries such as agriculture, construction, hospitality, manufacturing and car washes. Many women and girls are trafficked for sexual exploitation. Others, particularly children, are forced into crime such as cannabis production, petty theft or begging.

Typically, a person coming from a situation of poverty and lack of opportunity is offered an apparently good job in the UK. When the person arrives in Britain, the job and the conditions they were promised are completely different. Violence or threats are common practice, both against the victim and their family back home. The response of the UK Government to modern slavery has been slowly improving in the last few years. In 2009, the Government set up the National Referral Mechanism (NRM), to which potential cases are referred and through which victims can access relevant support. Unfortunately, the Mechanism wasn't fit for purpose as victims weren't receiving the appropriate support and offenders were escaping justice. Protests and calls for a new comprehensive law led to the passing of the new Modern Slavery Act in 2015.

There is no doubt that the Modern Slavery Act is a step in the right direction as it makes prosecution easier, increases sentences and bans the prosecution of victims for crimes they were forced to commit by their traffickers, amongst other measures. There is, however, still a concern that the law is too heavily focused on policing and doesn't afford enough protection for the victims. Only 1% of victims of slavery have the chance to see their exploiter brought to justice. There is clearly work still to be done but UK police forces are certainly now more aware of the challenges and are beginning to bring successful prosecutions against those who are exploiting the most vulnerable in our society.

Updated 2023

Victims of modern slavery will be identified earlier in criminal investigations, saving them from being wrongly prosecuted, following the publication of new legal guidance published in December 2021 by the Crown Prosecution Service (CPS). The CPS has previously carefully considered the claim of suspects who say that they offended due to being trafficked. The change in guidance shifts the focus of this consideration to before a suspect is charged and reminds prosecutors to assess the whole situation and to be alert to potential indicators of trafficking. The guidance states that where a person is suspected or claims to be a victim of modern slavery – that they were coerced or directed to commit a crime as a result – as far as possible, police or law enforcement should fully investigate suspects' situations before the CPS are able to make a charging decision.

It is expected that the updated Modern Slavery guidance, which is based on the experience of prosecutors over the past few years, will help continue to increase the number of prosecutions of criminals exploiting vulnerable people, while safeguarding against the criminalising of trafficked victims. Investigations into whether a person is a victim of modern slavery are often carried out after charge, which is likely to delay the case progression and increase the number of court appearances and adjournments whilst appropriate enquiries are made. The changes will mean that prosecutors will be able to make more informed decisions at the point of charge and should reduce the occasions where a claim is made halfway through a prosecution. It's worth noting that the law in *Section 45* of the *Modern Slavery Act 2015* (defence for slavery or trafficking victims who commit an offence) does not give people who have been trafficked blanket immunity. They will still face prosecution for the most serious crimes including murder, terrorism, serious violence or sexual offences. Of the modern slavery cases referred to the CPS by police in 2020/21 where the CPS decided, they prosecuted 81% with a conviction rate of nearly 80%. Full details of the new legal guidance can be viewed on the CPS website via the following link: https://www.cps.gov.uk/legal-guidance/modern-slavery-human-trafficking-and-smuggling

CASE STUDY – OPERATION POTTERY

Eleven people have been convicted of modern slavery and fraud as the result of a major investigation by Lincolnshire Police. Operation Pottery was one of the largest of its kind in the country and probed a group, largely from the same family of travellers, who targeted victims because they were vulnerable and homeless. Some of the 18 victims had learning disabilities, mental health issues or were dependent on alcohol or drugs. Others were forced to sign over their homes to their exploiters.

In September 2014, officers carried out seven raids across Lincolnshire, Nottingham and London which eventually led to convictions nearly one year later. The Senior Investigating Officer in the case explained "Through intelligence from partner agencies and the public, together with police intelligence, we knew these men were being kept in very poor conditions and made to work for little money. The extent of these conditions soon became apparent – the victims were 'accommodated' in caravans without running water or access to toilet facilities and, in some cases, the electricity to them was dangerously obtained from a nearby pylon. The victims were all adults aged between 18 and 63. They had been located and picked up by the defendants from all over the country and specifically targeted because they were vulnerable and homeless. They were promised that they would be looked after, sheltered and fed but were exploited and forced to work long hours laying tarmac and block paving for little or no money. This exploitation was illegally funding a lavish lifestyle which included luxury holidays, high performance cars and even cosmetic surgery. The victims living quarters were truly shocking and, at times, they lived in site stables next to the dog kennels. They were only provided food when they worked and this was often the family leftovers. They were not provided with any training for the manual labour and were financially, emotionally and physically abused, making any attempt to escape seem impossible. If they needed the toilet they often had no alternative but to use the nearby woods and fields. Some of their personal bank accounts were used to pay for gym membership and materials for the family business. After some considerable time, the victims have now begun to regain their trust and self-confidence enabling them to live independent lives again. The tragedy in this case is that the victims will never get those years back, we believe that one man was held for 26 years. Modern slavery is a cruel and demoralising crime and it's important that people understand that it isn't just forced labour such as this case, victims can be sexually exploited or forced into committing crimes".

Eleven members of the Rooney family were convicted of a number of offences including conspiracy to require a person to perform forced or compulsory labour and various assaults. They were sentenced to a total of nearly 80 years imprisonment with two members receiving more than 15 years each. A twelfth member of the family, who had flown to the USA, was eventually arrested and deported back to the UK. He was also convicted and sentenced to 11 years in prison.

MOTIVE

For the detective, working out why a crime has been committed is a main line of enquiry in any criminal investigation. Establishing a motive could help to identify the offender(s) and can be used by intelligence analysts to identify other offences which may have been committed by the same individual. If the motive is particularly unusual or specific, it could also help investigators to identify other people who may be potentially at risk. The motive for a crime isn't always clear and, on occasions, there may be more than one motive. In all criminal investigations, the detective must keep an open mind and not make assumptions about the reason why a crime has taken place.

Some of the more common motives are for gain (financial or otherwise), jealousy, revenge, gang-related (drugs, territory, power), hatred (racism, homophobia, religion) and sexual. Although this list is far from exhaustive, it hopefully gives you an idea of the type of reasons identified in many cases. Motives can link in with possible contributory causes of crime, such as drugs and alcohol. There is considerable evidence to suggest that offenders, particularly those who are violent, have taken or consumed either of these prior to committing a crime. It is possible, of course, that victims may have taken them too, which may provide an indication as to what sort of activity they were involved in prior to the crime or even why they were targeted. This can be useful information for building up an accurate picture on which to base a motive and to understand the background of a victim or offender.

I was the SIO for a murder investigation in Lincolnshire during which the motive remained unclear and was never fully revealed. The victim was a joiner who had a large workshop adjacent to where he lived in a bungalow with his female partner, who was also his business partner. One Sunday evening, in March 2011, they had both paid a visit to the workshop when they were attacked by two masked men. Following a struggle, his partner managed to run from the building but he was unable to fight the men off. The suspects set a fire in the building and he was trapped inside, tragically dying from smoke inhalation. In the early stages it looked as if it may have been a robbery which had got out of hand. The suspects had made off and there was very little evidence to identify them, partly due to the damage caused by the fire. Our investigation looked very closely at the financial aspects of the business and, over time, we were able to establish that there were significant debts owed by the business, to the point where bailiffs were preparing to visit to seize assets. There was no evidence that the victim knew about these debts as everything related to finances had been dealt with by his partner. Further enquiries revealed that the post had been re-directed to a nearby address and that the partner had been lying to financial authorities about the physical health of her partner. This information, together with other evidence gathered during the investigation, raised concerns to the point where the partner became a suspect and was subsequently arrested on suspicion of being involved in the murder.

To cut a long story short, it transpired that the two masked men never existed and she had invented this account to cover the fact that she had pushed her partner into a small storeroom, locked him in, then set a fire outside the door, ultimately resulting in the death of a well-respected member of the local community. Initially, she claimed that her actions were part of a pre-arranged suicide pact but then changed her account as the case progressed. She was convicted of murder, the circumstances described by the Judge as "premeditated and evil". He went on to say "her performance in the 999 call and to the emergency crews at the scene would have been worthy of the highest praise, had she been an actress in some fictional drama, and would have warranted an Oscar nomination". She was sentenced to life imprisonment with a minimum tariff of 23 years. To my knowledge, she has never confessed nor can we be sure exactly why she acted in such a calculated and heartless manner.

MURDER BAG

The contents of the murder bag have changed over the decades but it is still very much a part of the modern detective's toolkit. The bag, originally a forensic kit, was developed by Sir Bernard Spilsbury, a forensic pathologist, in conjunction with Scotland Yard in 1924. The Patrick Mahon murder case of that year identified that there was a requirement for such a kit. The murder scene was particularly gruesome as Mahon had dismembered his victim and had tried to burn the body parts. He was later caught throwing small body parts out of a train. Spilsbury was called to the scene to assist in finding the missing parts but when he arrived he found a detective using his bare hands to scoop up bloodied flesh and put them in a bucket. The detective confirmed to Spilsbury that he never wore gloves and that no-one he knew had done so, since the formation of the murder squad seventeen years before. Spilsbury updated the detective in charge of the murder squad who proposed a standardised kit to be carried by all detectives responding to a murder. The kit contained rubber gloves, tweezers, evidence bags, magnifying glass, compass, ruler and swabs.

The term 'murder bag' became recognisable to the British public after its use as the title of a popular television series which ran from 1957 to 1959. *Murder Bag* introduced Raymond Francis as Detective Superintendent Tom Lockhart of Scotland Yard. Apart from good old George Dixon (Dixon of Dock Green), Lockhart became probably the most respected television policeman in Britain over the next decade as *Murder Bag* was followed by *Crime Sheet* and *No Hiding Place*. Lockhart was assisted in his investigations by different police officers each week, but always present was the 'murder bag' – a black leather briefcase used on murder enquiries, which contained 42 items of equipment needed to gather forensic evidence, ranging from airtight jars to tweezers.

The modern-day detective is likely to have a murder bag full of useful items which you can never find elsewhere when you need them. These will probably include forensic suits, policy files, evidence bags, maps and a torch to name but a few. I used to keep my murder bag either in my office or the back of the car, depending on my commitments for that particular day. I used to take it home with me when I was on-call and also had an overnight bag packed because I didn't always know exactly when I was going to return.

MURDER INVESTIGATION MANUAL

The Murder Investigation Manual (MIM) was first published in September 1998. It was compiled by a group of experienced

Senior Investigating Officers (SIOs) supported by experts and other professionals working in the criminal justice system. They carried out extensive consultation within the police service and partner agencies to identify good practice in homicide investigation. The resulting manual is now seen as the definitive guide on homicide investigation, by practitioners and policy makers alike. It is used to underpin the training and development of SIO's and has become a reference point for all types of major crime. Two updated editions of the manual have been published to take account of the many changes in legislation and procedure. The extent of these changes has resulted in the most recent manual (2006) being substantially different from its predecessors. The manual addresses issues which are likely to be relevant to all criminal investigations as well as the individual strategies and techniques of homicide investigation. Topics covered in the manual include crime scenes, suspect management and family liaison. The manual, which is nearly 300 pages in total, is a useful guide for those tasked with the investigation of murder.

N

NEWTON COURT HEARING

A Newton hearing is a relatively modern legal procedure in English law, where the prosecution and defence offer such conflicting evidence that a judge sitting alone, without a jury, tries to establish which party is telling the truth. These hearings generally take place when a defendant pleads guilty to an offence, but there are factual issues that need to be resolved between the prosecution and defence.

The name stems from a 1983 case, *R v Newton*, in which the

defendant admitted buggery but claimed that his wife had given her consent to the act. The Court of Appeal ruled that, in such cases, there were three ways of resolving the issue. It may be possible to obtain the answer from a jury by directing them to consider whether there is the necessary intent for a specific offence or whether a lesser offence which does not require intent is made out. If that is not possible then either;

- evidence could be heard from both sides and a conclusion reached on the matter which was the root of the problem, or
- no evidence heard but submissions analysed and, where a substantial doubt still persisted, benefit be given to the defendant

The Newton hearing is similar to a trial, with a judge deciding the disputed points based upon testimony and submissions, rather than a jury. As with all criminal cases, the burden of proof is on the prosecution, who must prove their case 'beyond reasonable doubt'. From a criminal defence perspective, there are concerns about Newton hearings as they are time and resource consuming and, if they prove unsuccessful, they are likely to reduce any sentencing credit which may have already been obtained. For these reasons, many defence advocates avoid Newton hearings on the basis that they tend to favour the prosecution, who some may say have 'nothing to lose'.

I was involved in a Newton hearing which took place following a murder investigation. The defendant had admitted killing her partner but claimed that this was part of a suicide pact which they had both agreed together. The case for the prosecution was that no such pact ever existed and that there was no evidence uncovered throughout a detailed police investigation which indicated that the victim would have agreed to such a pact.

After hearing evidence from both sides, the judge decided that the murder was planned and that the account given by the defendant was "a pack of lies". He added "I am sure that this was not an assisted suicide. I am sure it was a premeditated killing". The defendant was sentenced to life imprisonment with a minimum term of 23 years.

NOVICHOK

Prior to March 2018 the term 'novichok' probably wouldn't have meant anything to a lot of people but the events in Salisbury brought it to our attention during a series of events which shocked the nation. During the afternoon of 4th March former Russian spy, Sergei Skripal, and his daughter Yulia were taken ill and had to be rushed to hospital with symptoms which suggested that they may have been poisoned. It was later established that they had come into contact with a nerve agent 'novichok' which had left them both in a critical condition. The area was cordoned off and the Metropolitan Police Counter Terror Command took over the investigation, working alongside Wiltshire Police. A local Detective Sergeant, who attended the home address of Mr. Skripal to check for further casualties, was also taken ill even though he had been wearing full protective clothing and gloves at the time. Fortunately, all three were eventually discharged from hospital after showing signs of recovery.

On June 27th, 2018, a local resident, Charlie Rowley found a perfume bottle which he took home and opened in the presence of Dawn Sturgess, who is believed to have sprayed some of the contents onto her wrists. Three days later they were both found unconscious at a house about eight miles from the original poisoning site. On 8th July Dawn Sturgess died as a result of the poisoning. Rowley recovered consciousness and was eventually discharged from hospital. Tests showed that the pair had also been poisoned by novichok. Scientists found that the liquid in the bottle contained a "significant amount of novichok" which could potentially have affected "thousands of people".

The police investigation established that the novichok was sprayed onto the front door handle and door of Mr. Skripal's house. CCTV identified two Russian men who arrived at Gatwick airport from Moscow on 2nd March and travelled to east London, where they stayed overnight in a hotel. The following day they carried out a reconnaissance of the Salisbury area. On March 4th they attended Mr. Skripal's address, sprayed the novichok on the front door handle and then left the area, discarding the perfume bottle containing the novichok in a bin. That same evening, they both flew back to Russia from Heathrow airport. Both suspects have been identified as members of the GRU (the military intelligence service of the Russian Federation) fuelling claims that the attack was co-ordinated by Russia. They have appeared on Russian television claiming to be 'tourists' on a sightseeing visit to Salisbury. They are wanted for questioning in the UK and both are the subject of International Arrest Warrants.

The name novichok means "newcomer" in Russian, and applies to a group of advanced nerve agents developed by the Soviet Union in the 1970's and 1980's. Some variants of novichok are thought to be five to eight times more toxic than the VX nerve agent (the chemical used to kill the half-brother of Kim Jong-un in 2017). Novichok agents act by blocking messages from the nerves to the muscles, causing a collapse of many bodily functions. Symptoms include convulsions, interrupted breathing and vomiting and can ultimately prove fatal. Novichoks were designed to be more toxic than other chemical weapons and exposure is likely to be through inhalation or ingestion, although absorption through the skin is also possible.

NUMBER SPOOFING

'Number spoofing' or 'caller id spoofing' is a tactic used by criminals when they ring people and pretend to be someone else, often a legitimate company. This type of 'scam' has been used for many years but in recent times it is being targeted at older, vulnerable people. If you have a phone with a caller display which tells you the number which is ringing you, it's likely to reassure you if you recognise the number calling and will probably encourage you to answer the call. Criminals are able to take advantage of this, as number spoofing allows them to show any number on the caller display when they are actually ringing from a completely different phone number. Your caller id display may indicate that the call is from a local number when in fact it's being made from a different area or even country. Criminals have also pretended to be from the recipient's bank and number spoofed the phone number of that bank onto the caller display. They are then able to reassure the person answering the call by advising them to check the caller display number with a bank statement or card to confirm their authenticity. Number spoofing can also be used for calls and text messages to mobile phones. Caller display is still a very useful facility to have on your phone but unfortunately the increase in number spoofing means that you can no longer assume that the call is being made from the number which is displayed. If you have any doubt at all that the caller may not be genuine, the call should be terminated and, if necessary, you can make the relevant enquiries by calling the numbers yourself. As an indication of how easy it can be to carry out number spoofing, there are websites available on the internet providing detailed instructions for a payment fee. They are promoted on the basis that you may wish to call a friend or family member to play a trick on them but, of course, number spoofing is also used by criminals for unlawful purposes.

CASE STUDIES – NUMBER SPOOFING

1) A man from Coventry was sent to prison after pleading guilty to three counts of blackmail committed in January 2018. Daniel Fox received 4 years and 10 months imprisonment when he appeared at Leicester Crown Court. Fox used a scamming technique known as 'spoofing' to disguise his own phone number with one that was familiar to his victims, before making demands for money of up to £10,000 accompanied by threats of violence if his demands were not met. In one offence, Fox disguised his number with that of the victim's wife and claimed to be holding her hostage. After the victim's wife was found to be safe and well, the police were informed and an investigation was launched. After the case, the investigating officer commented "It was clear from the start that this was an unusual technique, and that the offender could have been making these threats from anywhere in the country. The initial report came to us after the victim's wife returned home while the offender was still on the phone to the victim, claiming to be keeping her hostage and ringing from her phone. Enquiries were made at a very early stage to identify the phone that was being used to make the menacing calls, and from those enquiries we identified Daniel Fox. As part of the data we were able to retrieve, we were able to link him with two other very similar offences in Leicestershire. I would urge people to remain vigilant, particularly given the technology that is available to criminals to commit these offences".

2) A woman who was duped out of almost £40,000 is calling on banks to do more to protect customers of sophisticated scams. Sophie Briggs believed that fraudsters were actually calling from her bank's fraud team and alerting her to genuine suspicious activity on her account, because they appeared to

call from the legitimate number shown on the back of her bank card. Two transactions of £19,999, which she believed were going to a new account her bank had set up in her name, went through without being checked by the bank. Mrs. Briggs commented "If you don't know that scammers can set it up so their number is the same as your banks, how are you supposed to know you are being scammed". Mrs. Briggs described the con as a "clever, psychological set-up" which makes the victim feel vulnerable as they think that their money is at risk. She added "They even pretended to book me an appointment at my local branch with a fraud team member. I have no idea how they got hold of my mobile number". The bank stopped her third transaction attempt of £19,999 which is just under the limit for the maximum amount of money that can be transferred in this way. The bank sympathised with Mrs. Briggs and advised customers never to make a payment or divulge full security information, card reader codes or activation codes to anyone over the phone whom is purporting to be from their bank. They added "Customers should never respond to a request to move their money to keep it safe from scams or fraud. If a customer receives such a request, they should decline this and report it to their bank immediately on a phone number they can trust. We would also recommend that they call back from their mobile phone or wait 30 seconds before calling back from their landline".

In the first half of 2018, a total of £145 million was stolen through authorised push payment (APP) scams, where people are duped into authorising a payment to another account. Most victims of this type of fraud do not get their money back as banks argue that the customer is at fault for giving permission for the payment to go through. However, experts say that scams are becoming increasingly sophisticated and difficult to identify.

Banks have pledged to introduce new alerts and checks to prevent customers transferring their money to fraudsters.

O

ODONTOLOGY

Odontology is the term used for the scientific study of the structure and diseases of teeth. The unique marks of teeth have been used throughout history, as far back as the Roman Emperor Nero and William the Conqueror, who used to bite the wax seals on his letters with his crooked teeth to verify they were from him. The first formally reported case of dental identification was in relation to John Talbot, the Earl of Shrewsbury, who fell at the battle of Castillon in France in 1453. The American patriot Paul Revere was able to identify his friend, Dr Joseph Warren, 10 months after he was buried, a victim of the 1775 Battle of Bunker Hill in Massachusetts. This proved to be an easy identification because Revere had fashioned dentures for Warren. In 1865 a dental identification was made of John Wilkes Booth, the assassin of President Abraham Lincoln. The first disaster victims to be identified by their teeth were killed in a fire in 1849 at the Vienna Opera House. As you can see, people can be identified through their teeth and a comparison with dental records, if they exist, remains a primary means of identification, particularly when obtaining fingerprints is not possible.

Detectives may request the assistance of a number of experts during the course of a criminal investigation, particularly a murder. These could include a forensic anthropologist (study of bones) or a forensic palynologist (study of pollen and spores) who can provide expert advice which can help to solve a case.

Another type of expert, who may be invaluable if you are trying to identify a murder victim or the suspect in an assault case, is a forensic odontologist.

Forensic odontology is a branch of forensic medicine which, in the interests of justice, deals with the proper examination, handling and presentation of dental evidence in a court of law. The work of a forensic odontologist covers:

- Identification of unknown human remains through dental records and assisting at the scene of a mass disaster
- Age estimations of both living and deceased persons including neo-natal remains
- Analysis of bite marks found on victims of assault
- Identification of bite marks in other substances such as wood, leather and foodstuffs
- Analysis of weapon marks using the principle of bite mark analysis
- Presentation of bite and weapon mark evidence in court as an expert witness
- Assistance in building up a picture of lifestyle and diet at an archeological site

Identification of human remains

Unidentified bodies come to light frequently, having drowned, burned, been murdered, having committed suicide or dying from natural causes. Usually, sufficient evidence is apparent to positively identify the body, but from time to time, this identification will rely on dental evidence. All mouths are different and the trained eye of the forensic odontologist will offer a considerable amount of useful information, including an accurate charting of the teeth and any fillings to compare with dental records of missing persons. Even if only a few teeth are available, an opinion can still be offered on age, habits, oral hygiene, and individual features which may match with ante-mortem records. Where the subject has no teeth, useful information can still be gleaned from the study of any dentures and by x-raying the jaws and skull. Despite recent advances in DNA technology, dental identification still offers a rapid and cost-effective approach. In relevant cases it's important that the services of a forensic odontologist are secured at an early stage of the investigation.

CASE STUDY

The mummified remains of a female were discovered in the disused cellar of a hotel. During the postmortem the forensic odontologist, by studying the developments of the tooth roots, was able to determine the age at death to within 12 months. This led to a name being suggested by the Missing Persons Bureau and a positive identification using dental records within 48 hours.

Bite marks

Marks are frequently seen on the victims of assault, including child abuse, but not always recognised as bites. This vital evidence often goes unnoticed by the untrained person. Any 'curved' bruise should be treated as suspicious and the services of a forensic odontologist should be sought early in the investigation. As well as working with the photographer to record the evidence, the forensic odontolgist can take dental impressions of any suspects, be prepared to make a comparison and, if necessary, present the evidence in court as an expert witness. The shape of the bite mark can give useful clues about the person who caused it and may lead to the implication or exclusion of an individual under investigation. The forensic odontologist will also be able to recognise and record bite marks in other substances such as foodstuffs (apples, cheese, chocolate), leather (key rings, belts) and wood (pencils).

CASE STUDY
An assailant punched his victim and then threatened to kill her. During the struggle he bit her on the breast. A forensic odontologist directed the photography of the bite mark, took impressions of the suspect's teeth and prepared transparent overlays to make a comparison. This evidence convinced an Old Bailey jury that the accused was, indeed, the attacker. He was convicted and sentenced accordingly.

Weapon marks
Using the same digital imaging techniques as used for bite mark analysis, a forensic odontologist can make similar comparisons between offensive weapons and injuries seen on victims.

CASE STUDY
A forensic odontologist was asked to investigate a possible bite mark on the victim of a sexual assault. The mark proved to be too vague for comparison, but the bruise left by a belt buckle was clearly visible on the victim's thigh. By making a digital image of the suspect's belt and comparing this with a scaled photograph of the bruise, a direct link was established which resulted in the suspect pleading guilty to the offence.

OLD BAILEY
The Old Bailey, also known as the Central Criminal Court, is named after the street on which it stands in the western part of the City of London. Part of the present building stands on the site of the medieval Newgate gaol, on a road called Old

Bailey that follows the line of the City of London's fortified wall (or bailey).The original medieval court was first mentioned in 1585 but was destroyed during the Great Fire of London in 1666. It was rebuilt in 1673 as a three-storey brick building together with a Sessions House Yard, a place where litigants, witnesses and court personnel could gather. The area inside the wall, where prisoners awaited trial, was separated from the street by a brick wall with spikes on top to prevent escape. A surprising feature was that the ground floor of the building, where the courtroom was located, was open on one side to the weather. A wall had been left out to increase the supply of fresh air to reduce the risk that prisoners suffering from gaol fever (typhus) would infect others in court. The trials attracted a mixed audience of observers who would crowd into the yard. It was alleged that criminals attended in order to devise strategies to defend themselves should they be put on trial in the future. The crowd's presence could influence or intimidate the jurors sitting inside.

In 1737 the building was re-modelled and enclosed. Although this was purportedly to keep out the bad weather, the City authorities may also have wanted to keep out the influence of spectators. A passageway was constructed linking the courthouse with Newgate prison, to facilitate the transport of prisoners between the two buildings. The interior was rearranged so that the trial jury could sit together, since they were now expected to give their verdicts after each trial, without leaving the courtroom. With the courtroom now enclosed, the danger of infection increased, and at one sessions in 1750 an outbreak of typhus led to the deaths of sixty people, including the Lord Mayor and two judges. Spectators frequently came to see the trials, and courthouse officials had the right to charge fees for entry to the galleries.

In 1774 the court was rebuilt at a cost of £15,000 with a semi-circular brick wall in front of the courthouse, providing better security for the prisoners awaiting trial and limiting communication between prisoners and the public. The new courthouse still had only one courtroom but there was now a separate room for witnesses, so that they would not be obliged to wait their turn in a nearby pub. A grand jury room was appointed with eighteen leather chairs and three tables. During the Gordon riots of 1780 the courtroom was badly damaged, and the crowds carried away the furniture which they burned on the streets.

In order to accommodate the growing number of trials, a second courtroom was added in 1824 by converting a neighbouring building. In subsequent decades two additional courtrooms were added but conditions became rather cramped. The fourth courtroom contained little more room than was necessary for the judge, jury and prisoner's dock, with counsel and the clerk forced to sit in a narrow row of seats. There was no seating for the public, who had to stand in the gangway.

Between 1674 and 1834 over 100,000 criminal trials took place at the Old Bailey before it became known as the Central Criminal Court. The jurisdiction of the court was to extend beyond that of London and Middlesex to the whole of England for trials of major cases. In 1856 there was public revulsion against a doctor called William Palmer who was accused of poisoning and murder. This led to fears that he could not receive a fair trial in his native Staffordshire. The Central Criminal Court Act 1856 was passed to allow his trial to be held at the Old Bailey and opened the door for other cases from outside London.

As trials lengthened and the number of spectators increased during the nineteenth century, it became clear that the courthouse building was inadequate. In 1877 a fire forced the City of London to act and plans were drawn up for a new building. Owing to the dilapidated Newgate prison next door, which no longer held long-term prisoners, a decision was made to pull down both buildings to make room for a larger one. After many delays, the new building was finally opened by King Edward VII in 1907. A 12 foot gold leaf statue of a 'lady of justice' holding a sword in one hand and the scales of justice in the other, was built on top of the 67 foot high dome. The four courtrooms now had plenty of space for defendants, witnesses and lawyers with a number of separate rooms for each. The building was severely damaged during the Blitz of World War II in 1941 but was reconstructed during the 1950's. Although a modern extension was built around 1972 to accommodate more courts, the building remains to this day the structure which first opened in 1907.

The Old Bailey has 18 courts which are in regular use as Court 19 is mainly used as a press overflow or juror room. All judges who sit in the court should be addressed as "My Lord" or "My Lady" whether they are High Court, circuit judges or Recorders. The court deals with the most serious cases, not only from London, but also at times from the rest of England and Wales. Recently I read that someone had referred to the Old Bailey as "just another crown court and no different from other courts". I couldn't disagree more with that view. Having attended many crown courts across the country, I don't think that there is any experience that can match giving evidence at the Old Bailey, particularly, but not exclusively, in one of the old-fashioned courts where everything is wood-panelled and the room just emanates history and tradition. You can visit the Old Bailey and I would certainly recommend a look around inside if you ever get the opportunity.

OPERATIONAL NAMES

You may or may not be aware that major police investigations, whether pro-active or re-active, are often given operational names by the police. These names are randomly generated on a computer and can often contain words which require a quick search to establish their meaning. The aim is to select a name which is completely neutral and not inappropriate to the investigation. The names which include objects, animals and places are allocated to the investigation for its duration and will become the name by which the case is known internally. During my career I was involved in many investigations which had names such as Operation Gastard (a village in Wiltshire), Operation Barbel (a freshwater fish) and Operation Gam (a school of whales) amongst others. One of my murder investigations was given the apt name of Operation Roundup. This system has been in use since the 1980's and you will sometimes see or hear the operational name referred to in the media. You may be familiar with the names Operation Weeting (phone hacking), Operation Yewtree (sexual abuse) or Operation Elveden (inappropriate payments by journalists to police). One of the most well-known police investigations conducted in London between 1978 and 1982 was Operation Countryman, which investigated police corruption in the late 70's. The investigation was surrounded by controversy and, for a number of reasons, had limited success. So, if you're a writer and planning on making reference to a murder or other major enquiry in your book you may wish to give the investigation an operational name.

P

PASSIVE DATA DENERATORS

Although it sounds a bit like a 'dodgy' second-hand shop, 'passive data generators' is the term used to describe automated systems which gather information for purposes unconnected to criminal investigation, but which can be accessed by investigators. The term includes closed circuit television (CCTV), Automatic Number Plate Recognition (ANPR) and telephone billing systems. In a major criminal investigation, such as a murder, it will probably also include the collection of financial information, personal computer information and vehicle records, such as satellite navigation systems (SatNav) and tachographs. The number of different passive data generators which are now available to detectives has increased greatly during the last few decades with the advances in technology to the point where they now play a crucial role in criminal investigations.

What distinguishes passive data generators from other types of record keeping, such as patient records made by doctors and client information kept by accountants, is the fact that they are automated and require no judgement on the part of the person making them, hence the term 'passive'. They are also stored in systems that require technical expertise to access them. Records created by people are generally written or typed documents which are usually fairly easy to access, providing you have obtained consent or lawful authority.

There are two ways in which passive data generators can be used to assist detectives to understand the circumstances of a crime. The first, known as general material, is almost exclusively confined to locating, gathering and viewing images generated within particular locations for the purpose of identifying people and vehicles which may be significant to the investigation. This will involve locating CCTV systems, traffic safety cameras and ANPR sources. It may also involve the analysis of the telephone activity of relevant people, such as the victim of a murder, to identify contacts. In relation to a murder investigation, it is often the case that the only location known to be significant at an early stage is the scene where the body is found, and so the searches for CCTV will be confined to that immediate area and potential access and egress routes. As more material becomes available it may be possible to set new parameters which enable more images to be located. In relation to telephone activity, it is often the case that the only significant time that is known with any degree of certainty is the time that the body was discovered. The search for telephone activity will often begin there and work backwards. In the case of CCTV and telephone activity the priority will always be to locate the passive data generator and secure the material before it is deleted from the system. CCTV in particular is only available for a limited period and, as such, time is of the essence.

The second way in which passive data generators can assist during crime investigation, known as specific material, is where detectives are seeking material about specific circumstances that are relevant to the crime. These are likely to include the presence of victims, witnesses, suspects, vehicles or telephones at particular locations and the times they were there, the relationship between individuals and times of contact between individuals. The amount and type of passive data generators will vary and depend on the circumstances of the case and the people involved.

CASE STUDY – PASSIVE DATA
One Sunday afternoon a group of people had gathered in a pub to watch a televised football match. Two men wearing balaclavas

and carrying firearms entered the public area and opened fire, seriously wounding customers. After a struggle both men were chased out of the premises, having at some point also been shot in retaliation. They ran onto a grassed area where they collapsed and died. A third man approached and checked the bodies, then fled the scene in a black Ford Mondeo.

An important part of the investigation surrounded analysis of mobile phone use. Communications data indicated that, on the day of the incident, the phone attributed to the man in the Mondeo was in constant use. One of the numbers that featured in the recovered call data was attributed to a woman who had been in the pub when the attack took place. This information was confirmed through analysis of calls and cell-site data.

Analysis of the phone used by the man in the Mondeo showed a pattern of travel from his home address to other significant locations, culminating in the phone being located in the vicinity of the pub at the relevant time. The phone data also showed contact between him, the two deceased men and the woman before, during and immediately after the shootings occurred. No contact was identified at any other time.

Communications data, in the form of likely location, top-up information and call data records proved crucial to the prosecution case. It helped to show how the man in the Mondeo had arranged the attack, sending two armed men into the pub who had subsequently been shot dead while escaping. It also showed how the woman had acted as a 'spotter' inside the pub, helping to direct them to a target. Both were convicted of conspiracy to murder and received life sentences.

PHONETIC ALPHABET

The NATO phonetic alphabet is the most widely used radiotelephone spelling alphabet. Code words have been assigned acrophonically to the letters of the English alphabet, so that critical combinations of letters and numbers are most likely to be pronounced and understood by those who exchange voice messages by radio or telephone, regardless of language differences or the quality of the communication channel. The 26 code words in the phonetic alphabet are assigned to the 26 letters of the English alphabet in order. Police officers use the phonetic alphabet when spelling out words over their radios or phones to make it easier for other people to understand what they are saying. This practice avoids misunderstanding, particularly in a noisy environment, as it can be easy to mistake a letter B with an E or an S with an F. The phonetic alphabet used by police is as follows

A-ALPHA	J-JULIET	S-SIERRA
B-BRAVO	K-KILO	T-TANGO
C-CHARLIE	L-LIMA	U-UNIFORM
D-DELTA	M-MIKE	V-VICTOR
E-ECHO	N-NOVEMBER	W-WHISKEY
F-FOXTROT	O-OSCAR	X-XRAY
G-GOLF	P-PAPA	Y-YANKEE
H-HOTEL	Q-QUEBEC	Z-ZULU
I-INDIA	R-ROMEO	

For example, if police were carrying out a Police National Computer (PNC) check on a car which they had stopped in the street, displaying an index number of BH68 XYZ, the radio transmission message would request a check on "**B**ravo, **H**otel, six, eight, **X**-ray, **Y**ankee, **Z**ulu". A PNC person check on a Robert Faulkner would be transmitted as "**R**omeo, **O**scar, **B**ravo, **E**cho, **R**omeo, **T**ango" then "**F**oxtrot, **A**lpha, **U**niform, **L**ima, **K**ilo, **N**ovember, **E**cho, **R**omeo".

If you watch TV police dramas you may be familiar with a series called *Juliet Bravo* from the 1980's which was about female police Inspector, Jean Darbley. The title of the series was taken from the phonetic alphabet and denoted the call-sign of the Inspector, "J-B". Fans of *The Bill* will probably remember that the police station, Sun Hill, had the station code of "Sierra Oscar" which was frequently heard during radio transmissions.

The phonetic alphabet has been an important part of police communications for many years and continues to ensure that messages and information are accurately transmitted and understood. Occasionally it can also provide a bit of humour if someone forgets the phonetic equivalent, so you may end up with the zoological version including "E – elephant, M – monkey and Z – zebra" but it doesn't matter too much as long as the letters are correctly identified.

PHONETICS (AND LANGUAGE TEXTS)

In the detective's armoury today is a body of knowledge about language- its nature and its applications. This has become more important as the use of mobile phones has increased, with texting offering any number of clues to crimes committed.

Use the word 'phonetics' in conversation with the ordinary citizen and the word will not mean or suggest very much. He or she might possibly link it to something such as speech therapy or to the ever-expanding world of teaching English to speakers of other languages. These are quite valid reasons for understanding the word and its applications, but phonetics also has a fascinating place in crime detection. The science is about far more than 'The rain in Spain falls mainly on the plain' and people might be forgiven for relating it to the traditionally very important business of elocution.

The world knew all about the famous Ripper Tape back in

the days when the Yorkshire Ripper instilled fear into every woman in West Yorkshire. The taunting recording, goading the police chiefs into believing that they were near to catching their man. What they wanted to know was where did the speaker come from? Not just that he was vaguely a 'Geordie' – but where *exactly*. That is, almost to the street corner of the village, not just the city or the district. Who would be able to know such things?

The answer was the dialectologists, and at the University of Leeds, slap in the middle of the Ripper's hunting ground, academics Stanley Ellis and Jack Windsor Davies got to work on the voice of Wearside Jack. Ellis had worked on the Survey of English Dialects back in the 1950's and he was my tutor, telling me that he used to travel around his allotted shires of England on a motorbike, using questionnaires to elicit exactly what man from the land south of Lincoln would call the weakest pig in the litter. This was a way of working out linguistic boundaries.

This might seem like useless knowledge, but it was quite the opposite. Because Ellis could tell police where a speaker came from, very accurately, he was clearly useful in court. Yes, he pinpointed the speaker who tormented George Oldfield to the former pit village of Castletown, Sunderland. We have to recall that Ellis was aware that this did not mean that the voice was the voice of the Ripper – it was just information for the police to use.

In 1991, however, there was one of the strangest cases on record. This involved an author who was in debt, turning to a very clever device to sort out his problems. This was John Warrington, who bought a cheap electronic toy which he used to impose a half-million-pound ransom demand. He thought that the miniature speaker in the toy would distort voices so that they were undecipherable; it was actually part of his research for a thriller he planned to write. When the device was used against a certain Roger Smith, the Yard's experts got to work. *The Times* reported: 'The brief calls demanding a six-figure sum were barely understandable as Warrington juggled to hold the synthesizer close to the mouthpiece when he made his calls from public phone-boxes.'

PHONETIC SCIENCE

Today, the analysis of speech is very much more sophisticated than in the 1970s, as computer technology has enhanced analytical methods. The basis of this thinking is that we each have an *idiolect*: a very specific voice print, unique to us. It is merely a case of knowing how to study and log that voice print. Anyone who has used sound recordings, such as the Adobe programme, will know what the visual representation of the spoken voice looks like. Phoneticians work in several ways, but at the basis of the work is the minutely different ways we make sounds, from our vocal chords, through to our tongue, pallet, teeth and lips. We even use our nose of course. Most of us would recognise a Liverpool or a South Country accent – but accent is just a general feature. Person A and person B stating the same sentence, 'How are you today, Phil?' would have immense differences if studied closely. Our intonation patterns vary considerably and within a rising or falling intonation there are a number of other features which lend themselves to close study.

Police killer: David Bieber

When PC Ian Broadhurst was shot and killed near Dib Lane in Leeds in December, 2003, the accused was brought to trial and the jury heard recordings of a certain ' Nathan Coleman' placing bets on the phone. Dr John French was able to show that 'Coleman' and the man in the dock, David Bieber, were one and the same. Bieber is a Canadian, but he had been some time in West Yorkshire. The phonetic mix of those two components gave him distinctive features. Dr French studied the tiny speech utterances such as allophones- particular variants of each sound made – and concluded that the chances of the two voices being different to be 'very remote.' Fingerprint evidence backed this up too, and Bieber was convicted of murder.

The Coughing Offence

The TV show, *Who Wants to be a Millionaire?* provided its own very special challenge to the phonetics professional: the accused, Tecwen Whittock, had allegedly produced coughs while in the audience, to give aid to Major Charles Ingram, helping him reach the top prize. Dr French was called in once again, and the man on the show's mixing desk had noticed more coughs than usual from the location where Whittock sat, so the expert had plenty of coughs to study. The work done by the expert was summed up in his explanation: 'We have two ears which help us to determine directionality so a person receiving sound would have a very sharp indication where that sound comes from.'

That was one side of the problem, answering the question about whether Ingram could have heard the coughing guidance. As for the coughs themselves, even a short production of a sharp rush of air through the larynx will have certain characteristics, and these may be studied very closely. Though Dr French did say that 'the analysis of coughing is still in its infancy.'

Suicide Notes and a Gag

The same precision attained in the study of the spoken word extends to the written word. The classic example is the suicide note. In the case of the death of Mrs Sandra Weddell in 2008, there was an alleged suicide note, and the forensic linguists had to conduct an authorship study: this is now a very sophisticated area of their work, and they were able to show that the real author of the note was the husband, Garry Weddell, who had taken his own life after killing others. Psychologists had previously had a lot to say about the authenticity of supposed suicide notes, relating language to the reasons for wanting to take one's own life in the subject's mental profile. But modern linguistics offers something more precise. It can something as simple as a use of an ungrammatical past tense ('he scored - he *done* it with a banana shot') and that may related to other writings by the person in question. More general features help too, such as repetitions, particular vocabulary, or use of pronouns.

In contrast, the case of Eddie Gilfoyle offers a more complex study of how experts can get it wrong: a tale of wrongful imprisonment. Mr Gilfoyle was released in January 2010 and a gagging order imposed. In *The Times* on 25 February 2008, David Canter, famous for the development of crime mapping and a psychology professor, confessed that his previous opinion of Mr Gilfoyle's wife's suicide letter (that it was a fake) had changed. Mr Gilfoyle had been jailed for life, convicted for murder, in 1993, partly on the view that the letter was not a suicide note. We can all get it wrong, and linguistic analysis of the written word is a truly complex challenge for the most expert scholar. The complexity of the case was summed up in the fact that the jury had been asked to believe that the pregnant Mrs Gilfoyle had had the note dictated by her husband and had then hanged herself – with her husband present. This has been a terrible miscarriage of justice, but as the police spokesperson pointed out in 2010, there was a lot of evidence presented at the trial, and the linguistic analysis was just one element in that material.

When Was it Written?

The forensic linguist must be able to tackle any kind of language use in context. One of the latest is, of course, the language used in texting. The basis of study is the simple notion that we all write or speak differently in different situations and when doing different communication acts. This is called a *register*, and from that simple basis all kinds of individual features may be isolated. But above the register there is the totally individual use of words in sequences and in units. These may be studied very closely across a text, and the more text there is, the more chance of patterns and features emerging.

In the case of *R v. Bailey* (2007) at Lincoln Crown Court, the issue was whether or not a text in a diary was written at the time of the alleged offences, or whether it was written after the actions in question. The linguist used a range of other varieties of text to find out what language structures were used to express particular reference to present time as opposed to time in retrospect: the academic words being whether or not Bailey's words had 'contemporaneity' or 'historicity.' The diary was stated to have been written at the time of the events – and those events were those of arson, criminal damage and disconnecting an electricity supply to a residential home for elderly people.

Stanley Ellis and the Ripper Tape

Knowledge of a human voice played a part in a conviction as long ago as the execution of King Charles I. When his executors were later being charged and tried, a man was identified by the report of the nature of his voice (the axeman had worn a mask) and so charged.

But today the specialists are being more prominent as every day passes. The Forensic Linguistic Institute offers courses in all aspects of forensic linguistics, and universities such as Aston and Cardiff have established similar degrees. People may now specialise in a very specific area of this work and make a business out of it, of course, coaching other professionals. At the base of all this is the skill of transcription – being able to reproduce and construct a notation of the words uttered or written.

Stanley Ellis had recording equipment the size of a tank, and he was very familiar with a cassette player and its pause button. He had a very good 'ear' of course. Today, sound editing and recording can quickly identify and monitor a voice profile, and the exactness is perhaps beginning to rival the triumphs of DNA profiling. As a forensic tool in support of police investigations, phonetics and linguistics may still have their best work to come.

The science of forensics is now burgeoning in the universities, and young people are clearly attracted to the study, being inspired by the many television series so popular now, with their slick and wealthy protagonists. The voice and speech utterances play only a small part in that, but some high-profile cases have made the area of forensics one of the newest elements in the degree pathways in college. It is to be hoped, though, that students entering this academic discipline will widen their horizons, learning something about criminality itself, as well as the specialist pleasures of analysing discourse and studying the human voice on recordings. There is a particular delight and satisfaction in being able to transcribe every utterance from a Zulu click to a glottal stop in the speech production of a Yorkshireman. But Stanley Ellis, a quiet man with a fascinating ability, was far more than the man on the radio who could tell where the caller was born: he was a trailblazer in a new science with an exciting career trajectory. He and other analysts studied the Ripper tapes.

That foundation work was done long before the computer revolution. Today, lawbreakers must watch every word and be very careful when they write anything down.

PINKERTON, ALLAN

Maybe the name 'Pinkerton' became known universally after the huge success of the film, Butch Cassidy and the Sundance Kind, when, in the persistence of the men with white hats who were pursuing the villains, we were told that the key sleuth was a Pinkerton man. This relates to Glaswegian Allan Pinkerton who establishing his agency in 1850, with the famous motto 'We never sleep.'

He studied his profession closely and planned the trajectory of his career meticulously. From the start, it is clear that he saw the value of teamwork and efficient communication. What we would now call support networks and the employment of skilled people for specific jobs are two features that stand out as marking his methods of work. His reputation reached the point at which the phrase 'Pinkerton men' became a hallmark of professional reliance and efficiency.

The years in American history that cry out for being defined as the 'Wild West' were arguably the years between the end of the Civil War in 1865 and the 1890s. In that period, the expansion of trade and industry towards the west led to the vulnerability of the new banks, railroads and indeed private homes, out in the cattle towns, mining camps, ad railroad centres. Pinkerton stepped in and offered a protection and investigation service.

Pinkerton is perhaps best known for his discovery of a plot which was being hatched to kill Abraham Lincoln. He established a secret service which covered the American Northwest, and some of his major triumphs include the cracking of the notorious Reno gang, and the work one of his agents did against the brutal Molly Maguires in Denver. The hero of that very dangerous undercover operation was arguably one of the best detectives on record anywhere: James McParland.

The agents were not all as successful. In the work against the notorious James and Younger gang, in Missouri and beyond, one of Pinkerton's detectives, working undercover, was found out, and mercilessly killed.

Another celebrated detective out west was John B Hughes. Although he did not work for Pinkerton, he won fame by being the man who tracked down 'Black Bart' the stage coach robber.

When we look at the history of the Pinkertons today, what really stands out is the employment of women operatives, and in their ranks, the woman who stands out is Kate Warne. She worked undercover, and as a spy, and although she does not figure much in Pinkerton's memoirs, we are gradually learning more about her achievements.

They are still chasing rogues today, and one of their most recent escapades was in June, 1994, when it was reported that Pinkerton had 'set its sleuths on the trail of oil swindlers.' This was the announcement that the Agency was to open a massive centre in Aberdeen where, as one reporter put it, they would be 'at the sharp end of the battle to track down cheats in the multi-billion pound industry.'

Pinkerton characters will always figure in the literature and mythology of the American West.

PLOD

This is a derogatory term used by DCI Gene Hunt in *Life on Mars* when referring to his uniformed colleagues. He would often have some friendly advice for them and here are just two examples:

"Twenty per cent of the regional uniform division suffered some form of light injury last year (splinters from their pencils, cat scratches during rescue missions, scalded mouths from too many rushed cups of tea, that sort of thing). Yes, you can get yourself in dangerous situations, stop whinging!"

"Do yourself a favour. If you're out on duty (messing about on your bike, no doubt) and you see a beautiful copper-coloured Ford Cortina Mark III (2000E*) heading towards you at what you suspect to be above the speed limit, put your helmet over your face, count to five and when you look again, I'll be out of your way. Do not, under any circumstances, try and pull me over. I am probably in high pursuit and saving lives, like the hero I am. Even if I'm not, getting home while my tikka masala's still bubbling is a good reason."

* "The 'E' stands for 'executive' – even my car has a better rank than you"

There is no doubt that some detectives used these sort of terms many years ago but thankfully the relationship between CID and uniform is now much better, although the sense of humour, often referred to as 'gallows humour' is still very evident on both sides.

The term 'plod' is a reference to 'Mr Plod the Policeman', a fictional character in the *Noddy* children's series by Enid Blyton, who never let Toyland's crooks escape from the "long arm of the law." His catchphrase was "Halt, in the name of Plod!"

PRIVATE DETECTIVES

By the end of the nineteenth century, private detectives came on the scene, and their work was primarily in family, divorce and lost persons business. In the writings of John Mortimer, barrister and novelist, we have extensive details regarding the private sleuths and divorce problems. But there were other, more general difficulties when private detective work began to expand.

Being a 'detective' and finding work for the divorce courts was easy. Jesse Farbrother in Brighton (the place most celebrated for adultery evidence scenes) opened an account at Barclay's Bank under the name of The Gibbons Bureau. A client called Manning, just seventeen, then saw an advertisement in the local paper asking for 'a young lady with detective abilities.' Farbrother met his new recruit and told he had a big staff of 'eighteen permanent and twenty on reserve.' He detailed young Manning to follow a man from Brighton to London on five journeys, and also to watch a woman's flat. The whole business became farcical in court when the judge and jury learned that Farbrother had wandered the land trying to open detective agencies. Farbrother had even created a detective companion kit to be given to each agent, including a tab that had to be dropped on the ground if ever they were lost while on an assignment.

Crazy stories of 'detectives' proliferated as the popular media made them glamorous. Magazines such as *Union Jack* and the *Sexton Blake Library* (the latter started in 1915) had led to such innovations as 'The Dog Detective' and the blurb typified the appeal of the detective for readers: 'A Sexton Blake story means something really first class in the way of detective fiction. And you can get one every week! Stories that get you worked up with excitement, stories in which baffling mystery, non-stop action, brilliant detection and thrills are welded into one masterly whole...' Such was the impact that tales such as that of the 'sham detective 'William Martin was arrested for theft of thirty-two sides of bacon. He had carried out the theft by approaching a young boy who was in charge of the vanload of bacon, saying he was a detective and showing a badge. The boy said, 'I have seen detectives on the films wearing badges, so I believed him.'

Both private detectives on divorce cases and Scotland Yard men involved in special duties were bringing to light a whole tranche of new issues related to the morality of detective work. A detective had to encroach on personal liberties in the course of his or her work; investigative actions would sometimes border on crossing the line into criminality, at least as far as the letter of the law would define in a criminal law court. This whole area of detective work became apparent during the Great War when 'spy mania' meant that Vernon Kell and his new MI5 were intercepting letters; Kell, as we have noted, worked with the Yard, and Yard men would learn to act as agents, with a more military purpose.

These difficulties became more widely understood with the Janvier case of 1917, which went to the Court of Appeal in 1919. Henriette Janvier had come from Paris to London in 1908 to learn English, sent there by her employers. In London she met a German called Neumann. But the problem with this case is that the detectives in question were described as 'private enquiry agents.' They were almost certainly working for the Yard and for Kell. What happened was that, when the lodging house was almost empty one day in 1917, the agents arrived and told Henriette that another lodger called March was corresponding with a spy, but on his first appearance, one of the agents had said, 'I am a Detective Inspector from Scotland Yard and represent the military authorities, and you are the woman we want, as you have been corresponding with a German spy.'

There had clearly been a change of tack since the original trial, in which there had been no sentences given. The truth was either that the two men really were Yard officers doing the usual thing, intercepting suspect mail, or they were indeed private agents. If the latter, then they would have had no palpable reason for being on such a detail and to act as aggressively as they did. The incident illustrates the extent to which the presence of a Scotland Yard detective instilled awe and fear into private citizens. Of course, the affair with Henriette was in war time, but in effect the detectives were asking the girl to cooperate in an enquiry – and one that breached civil rights – without prior arrangement. Moreover, they did that after first terrifying her.

PROCEEDS OF CRIME ACT

Money is at the heart of all organised crime. The lifestyle and status it brings is the main motivation for most criminals and, just as legitimate businesses need funding to stay afloat, so does organised crime. Many such criminals fear attacks on their finances and lifestyle more than prison.

The Proceeds of Crime Act 2002 (often referred to as simply POCA) is a piece of legislation created to tackle organised crime, giving officers the power to seize cash and recover assets, such as cars and houses, bought by criminals through the proceeds of their criminal activity. POCA strikes directly at the main motive for crime, deterring offenders, disrupting organised crime and demonstrating that crime doesn't pay. The money recovered through the sale of a criminal's assets can be put back into community projects and can be used to assist future criminal investigations.

There are two ways in which the police can make it more difficult for criminals to get their hands on their money and launder the profits of their crimes –

Forfeiture order

A forfeiture order can be made against a person at a Magistrates Court using POCA. The order is only made against cash which is believed to be the proceeds of crime or intended for use in crime. A forfeiture order can be granted by the court even if the person concerned hasn't been charged or convicted of a criminal offence.

Confiscation order

A confiscation order can be granted by the Crown Court to deprive criminals of the benefit of their crimes. If it can be proven that a criminal has committed an acquisitive crime, such as theft, and they have benefitted from that crime, then an Accredited Financial Investigator working on behalf of the police or other enforcement agency can identify the value of any assets held by the criminal (bank accounts, houses, vehicles). This amount can then be used to pay back the financial benefits of their crimes, even if the assets are considered to be legally held by that person. Following a successful application for a confiscation order, the criminal will be given a specified timescale to pay the full amount or may be subject to a prison sentence.

POCA is a very effective piece of legislation and can be used to hit organised criminals where it hurts them the most – their pockets. So the drug dealer who is living in a luxurious house, driving a top of the range car and wearing designer clothes should bear in mind that they may well be on the radar of the financial experts who will seek to remove their ill-gotten gains.

CASE STUDIES – POCA

1) One of the biggest cash seizures in the last few years amounted to over £200,000 found in February 2018 on the

streets of Fulham in London. Police noticed a man pulling what appeared to be an empty suitcase and carrying a rucksack on his shoulder. He was seen to enter a communal area between two business premises before re-appearing minutes later with the suitcase and rucksack, both apparently full. The man was stopped by police and found to be in possession of a total of £240,000 which was contained in the suitcase and rucksack. He was arrested on suspicion of money laundering offences and later pleaded guilty to a charge of transferring criminal property for which he received a custodial sentence of two and a half years.

2) A man currently serving a jail sentence for offering to sell parts of endangered species has been ordered to pay back £100,642 within six months or face an additional three years in prison. Allawi Abbas from Hertfordshire was sentenced to 14 months imprisonment in November 2017 for keeping/offering for sale rhinoceros horns, elephant tusks and hippopotamus teeth. A financial investigation under POCA pursued by the Metropolitan Police Criminal Finance Team resulted in a criminal benefit agreed at £961,777. The available assets of Abbas were agreed to be £100,642. Any other major funds, valuables, or property up to the benefit amount, which he accumulates during his lifetime will be removed from him as and when they come to police notice.

3) A yacht seized by the Metropolitan Police from a man convicted of a £2.4 million fraud offence was sold for £58,000 in January 2017. The money has been used to pay off part of a £1.2 million confiscation order.

4) A man from Ipswich has been made subject to what is believed to be the first bank account forfeiture order in the

country, after new legislation was introduced earlier this year (2018), meaning that police can now seize almost £117,000 from his bank account. Legislation was introduced under the Proceeds of Crime Act (POCA) in March 2018 allowing police officers new powers in relation to the freezing and forfeiture of money which is suspected to have been derived from criminal activity. The powers are civil with a lower burden of proof with officers having to prove on the 'balance of probability' that the money is because of unlawful conduct. This is a lower level than the criminal burden which is 'beyond reasonable doubt'.

The case began when intelligence was received that suggested the man was 'laundering' suspiciously high amounts of money through his bank account. An 'account freezing order' was granted which prevented him from conducting any other transactions whilst his account was investigated. He was found to have deposited around £2.5 million, almost exclusively cash, into his account over a period of around eight months. This figure was far greater than his annual income as a freelance car mechanic. The circumstances led to an application for the forfeiture order by the Eastern Region Special Operations Unit (ERSOU) Economic Crime Unit. The forfeited money will be split between the Home Office and the five police forces represented by ERSOU. A senior detective commented "We want to maximise this new legislation to disrupt criminals across the region and will continue to use any powers available to show that crime does not pay".

POLICY FILE
One of the most important aspects of managing any serious criminal investigation, particularly a murder, is the systematic recording of the Senior Investigating Officer's (SIO) policies. SIO's should use a Policy File to record critical policy decisions. It

will become the definitive record upon which they will rely when subsequently asked to account for decisions at court or other proceedings some months, or perhaps even years, later. Policy files are sequentially numbered bound books which should be completed by the SIO or a person acting on their behalf. Each entry should be signed and dated. The book contains duplicate pages, one of which should be removed following completion for submission to the HOLMES incident room (see **H**) so that the decisions can be recorded onto the computer system. The book provides notes of guidance for completion and a detailed aide-memoire containing strategic, staffing and Human Rights information. It is likely that an SIO will complete a number of Policy Files during the course of an investigation. Key decisions and the reasons why you have or have not followed a particular course of action should be written down as the SIO is very unlikely to remember specific details some time later. It would be impossible to cover every potential type of policy decision but the following are just a few examples:

- the identification of crime scenes and their parameters
- the parameters of searches
- the parameters of a trawl for CCTV footage
- the appointment of trained forensic staff and a forensic recovery strategy
- the decision to arrest (or not) a suspect
- the decision to release (or not) specific information to the media
- the identification of key/significant witnesses (see **K**) and how their evidence will be recorded

Any policy decisions of a sensitive nature will be recorded in a separate Policy File which should be clearly marked as such. These will include sensitive intelligence issues, CHIS (see **C**), covert policing tactics and anything else which the SIO considers too sensitive to be recorded in the standard Policy File.

PROFILING

Psychological profiling began to take the form we now under-stand (through popular media) in the work of the Behavioural Science Unit within the FBI. But long before the recent development of such notions as psychopaths and sociopaths, and the mapping initiated by Professor David Canter, there was the 'foundation' case of the Mad Bomber in 1940–1941.

In November 1940 a bomb was discovered at the office of Consolidated Edison in New York. There was a note with it, which read, 'Con Edison Crooks, this is for you.' Other bombs and then a letter was received, followed by several letters during the war, but the unknown person had held back from further activity after the attack on Pearl Harbour. But that was not the end of the case, by any means. Between 1951 and 1955 fourteen bombs were found. Then, in 1956 one of the bombs exploded, and though nobody was killed, there were many casualties.

The result of all this was that a psychologist was called in to lead an analysis. This was Dr James Brussel, and he set to work on exploring what the personality of such a criminal might be. Brussel provided a 'profile' of the culprit. it was found that in the text of One specific letter- back in 1931 – there had been reference to something that had proved to be a major trigger to the lines of thought the bomber had taken up. A certain George Metesky, who had worked for the firm, was hurt in that industrial accident. He was tracked down, and at his home, detectives found details that lined up well with Brussel's profile. Amazingly, Brussel had said that the bomber would wear a double-breasted suit. He was right!

One of the consequences of this case was the cool profile of profiling. The basis of the approach was that characteristics of offenders could be gathered, systematized, and then applied to a range of types. Thus, it was thought, habits of thought and action, along with the *modus operandi* of an individual's crime, would be logged, assessed and acted upon. Psychological profiling had arrived.

This all became a massive influence on detective work as well as on crime fiction; the turn against its prestige came, perhaps, with the case of Robert Napper, who turned out to be the actual killer of Rachel Nickel, after profiling work and a police infiltration had settled upon another suspect. But it would be unfair and extreme to dismiss the claims of profiling after one media-hyped case. The basis of thought is compelling, taking notice of every specific detail of an offender's approach, down to the potential fetishism involved, and then also exploring the past influences on a particular offender.

There is no doubt that such notions as the progressive trajectory of an offender is an important part of a profile, and that such thinking is very useful and constructive. For instance, if one looks at the case of the Yorkshire Ripper, Peter Sutcliffe, there is a progression from failed hammer attacks, voyeurism, assault and then murder. The temptation for all writers concerned with profiling and this kind of thinking is that there will be a reliable template for a category of case, and this is patently untrue and unreliable.

It will always be appealing to readers and writers of detective fiction to think that a profile will be a major tool in an investigation; yet, as reality makes clear, it may be an egregious error to assume that a facile similarity in two cases assures the investigator that the same offender is involved, and modern criminal history shows that notions acquired from profiling have provided easy solutions to crime scene details and their questions. In other words, other approaches, combined with profiling, are just as valid.

Still, the American development of profiling, at first in the hands of John E Douglas, made behavioural assessment a definite arm of police investigation, and it is not difficult to find success stories in the records of that FBI approach.

We also have geographical profiling. This is based on notions of the extent of a suspect's movements, bearing in mind all the factors which might influence actions and mental or physical aspects of the nature of a specific crime. The most well-known example is arguably David Canter's interesting mapping of Peter Sutcliffe's movements across the Leeds/Bradford conurbation during his reign of terror. In some ways, the common sense of the approach stands out, in that the location of Sutcliffe's home in relation to the scenes of his attacks all form a circumscribed, manageable area for a man moving around in an extent of land he knew well. The topography of murder is of course, eminently definable – but in most cases this is with hindsight.

A similar instance occured in the hunt for Levi Bellfield in 2004–6 in West London. A look at the local map and the scenes of the crimes indicated immediately that when Bellfield first became a suspect, the map of his terrain stood out as being a hunting-ground entirely and intricately known to the man. Of course, other cases offer sharp contrasts to all this neatness. The case of Bible John is one, and also the possible murder catalogue of George Black. In these cases, crime scenes were a part of routes regularly traversed by suspects, so a similar but related analysis was undertaken in the investigations. There has, of course, been a determined application of such mapping to the infamous Jack the Ripper case. Suspects have been found whose movements in their daily work have taken them near to murder scenes, and then there is an enlargement of the investigation, as a matrix falls into place, mixing the murder itself and the immediate environs of the offence, with other, related aspects of a particular crime.

One popular result of profiling has been the psychopath test, which offers readers, in contexts of popular true crime publications, the chance to see how many aspects of a psychopathic profile fit their own nature. This is far from being a scientific tool, of course, but it does serve to highlight the idea of the 'psychopath among us' line of thought, which takes profiling from criminological contexts to everyday life. In other words, qualities linked to psychopathic killers are extended to such subjects as psychopathic personalities within business or any power structure.

PROMOTION

The police promotion system for Constables and Sergeants has changed fairly recently to include more of a work-based assessment approach. Since 1991 police forces in England and Wales had been using the Objective Structured Performance Related Examination (known as OSPRE) which consisted of two stages. OSPRE Part I was a multiple-choice written examination and Part II consisted of a series of scenario based role-playing exercises. In order to qualify for promotion to the next rank, an officer would need to pass both Parts and would then have to attend some form of selection process, normally a formal interview, in their home force. Successful candidates would then be promoted as and when suitable vacancies arose.

OSPRE has been replaced by the National Police Promotion Framework (NPPF) which is a continuous four step process aimed at promoting officers to the rank of Sergeant and Inspector. Promotion can only be attained once an officer has successfully completed all four steps.

Step one – competence in current rank (the purpose of this step is to ensure that candidates are suitable to enter the promotion process. This means establishing that they are competent in their current rank, rather than assessing potential for temporary promotion to another rank. They must have completed the probation period in their current rank, demonstrated competence and be endorsed by their line manager).

Step two – written examination of law and procedure (the purpose of this step is to ensure that candidates have the appropriate legal knowledge relevant to the rank of Sergeant or Inspector. This is the same type of examination as OSPRE Part I and, if passed, is valid for 5 years from the date of the examination. Candidates who are unsuccessful and don't achieve the pass mark will return to NPPF Step one).

Step three – local selection process to evaluate suitability (the structure of this process will probably differ between forces but is likely to always include a formal interview. The process is intended to match suitable candidates with existing vacancies in that force).

Step four – work-based assessment on temporary promotion for a 12 month period (candidates are assessed in the workplace against selected competencies for the next rank. They need to pass the academic assessment and be able to evidence satisfactory performance in that rank before they can be substantively promoted).

The NPPF only applies to promotion to the rank of Sergeant or Inspector. All ranks of Chief Inspector and above are likely to be subject to local force selection procedures which will normally include a written application form and a formal interview which may also include a presentation to the interview panel.

Detectives are required to follow the same promotion process as their uniformed colleagues. It is a complete myth that detectives are of a higher rank. A Police Constable is the same rank as a Detective Constable, a Police Sergeant is the same rank as a Detective Sergeant and so on. Detectives receive specialist training to enable them to carry out their role effectively but the rank is equal.

When I transferred from the Metropolitan Police to Lincoln-shire Police in the year 2000, I was posted as a uniformed PC. This was despite the fact that I had served as a DC and Acting DS for several years prior to my transfer. I was qualified (via OSPRE Parts I and II) to be a Sergeant but had to wait for the opportunity to apply to become a DC in my new force. When I was promoted to Sergeant in Lincolnshire, I was posted as a uniformed Sergeant and had to wait for the opportunity to apply to become a Detective Sergeant along with others in a similar position. I was able to secure promotion from Detective Sergeant to Detective Inspector and then to Detective Chief Inspector without the requirement to carry out uniformed duties in those ranks which made perfect sense, taking into account my skills and experience. I enjoyed the challenges presented in a uniformed role and it certainly did me no harm, but continuity as a detective made a lot of sense. Forces tend to be more flexible when promoting detectives these days and don't always insist on a return to uniformed duties unless there are sound operational or personal reasons.

PSYCHICS IN CRIME DETECTION

In December 1990, police were called to a house at Westcliff-on-Sea in Essex. There had been a desperate confrontation inside those walls: Martin Rivers was facing what he was sure was a phenomenon known to paranormal investigators as a poltergeist – a 'noisy spirit' in the literal translation of the German words.

Martin told *The Times* reporter that 'an evil spirit' had come into his home in Gainsborough Drive. The presence had been extremely violent, as the reporter put it, in this account, the thing, '...threw his son Daniel out of bed, moved furniture, and attacked the dog. Neighbours woken by screams, wails and barking confirmed that the noises were spine-chilling.'

The police were at a loss as to how to proceed. They simply confirmed that they would try to protect the house and its family. But the press summed up the dilemma: 'Poltergeist raid puzzles detectives.' It certainly did.

Paranormal events and alleged beings naturally present a huge problem for detectives. But what about the other side of the coin- the assistance given to detectives by psychics and mediums? There is a fair amount of evidence on record to suggest that such approaches have a place in the teamwork. Despite this, Britain appears to be the state with most resistance to the use of psychics in investigations. Elsewhere, there have been numerous cases in which the participation of psychic investigators had led to impressive outcomes, though of course there are probably more failures than successes, and the media tend to fasten onto the more sensational stories.

A few examples may show the nature of some claims made to the success and viability of psychics' approaches in this context. In 1983, for instance, pilot Arthur Herbert went missing. He had three passengers in his plane, and the craft disappeared. A police search came to nothing, but then psychic Noreen Renier was asked to help and she provided perfect co-ordinates for the location of the crash site. Again, in Sydney in 1996, psychic Phillipe Durant was brought in to help find the missing Paula Brown somewhere around Port Botany. Using a map, a plumb-bob and some of Pauline's hair, he came very close to finding the location. As it happened, a lorry driver passed the body and stopped, in order to check it out. The body was very close to Phillipe's suggested findings.

Obviously there will be scepticism regarding this subject. The reasons why such investigations are often rejected are not hard to find. For one thing, there is always suspicion on any methods using non-rational approaches; police work is systematic; it is professional in planning and in applications of procedures. Detectives must rely on a set sequence of measures, and any deviation from that could cramp the progress of a case.

In popular culture, we may see the result of that desire to add a paranormal perspective to the rationality; when Hollywood fastened onto the Sherlock Holmes phenomenon, for instance, when it ran out of solid police detection methods, it sprang into Holmes psychic tales with alacrity. The result was usually farcical. The entire subject seems to offer something utterly opposed to dogged, deductive and organised detective work. Yet there will always be people who will back the off-beat and innovative in detective work, and the number of worthwhile results on record will always encourage such initiatives.

Q

QUALITIES OF A DETECTIVE

I've thought long and hard about what I think are the sort of qualities which make a good detective and there are lots. You certainly need to be omnicompetent and a 'jack of all trades' as there are so many different areas of policing where you need to have a good working knowledge. These include criminal investigation, law, procedures and the prosecution process, to

THE A–Z OF DETECTIVE WORK

name but a few. If you're working as a detective in a specialist role such as child abuse investigation, counter-terrorism or murder investigation, then your knowledge and skills are likely to be concentrated towards that role, but as a detective working in a Divisional or Borough CID office you may be the first detective to attend the scene or advise on any occurrence, from a suspicious death to a suspected terrorist incident, and as such, you need to have some understanding of what is required at that time. I have chosen just six qualities which I think are essential for a detective but it's fair to say that there are more and, no doubt, you may come up with your own.

Attention to detail

This is a vital quality which every detective needs as they will be investigating serious crimes which will always require high levels of concentration and patience. There may be a piece of evidence in the middle of a mass of other information which could be missed if the examination of that material isn't thorough and systematic. A detective may need to review hours of CCTV footage, examine masses of phone data or interrogate several databases during the course of each investigation. Although the key elements of their enquiries will be updated on the relevant computer crime report, they will make notes in a 'rough' book, a lined notebook, which they will normally carry with them whilst out making enquiries.

During one of my investigations, I still clearly recall spending months looking at phone data in an effort to identify the suspect. A young girl had been attacked and injured with a knife in her own bedroom by a man who had made off from the scene and was at large. Despite a thorough forensic examination and a feature on *Crimewatch*, we were unable to identify the offender. I looked through a huge quantity of phone data over the course of several months, looking for clues which might benefit the investigation. It got to the point where I would sometimes wake up in the middle of the night with numbers flying around inside my head. The long hours spent looking through phone numbers and call data was worth it in the end as we were able to use some of it as evidence when the offender was eventually identified. He was convicted at court and sent to prison.

Communication skills

As a detective you need to have effective communication skills as you will be required to interact with many different people in a range of varied circumstances. You will need to be able to adapt your approach depending on the person you are communicating with and how. A stop in the street or a taped interview with a seasoned criminal will require a different approach from a case conference with a barrister or a visit to a Magistrates house to apply for a search warrant. This may seem quite obvious but your attitude, body language and the words you use will always impact on how you make sure that you are understood and how you are able to elicit the information you require.

Intuition

Sometimes you can't always explain why something doesn't feel quite right or why you acted in a certain way but for a detective, intuition can be very important. It can't be taught on a training course, but it is right to say that if something appears unusual or out of place, there's every chance that further investigation could prove beneficial. Taking the initiative and going with your 'gut instinct' can often lead to the detection of major crime. Attending reports of sudden deaths, suicides or missing persons requires a sensitive but tenacious approach. The latter category, in particular, will be a test for any investigator should there be something more than meets the eye. For example, a man who reports his female partner missing and has in fact murdered her, may leave some clues around their home. Things that look out of place, such as missing or broken items of furniture or ornaments (indicating a struggle may have taken place), signs of recent cleaning, disinfectant, a small bonfire in the garden, or a missing shower curtain, bedding or rug (to wrap up a body), are examples. During the investigation into the disappearance of Holly Wells and Jessica Chapman (Soham, 2002) the police who went into the house of Ian Huntley (later convicted of their murders) during the early stages of the investigation, noticed a strong smell of lemon disinfectant. It transpired that Huntley had killed both girls in the house and had thoroughly cleaned the interior in an effort to remove any forensic evidence which may have implicated him.

CASE STUDY – INTUITION

At 10.50pm on Friday 2nd January 1981 Sergeant Robert Ring and PC Robert Hydes were on patrol off Melbourne Avenue in Sheffield when they saw a V8 Rover 3500 parked up with a man and woman inside. When the male driver got out of the car, which was bearing false number plates, he went to urinate behind a nearby stone porch and oil storage tank. He was later arrested on suspicion of theft of the car number plates and taken away. However, the Sergeant later made the most crucial decision of his career when he returned to the scene and searched the area around the storage tank. He shone his torch on the ground and lying near the wall was a ball-pein hammer and a knife. When the driver, who gave his name as Peter William Sutcliffe, was confronted with this evidence he confessed to being the man known as the 'Yorkshire Ripper' and having been responsible for murdering 13 women and attempting to murder 7 others, for which he was later convicted. The woman in the car with him that night, Olivia Reivers, would undoubtedly have been another of his victims had the police not arrived. Largely through the instinctive actions of the officers, Sutcliffe was caught and was to enter the history books as one of the UK's most notorious serial killers.

Knowledge of the law

A good working knowledge of criminal law is a must for a detective. During your initial training to become a detective you will be studying law and procedures to prepare you for the National Investigators Examination, but you need to keep yourself updated with new legislation and changes to the current laws as your career in CID progresses. This isn't an easy task as, due to limited funding and resource issues, the training departments in a lot of forces have been dramatically cut and, in some cases, removed altogether. It now falls on the CID supervisors and the detectives themselves to make sure that they are appraised, particularly in relation to changes which will have an effect on their current role. You will often see piles of books on the desks in the CID office in relation to criminal law and legislation such as the Police and Criminal Evidence Act (PACE) which are so important to the daily work of a detective. Blackstone's Police Manuals are popular with detectives, particularly those who are seeking promotion. There are specific manuals covering all aspects of *Crime* and *Evidence and Procedure* which are updated regularly to include changes and new legislation. A detective may have to investigate a serious assault, sexual offence, fraud, robbery, drugs offence or another serious or complex case and so they really do need to know their criminal law.

Persistence

Persistence is 'to continue in an opinion or course of action in spite of difficulty or opposition.' It is a great quality to have and one which makes for a good detective. When I think of this quality, I have to mention a former colleague of mine, DC Garrie 'Taff' Roberts, who had it in abundance. 'Taff' was one of the DCs in our CID office in a rural town in South Lincolnshire. We gave him the nickname of 'The Beagle' because he was like a 'dog with a bone' and could sniff out clues. I knew that 'Taff' would never submit an investigation as complete unless every possible lead had been exhausted and he was a real asset to our little team. 'Taff' was ex-RAF and used to refer to me, his DS, as 'Red One' (the Team Leader of the Red Arrows). Earlier this year (2018) 'Taff' passed away, far too early and only a few years after retirement from the police. He will be sorely missed but will no doubt still be solving crime in his unique way. RIP mate.

Sense of humour

Last, but certainly not least, every detective has to have a sense of humour as I don't think you'd manage without one. Humour within emergency service workers is often referred to as "gallows humour" as it can, at times, seem rather inappropriate. It is a coping mechanism to help people deal with the stressful and tragic circumstances they are often faced with. The examples I'm going to quote certainly don't fall into that category, more the mischievous pranks designed to embarrass new detectives in the office.

The first dates back many years and involves a message left on the trainee's desk asking them to contact Mr. C Lyon on a phone number. You may already see it coming, but many didn't. When the call was answered by a representative at London

Zoo, they probably guessed who was calling when they asked to speak with Mr. Sea lion! Another phone call prank involved a request to contact Detective Constable Tenn on a phone number. Inevitably the trainee would shorten the rank without thinking and say "Can I speak to DC Tenn please?" The number related to Heathrow Airport and the DC-10 was, at the time, a type of aeroplane in use there. There are many others, as you can imagine, not all of which are suitable for print, but hopefully you get the picture.

Q CAR

The term 'Q-car' was first used way back in 1933 in the Metropolitan Police to describe unmarked cars used for detective work. The name was taken from the 'Q boats' used by the Royal Navy, heavily armed merchant ships with concealed weaponry, which were designed to lure submarines into making surface attacks. Throughout the decades the 'Q-car' came to be recognised as a pro-active element of crime investigation. Back in 1964 the British magazine *Motorcycle Mechanics* reported "If you drive down the A20 between London and Maidstone, keep a careful eye on the four-wheel boys... because there are several police vehicles in the area disguised as normal vehicles. Watch out particularly for a black Daimler SP250 sports car and a green Farina A40... I've no doubt that these police 'Q-cars'- the Daimler particularly – pick up dozens of offenders every day... Everyone concerned in any way with motoring should clamour against 'Q-cars' and hidden radar traps too". In 1966 the crew of the 'Q-car' call-sign Foxtrot One-One were all killed by a group of criminals in West London (see **F**).

The 'Q-car' was generally a high-performance vehicle which usually had a crew of three police officers. It was common practice for two of those officers to be detectives and the third would be an advanced driver from the uniformed branch, all in plain clothes. Their brief was to patrol the streets in their vehicle to detect crime. A posting to the 'Q-car' was highly sought after, due to the fact that it gave officers the chance to work as part of a small team and also provided a respite from the routine daily CID office work. As the car looked just like many other vehicles on the streets, it provided the occupants with the opportunity to watch and get close to people without necessarily being recognised as police officers.

Although there are many unmarked police vehicles in London and across the country today, they are not generally used in the same way as the 'Q-car' used to be. This is partly due to resource issues and a change in the way police now investigate crime. The concept of a 'Q-car' is a thing of the past and the name is rarely, if ever, used in modern policing.

QUEEN'S COUNSEL (QC) now KINGS COUNSEL (KC)

A Queen's Counsel (QC) was an eminent lawyer or advocate who was appointed by the current monarch to be "one of Her Majesty's Counsel learned in the law". Members wear silk gowns of a particular design and the award of Queen's Counsel was known informally as "taking silk". As a result, QCs were sometimes referred to as "silks". Appointments were made from within the legal profession based on merit with successful applicants tending to be barristers, or (in Scotland) advocates, with at least 15 years of experience.

The first Queen's Counsel *Extraordinary* was Sir Francis Bacon who was given a patent giving him precedence at the Bar in 1597, and formally styled King's Counsel in 1603. It wasn't really until the early 1830's that King's Counsel emerged into eminence and the numbers began to increase. It became the standard means in which to recognise a barrister as a senior member of the profession. The earliest English law list, published in 1775, lists 165 members of the Bar, of whom 14 were King's Counsel. There are now thousands of QC's qualified to practice in the UK.

QCs would generally be involved in the presentation of the most serious and complex cases heard in the Crown Court. In a murder trial with six defendants there would probably be seven QCs involved, one for each of the defendants and counsel for the prosecution. Each QC would probably be supported by a junior barrister who would present certain parts of the case. In such a trial, you could well see up to fourteen barristers inside the courtroom. As a detective you are likely to come into contact with these barristers when they prosecute a case which you have prepared for trial.

It's common for the police, Crown Prosecution Service (CPS) and barrister(s) to hold a case conference in advance of the trial to discuss the case. You will also see them at the Crown Court throughout the criminal trial.

Updated 2023

Following the passing of Her Majesty Queen Elizabeth II on 8th September 2022, all Queen's Counsel (QC) have now become King's Counsel (KC). The first case to be seen by a KC since 1950 at the Old Bailey took place on Friday 9th September, the day after the death of the Queen. Like QC's, KCs are well-established lawyers appointed by the monarch who take on cases that require a high level of experience. Becoming a KC (formerly QC) is referred to as 'taking silk' and although merit-based, requires many years of experience and selection founded on particular areas of expertise.

There will be no change to the way that the Crown is referred to during criminal prosecutions (it will still be R v Smith, for example) but the initial 'R' will change its meaning from Queen, Regina to King, Rex. In addition to the title changes, the Queen's Bench Division of the High Court will become the King's Bench Division, forming the largest of the High Court divisions, overseeing disputes including negligence, libel and personal injury claims.

Academic manager at the University of Law commented 'For some 70 years the term Queen's Counsel or QC has been used with great pride for those taking silk in the legal profession. It will take a bit of time to get used to the new term KC's, as King's Counsels will be known, but they will of course be just as revered.'

R

RANK STRUCTURE

The rank structure for detectives, whether in a CID office or a specialist team investigating murders, is pretty much the same. In order of seniority, it is as follows

Detective Superintendent – D/Supt or Det./Supt
Detective Chief Inspector – DCI
Detective Inspector – DI
Detective Sergeant – DS
Detective Constable – DC

There are also likely to be some trainee detectives, particularly in a CID office or working in a specialist role, such as child abuse investigation. They may be referred to as DC's but may also be called Trainee Investigators (T/I) or Trainee Detective Constables (T/DC). There may be a Detective Chief Superintendent in overall charge of crime and part of the

Command Team in the force. They will normally be based at the force headquarters and will adopt a strategic management role rather than investigative. Due to the current resource and finance issues, some forces have started to consider the removal of the ranks of Chief Superintendent and Chief Inspector. If this happens, which is not certain at this time, it will be through non-replacement after retirement rather than any form of redundancy.

The rank structure for uniformed officers is exactly the same as detectives, simply remove the word 'detective' for the more senior ranks and replace it with the word 'police' for Sergeant and Constable

Superintendent – Supt.
Chief Inspector – C/I or Ch./Insp.
Inspector – Insp.
Police Sergeant – PS
Police Constable – PC

RECRUITMENT AND TRAINING (Historical)

From the early days, that is the 1840s, professional detectives were recruited from the ranks, as it were. It was understood in the first decades of the professional force that plain clothes operations were of primary interest. Consequently, as 'narks' had always been cultivated since the century before when the Fielding brothers operated out of Bow Street, the detectives learned as they progressed, working with a circle or network of contacts.

It was when, towards the end of Victoria's reign, that increased professionalism came along, linked to advances in forensics and in wider developments of espionage and terrorism, that detectives became more specialised.

In the years immediately after the Great War there was serious trouble related to police strikes; issues around pensions and employment conditions led to a shake-up in all areas of police work.

Then in the mid 30s, the Home Office commissioned a major enquiry into detective work, and the result was the report of the *Departmental Committee on Detective Work and Procedure* (1938). This had a great deal to say about training and recruitment. In the second volume of that publication, we have a criticism of the situation before c. 1935:

'We have not found any existing course of instruction for detectives which we would regard as satisfactory meeting of all requirement....the experience of local officers has been too circumscribed and there has been no machinery by which the results of their good work and original thought could be made available beyond the local force boundaries.'

The authors of the report did go on to prioritise certain skills which they argued formed the core of the ideal detective's profile:

- *Loyalty to the service, superiors and colleagues*
- *Dealing with the public*
- *Conduct at the scene of the crime*
- *Behaviour in the charge room, station and offices*
- *Conduct in the courts and witness box*
- *The necessity for strict fairness when dealing with prisoners and their relatives*
- *The dangers of improper associations when endeavouring to obtain information*

What the report shows us today is that the top brass in the police were looking for ways to amalgamate the 'school of the street' with the classroom study they were developing. The recruits to the force at this time had to be assiduous students. Their work entailed visits to laboratories, a viva voce examination, Descriptive and Identification test, and a final written examination.

REGIONAL DETECTIVES: PRE-1900

There was no professional detective force in England until 1842, and that was only the start of it, being formed in the Metropolitan Police. But as the century went on and regional forces were formed, there were small detective branches and plain clothes men across the land. It had formerly been common practice to ask Scotland Yard men to come out to the provinces when there was something that was beyond the resources of the regional force, such as Chartism or Luddites problems. There had been special constables and the police of course, but when it came to the special skills of detective work, specialists were needed.

The regional detectives in Victorian Britain are not well known, and the publications are few. One Manchester man, who was famous at the time, was Jerome Caminada, (see separate entry) who worked mostly in Manchester and who wrote his memoirs at the end of the century. He explained that drink and crime were inextricably mixed: 'Much of my work over 27 years as a detective was aimed at closing down illegal beer houses and putting an end to criminal activities that happened on licensed premises.' He had something of a crusade in his later writings, asking the question, how come the worst criminals are the ones with the longest records?

The new detectives in places like Doncaster and Sheffield had to practise what had been learned in London at the beginning: forming a string of contacts and snitches, using plain clothes disguises, and being as observant as we are asked to believe Sherlock Holmes was. They also had to learn how to cope with the more subtle types of crime – the non-violent ones that involved swindles, frauds and deception.

In the Doncaster area, the detective who stole the limelight in all kinds of contexts was Detective Officer Winn. He was based in Sheffield but often found himself at work in Doncaster and beyond. In 1858 he found himself on the tail of a forger who worked across South Yorkshire, going to horse fairs and passing dud cheques and forged notes. He had the same name as a very famous man of Victorian times – William Morris – and he was caught courtesy of the *Police Gazette*. This publication, still going well today, was originally called *Hue and Cry,* and was circulated across London at first and then further afield, with descriptions of wanted criminals, lists of army deserters and short accounts of crimes.

One day in April 1858, Detective Wetherall of Sheffield was on the hunt for Morris and when he went into one of the public houses where villains tended to congregate he saw a copy of the Police Gazette on a table. It couldn't have been a more significant clue: the publication was folded just as it had arrived, and there was a line drawing of Morris, visible. Wetherall knew that the best bet was that Morris had, through sheer crook's vanity, wanted to see how he was described in print.

It didn't take long to find out that Morris was lodging in a room upstairs and was in his room at that moment. Issuing false bank notes was a very serious offence: thirty years before this, it had been a hanging offence and even in the 1850s it had a likely sentence of many years' penal servitude. In those days when the police communication was still with whistles or feet, Wetherall had to run to the nearest police station for help. He knew that Officer Winn was a good man and he was there, so the two detectives went to get their man. They were soon entering the room where Morris was sitting. Wetherall identified him as the man he was searching for, and Winn at once seized him.

Detectives Winn and Wetherall knew that Morris had tried to drop a parcel in the corner of the room, and when they retrieved it, they found a roll of forged notes. Winn looked closely at them, and he knew that although they were cleverly done, with a correct watermark and excellent reproduction, his skilful eye could see that they were forged. Morris also had a bag of forged sovereigns on him, called 'jacks'

The full story about Morris came out then: he had been a convict for many years and had returned on a ticket of leave. His life was transient and reckless, even though he had married recently – to a woman he had known only a short time.

Also in Sheffield, Winn collared another man who had been at work around Doncaster, and who had called at a butcher's saying he had several 'fat beasts' for sale. The normal price would have been around £20 but the man was asking for just six pounds. Clearly, this was a case of stolen cattle being shifted very quickly, and the rogue would have moved on elsewhere with a quick profit. The man was to gather his animals in the Sheffield Shambles and sell them there: Winn had learned that from a contact. The detective was soon there, in plain clothes, and he took the man in charge and had the cattle taken to the *Yellow Lion.*

George Winn was becoming a very smart professional by the early 1860s. In 1864 he was involved in one of his most high-profile cases, and one of Doncaster's most large-scale burglaries in the nineteenth century. The crooks in the case were George Harris and George Perry from Huddersfield; they travelled across Yorkshire, 'casing' likely easy targets for burglary, and then worked as a team. They were adroit and cunning, and planned the work well, but on this occasion, they met Winn and were taken into custody.

On the 12th of September in this year the two men loitered on Christchurch Terrace by a house owned by a Miss Drabwell. She had gone away for a while to stay with her niece but left her niece to look in and check the property when she could. But on the 20th the police were told that there had been 'an extensive burglary' there. Miss Drabwell was telegraphed and informed and she returned.

The thieves had broken into the house from the rear and then worked recklessly through the place, ransacking everything and going from room to room. Miss Drabwell was wealthy, and she kept a wine cellar. The thieves had discovered this and had a good time. Police found that several bottles had been drunk, two bottles of brandy had been drunk, and the burglars had also smoked cigars there. As to the booty the crooks went away with, the list was massive, including silver spoons, candlesticks, a silk mantle, silk jackets, a cashmere tablecloth and all kinds of silver items. They had also found and taken thirty yards of satin and all kinds of jewellery.

But the burglars had a 'fence; called Charles Walker, and detectives kept an eye on him. Sure enough, at a shop belonging to a Mr Cash in Sheffield, a man who was working with the burglars went in and offered two seals. These had a crest on them, and Mr Cash was suspicious. Cash was used to helping police catch up with the rogues trying to unload their booty, so he asked the man to come back with more items and he would by them as a job lot. But Cash also told police, and who was waiting for the man in the afternoon? George Winn.

Charles Walker came to the shop, with the burglars behind; Walker had a bag under his coat, and Winn grabbed him. The other crooks ran away. But Walker spilled the beans under pressure and led Winn and officers to the lodging house where all the stolen goods were kept.

What is particularly interesting in the way the case ends, and the success of the hunt for the Doncaster burglars, is the Yorkshire detective network. The burglars returned to Huddersfield but descriptions had been sent on, and police were waiting for them. They were in the dock at Doncaster police court and sent on to Leeds Assizes, and from there to a long time behind bars.

We have a confirmation of Caminada's comments about drink and crime. When any kind of new or refurbished pub or 'eating house' was established, it was checked out. Obviously, known criminals would always be out to settle in a fresh den, and often with a 'legitimate' front. Winn was often the man called in to help give these places a clean bill of health in terms of criminal potential. A typical example was the Alexandra Music Hall in Sheffield, where the magistrates were opposing a licence to the owner who was trying to import foreign wines. Winn was called; he had clearly been to visit the place and also walked past it at different times of day, and he gave testimony to say that he had no grounds to be suspicious of the owner and staff.

This shows that the new detectives in the shires were powerful, influential men in some areas of urban life; the career of George Winn, Detective Officer, shows just how adaptable and resourceful these officers had to be, dealing both with the usual physical force side of policing and with white collar crime in that restless, pushy society which was opening up all kinds of new areas of crime as population expanded and industry diversified.

RETIREMENT

The Police Pension Scheme 1987 allowed for detectives to retire, if they wished, after serving as a police officer for 30 years.

Not everybody took that option but it did mean that those who joined the police service at a relatively young age could retire at aged 50 or possibly even younger. The New Police Pension Scheme 2006 raised the retirement age to 55 years and in 2015 it became apparent that, due to people tending to live longer, the age could be increased to 60 years. The latest Career Average scheme still allows an officer to retire at 55 but with a reduced police pension when compared to an officer retiring at 60.

Quite a lot of detectives work beyond the 30 years and others may retire from the police service only to return as a member of police staff. The role of a detective is very intense, particularly for those working shifts, on-call or in a challenging role such as child abuse investigation. For this reason, you tend to find that some detectives are ready for a change of environment after a number of years investigating crime. Some detectives want to remain part of the investigation world whereas others just want a complete change of direction. A chauffeur, vicar and chimney sweep are just three of the occupations which spring to mind when I think of former colleagues of mine who chose something completely different following retirement from the police service.

RIPA

The Regulation of Investigatory Powers Act 2000 (known as RIPA – pronounced 'reaper') is an Act of Parliament regulating the powers of public bodies to carry out surveillance and access a person's electronic communications. The Act also covers the use of informants (**CHIS** – see **I**). There are a large number of public bodies who are entitled to use the powers as long as they are correctly authorised. Interception of a communication such as a phone call or letter (wire tapping or reading post) can only be carried out by the Security Services, HM Revenue & Customs and the police in serious cases and only when authorised by a warrant issued by the Home Secretary or, in Scotland, the Justice Secretary. On the other hand, the use of communications data (information about a communication, but not the actual content) can be carried out by a representative of a number of public bodies with the authorisation of a senior member of the respective body. The list of public bodies includes local councils, Health and Safety Executive, Food Standards Agency and the Environment Agency.

RIPA has no shortage of critics who claim that the Act was passed with little debate and is a threat to civil liberties in the UK. Campaign group *Big Brother Watch* published a report in 2010 in relation to the alleged improper use of RIPA by local councils. Some MPs have expressed concern that the Act is being abused on "petty and vindictive" cases, one particular member accusing councils of acting like comic strip detective Dick Tracy. In April 2008, it came to light that council officials in Poole, Dorset had put three children and their parents under surveillance, using RIPA, at home and during their daily routine to check whether they lived in a particular school catchment area. This was in the context of rules which allow people who live in the school catchment area to enjoy advantages in obtaining a place at a popular school. The council was later admonished by the Investigatory Powers Tribunal for improper use of surveillance powers. The same council put fishermen under surveillance, using RIPA, to check for the illegal harvesting of cockles and clams. Other councils in the UK have conducted undercover operations regulated by RIPA in relation to dog fouling, fly tipping and waste disposal.

There have been a number of prosecutions resulting from an abuse of the powers conferred by RIPA. In 2005, two men pleaded guilty to the interception of company e-mails. In 2007,

News of the World royal editor Clive Goodman was sentenced to four months in prison for intercepting the voicemail ('phone hacking') of members of the Royal Family. In the same year, a police investigation named 'Operation Barbatus' exposed a sophisticated criminal surveillance business run by corrupt police officers. Five former police officers and a private detective were sent to prison in relation to various offences including conspiracy to intercept communications unlawfully. In 2010, a 19 year old takeaway worker, subject of a police investigation into a child exploitation network, was sentenced to four months imprisonment having failed to provide his 50-character encryption key when requested to do so, a requirement under RIPA.

CASE STUDY – RIPA

Surveillance court Judges ruled that a police force's use of 'spying powers' on two former officers, in a bid to find the source of information leaks to journalists, was "unlawful". The Investigatory Powers Tribunal (IPT) also said that two of the seven applications made under RIPA by Cleveland Police in 2012 "must be quashed". The panel of serving and former High Court Judges added that there had been "no consideration at all of the impact of Article 10 (of the European Convention on Human Rights – freedom of expression) by way of targeting the communications with journalists" in the RIPA applications. The case against the force was brought by two former Cleveland police officers who argued that the force had breached their right to privacy under Article 8 of ECHR by covertly accessing their phone records. Following the authorisation of one particular RIPA application, Cleveland Police accessed the phone records of the officers, a solicitor and several journalists. They told the IPT that the force had applied to use surveillance powers following three successive leaks to the Northern Echo newspaper in April 2012, in relation to an internal grievance report, an equality report and a murder enquiry.

Judges heard how Cleveland Police relied upon legal advice indicating that the leaking of information by officers could amount to the crime of 'misconduct in a public office' and that this advice had been the basis for the RIPA applications. In their ruling, the judges commented "The reality is that there was no legal advice at all, upon which the [police] could rely, whether on the facts or otherwise, as to whether there was a case (with regard to either officer) by reference to misconduct in a public office or Section 55 of the Data Protection Act, nor any analysis of the requirements of either offence." Under its use of RIPA powers, Cleveland Police examined four months of call data and monitored the entire switchboard of the Northern Echo during a 48-hour period. The scale of the surveillance was said to be 35-times the size of that used in the 'Plebgate' scandal, which saw RIPA used to access the records of three *Sun* journalists.

The judges found that there was "no lawful basis" for obtaining the RIPA applications against the two former police officers. They added "Other steps could have been taken but were not even considered prior to any application for communications data being made. Had they been taken, it might have become apparent that any application for communications data would be unjustified, or alternatively it might have provided some justification for the making of such application, although on any basis the duration and extent of the applications, and the involvement, without any consideration or legal advice, of journalists and a solicitor would have been most unlikely to have been justified. The IPT judges said that they would hear submissions from those involved in the case "as to remedies and the consequences of our findings". The Chief Constable of Cleveland Police has apologised to those targeted and announced a major overhaul of the force's Professional Standards Department.

ROGUE TRADERS

You may be familiar with the term 'rogue trader' particularly if you ever watch TV programmes such as *Watchdog* or *Rip off Britain* as they tend to feature quite regularly. 'Rogue traders' are criminals who will try to 'rip you off' by offering a service which falls way below a satisfactory standard. There are many different ways in which they operate but I'm going to cover one of the more popular methods.

They will target an area which appears to contain houses occupied by elderly and/or vulnerable people and knock-on doors (known as 'cold-calling'). They may offer gardening help (lawn mowing, tree pruning, weeding), a resurface of the driveway or path (normally with tarmac) or replacement tiles for the roof. This work is often not actually required but, by using 'pressure' tactics and sometimes intimidation, the occupier may agree to the work. The 'rogue trader' may quote a price but will probably inflate this by the time payment is required. It's not unheard of for a quote of £100 to become £500 and sometimes even more. The 'rogue trader' will either do no work at all or some work which is of a poor standard, certainly not worth the prices quoted. I have previously investigated cases where the 'trader' has driven the elderly occupier (victim) to the bank or building society and waited outside, or even gone in with them, while they withdraw a large quantity of cash for payment. The 'trader' will only accept cash as it's more difficult to trace, when compared to a cheque or bank transfer. To falsely reassure the victim that they are genuine, the 'trader' may provide them with a mobile phone number in case they wish to get in touch about the work after completion. This number will relate to a

'Pay as you go' phone which will be very difficult for the police to trace. These criminals target the most vulnerable members of our community and will show total disregard for their victims. The criminal offences committed by 'rogue traders' will often involve some type of fraud and, if threats and intimidation are used, an offence of blackmail. The investigation of 'rogue trader' incidents will usually be carried out by detectives, often as part of a dedicated team.

CASE STUDIES – ROGUE TRADERS

1) In June 2018 police in Cumbria were advising the public to be vigilant, and to speak to vulnerable family and friends following reports of rogue traders. Two men had approached a local man in his 80's asking to clean his driveway. They then claimed that his garage door needed repairing and offered to fix it for him. The man paid the offenders £800 to fix the door but they then returned on two further occasions, on the last visit demanding a further £600. They subsequently took the victim to the bank to withdraw the money. The victim handed over a total of £1,400 in cash. No work was carried out and the offenders did not return. A police spokesman commented "We would advise the public never to agree to have work carried out by a stranger knocking on your door. Also, we advise never to agree to have work carried out because you are made to feel pressured. If you feel you need the work carried out, look for official traders yourself or ask friends and family for recommendations. If you are ever made to feel intimidated or uncomfortable, please call police on 101 with a description and details. Always dial 999 if a crime is in progress or in an emergency. We are here to help."

2) In September 2018 West Midlands Police appealed for help to find a man suspected of being part of a heartless gang that

conned pensioners out of their savings. The force secured convictions against brothers Errol and Timmy Flynn, Karl Bean and Steven Craven for conning almost £60,000 out of elderly residents with a rogue trader scam that saw them pose as roofers. Another man related to one of the gang, Brian Williams-Craven, is believed to have joined them in defrauding a couple who were stung for £24,000 after being told their roof needed urgent repairs, including replacement beams. An inspection later showed that the men had pulled up tiles themselves and merely painted part of the roof to make it appear they had carried out work, with some of the paint dripping down onto guttering and window frames. Police suspected that Williams-Craven had paid some of the money into his bank account but, after being arrested and released, he failed to answer his bail and is now wanted by the police. A police officer involved in the case commented "It's important we know what's happened to him as he's wanted in connection with a truly awful fraud that left an elderly couple traumatised, not to mention hugely out of pocket."

3) In November 2018 two men were jailed at Teesside Crown Court for three years and nine months following a police investigation which began in February 2017. The men were sentenced after pleading guilty to conspiring to defraud elderly and vulnerable victims in relation to property repairs carried out at their homes. The investigation began after concerned relatives reported works conducted at the home of their 80 year old relative who lived alone at an address in North Yorkshire. Following her admission to hospital and subsequent residential care, the relatives discovered cheques for £94,500 had been paid to the pair, between January and October 2016, for work carried out to her drive, gardens and roof. The investigation

was carried out by Operation Gauntlet, the multi-agency safeguarding team hosted at North Yorkshire County Council Trading Standards Service. The work carried out by the pair consisted of laying rubber crumb to various areas, landscaping, power washing, painting and other minor works. An expert surveyor examined the works and concluded that they were worth no more than £25,000. The investigation also identified two additional victims in the Lincolnshire area. A disabled couple in their 60's paid £56,000 and a couple in their 70's paid £35,000, both considerably more than the value of the work carried out.

The victim sadly passed away in July 2017 and did not get the chance to see the pair, Riley Smith and William Gaskin, brought to justice. Both men had previous convictions for similar defrauding of householders in relation to property repairs. Sentencing the pair, the Recorder of Middlesbrough said "Once you realised they were elderly and vulnerable you took full advantage of them, in a way which was utterly dishonest and callous. You used them for greed, ripping them off without any thought at all. Once you had persuaded them to allow you to carry out the work, you went back and back and continued until all the money was gone, until there was nothing left, until the pot had run dry."

S

SCAMS

A scam is a fraud or con designed to steal your money or personal details so that criminals can profit. There are so many different types of scams that it's very difficult to keep up to date, particularly as the fraudsters tend to change their tactics regularly. A scam can be carried out in person but the most popular methods are by post to your address, via your computer or your telephone (see **T**). I'm going to cover one or two but, if you want to find out more information about scams there are websites you can visit such as Action Fraud and Friends Against Scams.

Scam mail

Criminals worldwide are sending letters which trick millions of people into parting with billions of pounds every year. Older and vulnerable people can often be bombarded by scam mail sent to their address. If they respond to any of this mail, they may be put on what is known as a 'suckers list' which is circulated to criminals all over the world. The result is that they will then receive even more scam mail and the situation can quickly escalate. The criminals who send this mail are known as 'scammers'. Modern technology means that scam letters can be mass-produced and made to look like personal letters or important documents, in the hope of tricking the recipient into sending cash, making money transfers or disclosing personal information such as bank details.

Two of the most common scams are lottery and prize draw scams. Victims are told they have won a large cash prize, but are asked to send some sort of fee to release it. No genuine lottery or competition would ask for money to claim a prize but the mail can be so convincing that people will think it's genuine and comply with the instructions. Clairvoyant scams are also very popular with scammers. They have no idea who will read their letters but show false concern and pretend they are going to a lot of trouble to give the reader good health, wealth and happiness. They weave some very imaginative stories, including performing rituals and sensing danger. They often blackmail victims by telling them "Bad luck will befall you if you don't pay up." Scammers also send out literature selling a variety of different products including food, pills, beauty products, jewellery and clothes. They guarantee prizes to those who order, but they never send the prize. Instead, they send out more promises to get more orders.

A charity called 'TH!NK JESSICA' has been set up by the daughter of a scam mail victim. The charity helps victims, provides advice and raises awareness of postal scams and criminal phone calls. Jessica was a victim who was repeatedly tricked into sending cash and making money transfers to criminals over a period of five years. Her family tried, without success, to make her understand she was being scammed, but the psychology used by the criminals was so powerful that she refused to accept this. She lived in a delusional world, totally believing everything the scammers told her. She thought that the bogus 'clairvoyants' and 'officials' were her friends. Jessica died at the age of 83 in 2007. She was still waiting for her promised prizes. Approximately 30,000 scam letters were removed from her home. The scale of the number of scam mail victims isn't totally clear as victims are often too embarrassed to tell anyone but it is a crime which devastates families and, once again, targets the most vulnerable in our communities.

Phishing

Phishing involves an e-mail scam where you receive a message which appears to be from a legitimate source such as your bank, HM Revenue & Customs, PayPal, Apple or Amazon. The message will encourage you to click on a link within the e-mail to log into your account, normally by telling you that your account has been locked, unlawfully accessed or there is a large transfer of money. In reality, the link in the e-mail takes you to a fake website which collects your personal information as you enter it. Another version of this scam involves an e-mail attachment (perhaps a coupon or form you need to fill in), which is in fact a computer virus. Phishing e-mails will often be addressed to you as Sir, Madam or Customer rather than using your name (as they probably don't actually know this information). If you look closely at the sender's e-mail address you may also notice that it doesn't appear correct or may have a letter missing or in the wrong order. Finally, if you hover your computer mouse over any links (without clicking) you will see further details which may help you to identify it as a scam. If the e-mail is allegedly from an organisation which you have dealings with such as your bank then you have to be extra careful when deciding whether it could be a scam. If in any doubt whatsoever, please don't click on any link or reply to an e-mail, simply contact them in some other way. I recently received an e-mail, purportedly from Lloyds Bank, titled 'Security issue with your account' which informed me that they had detected an issue and instructed me to clink on the link then enter my User ID and Password. The e-mail address appeared incorrect but the real giveaway was the fact that I don't have a bank account with Lloyds Bank!

Smishing

Smishing is the commonly used name for SMS phishing, an activity which enables criminals to steal a person's money, identity or both as a result of a response to a text message sent to your mobile phone. The text message will claim to be from a trusted organisation or individual and will ask you to carry out some sort of action such as clicking on a link within the message, visiting a website or making a phone call. They may pretend to be your bank informing you of a problem with your account, a retailer offering 'vouchers' or 'gift cards', a technology provider such as Apple or Google requesting validation of an account, a parcel delivery company requesting confirmation of a delivery or HMRC advising you that you are due a tax refund. This list isn't exhaustive but gives you an idea of some of the tactics used. Smishing messages generally state or imply the need for urgent action to either avoid an issue or take advantage of an offer. They also play on your emotions and needs such as trust, safety, fear of losing money, getting something for nothing, eagerness to find a bargain or desire to find love, popularity/status. As with all scams 'if it sounds too good to be true, it probably is'. The best advice is to not respond, reply or click on any links/attachments contained in unsolicited communications.

SCOTCH

Well-known fictional detectives including John Rebus, DI Jack Regan (*The Sweeney*), and DCI Gene Hunt (*Life on Mars*) were all partial to a drop of the old scotch now and then, but is it a myth that detectives always had a bottle in their bottom drawer at work? As I've alluded to elsewhere in this book, there was a bit of a drinking culture, particularly in CID, back in the 80's and there were quite a lot of detectives who had 'emergency rations' to hand for occasions of impromptu celebrations or to provide that moment of inspiration. One or two had supplies which would put the local alehouse to shame, as scotch wasn't everybody's 'cup of tea'. When I had my own office, I have to admit that a bottle of scotch somehow found itself in my set of drawers, lockable I might add. It made the odd appearance for debriefings but nowhere near as regularly as in years gone by. So, no, it isn't a myth, although times are very different these days. I'll leave the last word to DCI Gene Hunt and his definition of 'scotch' – "What you buy the Guv' whenever you like. Single, mind you, none of that blended crap."

SCOTLAND YARD

These two words immediately suggest something special, but not necessarily anything specific. To some, the words might suggest a gaunt, impressive building, whereas to others they might denote images of detectives in hats and raincoats leaping into action on London's mean streets. A prosaic definition would be that it is the name given to the HQ of the Metropolitan Police. This famous address was the place where, in 1829 when professional police in London were established, the new Commissioners put down roots. Originally, it was the location of London provision for the Scottish royals when they were in town.

In 1890 after a move, we had the first use of the words, 'New Scotland Yard' and today it is in Westminster and is the fourth HQ of the Met. Formerly, it was called the Curtis Green Building, being designed by the architect, William Curtis Green, and this was where, during World War 2, the forensics and technology sections of the force were centred.

Of course, to anyone who enjoys detective fiction or the social history of police and crime, Scotland Yard is a phrase that suggests excellence, and also a certain level of drama. After all, when there was a particularly knotty regional crime, the 'Yard' were called in to help, and they still are today. It is odd that the words link immediately to detectives, when all kinds of police personnel are there. But with the ever-increasing popularity of crime dramas on film and television featuring the detective pairing of Inspector and Sergeant, the 'Yard' will always relate as much to fiction as to fact.

It has become, if we have to use a word which arises in all kinds of concepts in modernity, an *iconic* concept. Since Arthur Conan Doyle had some fun at the expense of his Yard men (always inferior to Sherlock Holmes of course) there has been a complete revision of the Yard detective and his status, along with his or her interest in the fictional guises we now love so much.

SHOULDER SURFING

Shoulder surfing is a form of data theft where criminals steal personal information by observing victims when they're using devices such as ATM's, computers, mobile phones, or other electronic devices. The term refers to the act of someone looking over your shoulder trying to watch you as you enter personal information such as a password or account number. Shoulder surfing is a criminal speciality which began before the existence of the Internet and smartphones. Its originators became adept at spying on people as they used public telephones to enter information such as their credit card numbers into the phone keypad. The skill, which can often involve the interpretation of subtle finger movements of the user, rather than just actually reading pressed keys, is now something which users of bank machines should be aware of. The 'surfers' will stand behind the user and try to identify the PIN number as it is entered. This is more likely to happen in a shop or retail outlet than at a bank but there have been cases in the UK where criminals have positioned themselves inside the bank to watch people as they use the machines and have been successful in their efforts. So many people pay for items with bank cards these days that the number of Chip and Pin machines have increased considerably as it becomes the preferred method of payment. Busy shops and supermarkets are ideal environments for the 'surfers' to frequent. They may stand directly behind you in a queue or stand at the end of the checkout pretending to wait for someone. The vast majority of card users do nothing to protect their PIN number as they enter it into the bank machine so if a criminal can get close enough, they have a good chance of being able to work out your number as you enter it. The hardest part for a criminal is to obtain your PIN number, stealing your bank card won't be too much of a problem for experienced criminals who do this sort of thing as a job. The best advice I can give people who use bank machines is to cover the keypad with your hand or anything in your hand as you enter your PIN. You need to make sure that, if anybody is standing behind you, they have no chance of seeing you enter the number. This is really important, whether you're using an ATM at the bank or a machine in a shop or other location. If I told you that I once investigated a team of criminals who had been able to place a miniature camera into the top of the ATM to record the PIN numbers of every user as they entered them, you'll understand why I'm so paranoid about this type of criminal activity. Every time I use any type of bank machine, I always remember this tactic and place my hand a couple of inches above the keypad. It is rare, but if there ever was a camera then it would only record the back of my hand rather than any personal information. You should also be careful when using your mobile phone or tablet in public, particularly in busy areas or where people can stand or sit behind you.

CASE STUDY – SHOULDER SURFERS

This example happened during the day in a supermarket in Lincolnshire. A man spent some time loitering in the store, paying particular attention to the self-service checkout area. Each checkout has a Chip and Pin machine positioned around shoulder height for the benefit of customers paying by bank card. The man was pretending to look at his mobile phone which he held in front of him but he was actually looking over people's shoulders and entering their PIN numbers into his phone as customers used the bank machine. As I've already alluded to, the vast majority of people do nothing to protect their PIN numbers which made things a little easier for him. Outside in the car park the same man, accompanied by another man, approached a lady who had just put her shopping and bag into her car. She didn't have time to get into the car nor to lock it before she was asked where the local hospital was. One of the men produced a large map and placed it on the car bonnet, a clear distraction tactic often used by criminals when they are trying to steal from you. As the lady spoke with the first man, the other one was able to open her car door, rifle carefully through her handbag, and remove her bank card before leaving everything exactly as it had been. At the end of the conversation, the lady drove off in her car completely unaware that her card had been stolen. In fact, it was some time before she realised what had happened. In the meantime, the criminals made their way straight to the cashpoint machine outside the supermarket. As they knew the PIN number and now had the card, they were able to withdraw a large amount of cash and make off undetected. There was CCTV footage of the individuals but they were very unlikely to be local and may not be traced. On the same day, another lady was the victim of exactly the same theft, having used the self-service checkout and paid by bank card. I'm sure this happens more frequently than we are aware, so the importance of protecting your PIN and being aware of people in the vicinity when you use bank machines cannot be overstated.

SIO

The Senior Investigating Officer (SIO) is the title given to the lead detective who is in overall charge of a particular serious crime investigation. This could be a murder, kidnap, rape, robbery, or any other major crime which is likely to attract

THE A-Z OF DETECTIVE WORK

media and public interest. The SIO will be responsible for all decisions made during the investigation, although a lot of the actions may be carried out by other officers who are part of that investigation. The SIO will be the person who will have to justify why they did or didn't do something when they face questions at a criminal trial or coroners hearing. This could take place months, possibly years, after the event which is why it's so important for the SIO to keep a record of their key decisions and the rationale behind those decisions. This information will normally be written in a Policy File (see **P**) which will be updated regularly by the SIO throughout the investigation. The Policy File is a book with duplicated pages which will need to be retained for many years after the investigation in case it needs to be referred to. In a murder investigation the SIO will complete many Policy Files as each book only contains a limited number of pages. In addition to the standard Policy File, the SIO will also keep a sensitive Policy File which, as the name suggests, should be used for sensitive information and decisions in relation to confidential matters such as covert policing tactics, CHIS (see **Informants**) or sensitive intelligence.

At one time the SIO for a murder investigation would have been either a Detective Superintendent or a Detective Chief Inspector (DCI). Cases involving a serial killer or high-profile in some way would be led by the higher rank and a number of the more, so to speak, straightforward investigations would be managed by a DCI. In some areas this is still the case but, due to limited resources and other operational commitments, there is a possibility that the SIO for some murder cases could be a Detective Inspector (DI). The SIO should always have a deputy (D/SIO) who will normally be a rank below that of the SIO. If a Detective Superintendent was running the investigation, then the deputy would probably be a DCI, the deputy for a DCI would be a DI and the deputy for a DI would be a Detective Sergeant (DS). As the name suggests, the deputy SIO carries out the role of the SIO when they are not available and will also be allocated the management of specific investigative areas such as forensics, family liaison or house to house enquiries. The larger and more serious crime investigations usually have a deputy SIO but in some cases of rape, robbery, or assault (GBH) the SIO may not have a deputy. It's also possible, depending on available resources, that these types of crimes may be managed by a DS or DC.

SPECIAL BRANCH

Today, this is referred to as SO12, and its primary role is in the context of national security. The structure is based on operational command units. There are related units which concentrate on Royal and Diplomatic Protection.

This began life back in 1883 with a staff of four CID men and eight in uniform, and the first commander was Howard Vincent. But at its inception, it was the Special Irish Branch. What prompted this was the Fenian bombing campaigns in Manchester and London. Through most of the nineteenth century, various threats to the sparsely defended centres of Irish immigration in England had been vulnerable to disorder because of the tendency for the newly settled Irish communities to bring with them across the Irish Sea the dissensions and the enmity fuelled by religious sectarianism.

Earlier in the century, there had been disturbances at parades linked to the Orange celebrations, or to other movements such as the 'Ribbon Men.' But matters escalated into serious terrorism in the Manchester bombings and the Clerkenwell explosion. In Manchester there had been a serious incident when a police van carrying three Fenians who were subsequently labelled

'The Manchester Martyrs' was attacked, and Sergeant Charles Brett was killed.

Vincent's fondness for what we would now call 'entrapment' was made apparent in the case of a chemist called Titley who was involved in illegal abortion activities. A 'plant' who was in fact the wife of a police officer posed as a customer for Titley; he sold her the requisite drugs and he was entrapped and charged. This was a very un-English move. There was such an outcry that the Home Secretary had to go through the motions of indicting the officers in plain clothes, but that fizzled out.

Vincent had shown these predilections before coming to power, having written a report on the French detective system, the brainchild of the great Vidocq (see separate entry) in the previous generation, and the first stage in an inevitable change of identity was taking place under Vincent's leadership.

This new, more cosmopolitan and less restrained form of detective work was to meet with criticism and opposition, being slated by one writer as 'an entire failure in every respect,' but the signs of the times were wholly apparent after the Fenian bombing at Clerkenwell in 1867, ten years before the Trial of the Detectives, criticisms had been levelled at Mayne, who had done thirty-eight years of service by then. The Earl of Derby wrote: 'It is really lamentable that the peace of the Metropolis, and its immunity from wilful destruction, should depend on a body of police who, as detectives, are manifestly incompetent; and under a chief who, whatever may be his other merits, has not the energy nor apparently the skill to find out and employ men fitted for peculiar duties.' The Clerkenwell bombing had killed twelve people and injured another 120. A small detail that would today command the attention of every passing constable allowed the Fenians to do that mass killing – a barrel left against the wall of the House of Correction. The disaster was not really the result of poor detective work on the part of the new CID: it was poor everyday policing of the streets.

But the new professionalism of the CID was clearly apparent in the structure and the staff: the new outfit, under solicitor J E Davis for administration and Vincent for general control, had sixty divisional detective patrols and twenty special patrols. There were a regulating body of sergeants – 159 in number. A shift system would operate and there would be tighter supervision down the ranks, with fifteen Detective Inspectors at the top. A division between the Yard and the CID men was established and that tradition, whereby the CID men stayed with the CID, remained in place until Sir Robert Mark's regime changed things in the 1970s.

There had been a significant step forward in terms of the more political arm of detective work back in 1867 when an army man, Lt. Col. W H A Fielding started a secret service operation. It was clear from that point that there were going to be increasing specialisms within the range of detective work. The whole profession was becoming demanding in different ways, and this is exemplified by the footnote to police history that relates to a Sergeant Lear from Shropshire, a man who had to track his suspect for a hundred miles, travelling on foot, in 1871.

The 'peculiar duties' referred to by the Earl of Derby in his criticisms were to be far more onerous, demanding and radically different from past procedures than anyone realised, with the coming of the phenomenon of the serial killers Jack the Ripper and Charles Peace. Both cases illustrate the nature of this more accelerated, mobile and highly populated world they had to police. The police corruption had taught the top brass about internal disintegration and the challenge from inside the Yard's own structures: now in Whitechapel and in the regions, there was a new threat to their competence and organisation. What was about to be tested, more than anything else in the responsibilities and structures of the detective force, was the efficiency of their work at two important levels: first in their communication methods across city and provinces, and second, in their supervision and monitoring of the population in those city areas in which dissidents, radicals and alienated individuals resided.

'Peculiar duties' were soon to become far more specialised than Derby ever dreamed or Vincent himself could have imagined, though his knowledge of Paris and the methods of the police in the Napoleonic period would be an asset.

SPECIALIST ROLES

As a detective you may work in a Divisional or Borough CID office where your role will be to investigate a number of different offences including burglary, robbery and serious assault (GBH) and to interview witnesses and suspects involved in those offences. On the other hand, you may be employed in a specialist role where you deal with specific offence types. When I was a Detective Inspector working in public protection, there were a number of detectives working in the unit carrying out different investigative roles including domestic abuse, child abuse, adult abuse and sex offender management. Forces now also tend to have dedicated teams which investigate rape and serious sexual assault. These teams will normally consist of a mixture of uniformed constables (working in plain clothes) and detectives. The increase in cyber crime has resulted in forces creating specialist teams to investigate child sexual exploitation and offences related to the use of the internet. Detectives will also be used to carry out investigative work within such teams. You will also find detectives working in Special Branch, Counterterrorism and Fraud investigation. Due to the nature of these roles they tend to be carried out on a regional or national level.

As you would expect, you will also find a number of detectives, of various ranks, working on murder investigation teams which are now, with the exception of the Metropolitan Police, regional units. I was the DCI for major crime working in Lincolnshire Police when the East Midlands Special Operations Unit – Major Crime (EMSOU-MC) was launched in the county. This meant that all five forces in the East Midlands (Lincolnshire, Nottinghamshire, Leicestershire, Derbyshire nand Northamptonshire) had their own resources to investigate murders in their own force areas but could also support other forces in the region with additional resources if and when required. In 2011, I was the SIO for a murder in Boston, Lincolnshire where a Polish man had been stabbed to death in the street. It was the first murder case with the force officially part of EMSOU-MC which meant that I was able to contact my counterparts in some of the other regional forces for support. This support was provided in the form of additional detectives which was really helpful in those critical early days of the investigation. The arrangement was mutually beneficial as I would also send detectives from our unit to other force hubs when they required support. A lot of forces around the country have now joined together with others in their region to provide an effective response to murder investigation.

SUPER RECOGNISER

An elite team of police officers in London known as 'super-recognisers' are using their remarkable ability to identify criminals by viewing CCTV footage. They have helped to catch people for a number of offences including murder and sex crimes. The small team scan hundreds of hours of CCTV and are able to recall the faces of people they have seen before, sometimes years ago. Among the successes of the team is the arrest and conviction of a man who had been attacking women on London buses. The team were able to examine CCTV footage and identify Camden station as a focal point for the investigation. When a super recogniser visited the area she spotted the suspect and he was detained. In 2011 after the London riots, a super recogniser who was focusing on gangs, studied the grainy CCTV image of a young man who had thrown petrol bombs and set fire to cars. The rioter wore a woollen hat and a red bandana, leaving only a very small part of his face uncovered. The man had been arrested years earlier and the super recogniser was able to identify him, particularly his eyes, from that earlier sighting at the police station. He was convicted of arson and robbery, for which he received a six-year prison sentence. The success of the unit is quite staggering, one officer making 600 identifications in just six months and as many as five arrests a week when off-duty. When schoolgirl Alice Gross was murdered in 2014, the super recognisers helped to track a man seen on CCTV cycling after her, who turned out to be her killer. They have also helped the German authorities to solve a series of sexual assaults in Cologne during New Year celebrations. Many of the positive identifications come from an online bulletin "Caught on camera" which is issued three times a week by the Metropolitan Police and features video stills of unidentified suspects committing crimes.

DCI Mick Neville led the team of talented police officers who, in one year alone, solved 2,500 crimes in London. By some estimates, there are as many as one million CCTV cameras installed in London, but with more than eight million residents in the city, the task of identifying people who commit crime is a challenging one. In 2006, DCI Neville set up a dedicated unit to comb through CCTV footage and make identifications. Some officers excelled at the task which he initially attributed to their motivation, until he heard about a Harvard University paper on 'super-recognisers', which concluded that there is a broad distribution of the facial-recognition capability. While some people have 'prosopagnosia', a rare condition in which patients are unable to recognise human faces, others have preternatural (beyond normal) ability. DCI Neville collaborated with Josh Davis, a psychologist whose dissertation focused on forensic analysis of CCTV footage, and on the risks associated with misidentifications. Davis was initially dubious of the capabilities of some of the officers, commenting at the time "I knew about prosopagnosia but I hadn't known that there was anyone at the other end of the scale." To prove that the super-recognisers were effective, Davis subjected officers who were particularly good at making identifications to facial-recognition exams. Those who performed well were asked, from time to time, to carry out an identification. This proved so successful that DCI Neville was granted permission to create a dedicated unit of super-recognisers. The unit now includes well over 100 officers and is one of only a few in the world. It can identify suspects based on poor quality CCTV footage, dim lighting and oblique angles. They have, for instance, identified 16 victims of the Hillsborough football stadium disaster, based on footage from the stadium, decades after the event. The super-recognisers can remember more than 95% of the faces they have seen before, while most of us are only able to identify a fifth.

It's estimated that only two percent of the population is a super-recogniser. Of course, there will always be cases where a person is mistakenly identified and so the unit has implemented a peer-review process, in which a second super-recogniser provides an independent opinion. As a Detective Sergeant from the unit clarified "It's never our word alone that puts someone away. What we do, by identifying suspects, is help direct the investigation."

T

TACTICAL CONTACT

From January to October 2017, there were 19,455 moped-enabled offences across London, a figure which was reduced by 36 per cent to 12,419 offences in the same monthly period of 2018. The Metropolitan Police has adopted a dedicated team approach (Operation Venice) following a dramatic increase in the use of scooters to commit crimes such as armed robbery, mobile phone snatches and smash-and-grab raids in the capital. Police have also confirmed that the use of a 'tactical contact' strategy has helped to reduce the number of offences. This tactic involves a specially trained police driver, known as a 'scorpion' driver, initiating contact with the offending moped with the intention of knocking the rider(s) off and bringing any pursuit to a safe conclusion. Officers feared being prosecuted or disciplined if moped riders were injured during high-speed chases in the past, while criminals have often taken their helmets off in the belief that this will prevent a pursuit. The Government has now backed new legal protections for officers, and the Metropolitan Police have confirmed that it will continue to target moped criminals "even when they ride dangerously, discard their helmets and disguise themselves in the belief that this will prevent pursuit and their capture." Police have released footage showing their vehicles knocking riders from mopeds in the hope that their "hard line approach" will make potential offenders think twice. A Metropolitan Police

Commander commented "Operation Venice is multi-faceted, and we can call on all manner of tactics from an experienced investigation team to police helicopters. There is a perception that if you remove your helmet or fail to stop for police when requested to do so, we will not take any further course of action. This is untrue. The public quite rightly expects us to intervene to keep London safe. Our highly trained police drivers weigh up the risks and decide upon the most appropriate tactics in those circumstances. Offenders on mopeds and motorcycles who attempt to evade the police are making a choice that puts themselves and others at risk. So our message is clear: we can, we will and we do target those involved in moped and motorcycle crime at every opportunity."

My personal view is that this approach is long overdue but I do hope that the drivers who make these split-second decisions are supported by their force, particularly in cases where the person being pursued is seriously injured or worse.

TELEPHONE SCAMS

Telephone scams are one of the biggest problems being faced by people who answer their phone these days. As with other scams, it's often the older and vulnerable who are targeted by criminals who use pressure and sophisticated methods to trick people. I'm going to cover a couple of the more prevalent phone scams which have been used for the past few years and show little sign of stopping.

Impersonation fraud

The caller will tell you that they are from your bank and that there is a problem with your account. Often, they will have already established which bank you are with prior to calling and will pretend to be from the fraud department of that bank.

THE A–Z OF DETECTIVE WORK

They will tell you that you need to transfer all funds into a 'safe' bank account immediately to avoid losing it to criminals. They will give you the sort code and account number of that account and emphasise the importance of swift action. The banks don't have 'safe' accounts and the money, if transferred, will be quickly moved on to another criminal account. They may use this tactic persistently, ringing you on several occasions if the first attempt is unsuccessful. A genuine bank would never ask you to transfer money in this way.

Courier fraud

You will receive a call from a person who pretends to be from the bank or the police. They will tell you that there has been an issue with your bank card/account and request that you attend your local bank branch and withdraw cash (often several thousand pounds). They will emphasise the need for confidentiality, often advising you not to discuss the withdrawal with bank staff as they may be complicit in the fraud. They will sometimes even keep you on an open telephone line when you attend, so that they can hear what you say at the bank. Once you have returned home with the cash, having confirmed your address, they will send someone to collect the cash "on behalf of the bank", hence the term 'courier fraud'. If they are pretending to be the police, they may tell you that the cash needs to be fingerprinted or that they will send someone to take possession of the cash for safekeeping. The person who attends will be a criminal posing as a police officer.

An alternative 'courier fraud' scam will involve a call to you by a person posing as the bank who will ask you to phone your local branch as they terminate the call. Even though you may hang up, they stay on the line which can keep the line open for a short time. When you dial the number for your branch and speak to a person, it's understandable that you think it's your bank as you have dialled their number. In actual fact, you will be speaking to the same or another criminal as the line has remained open and they have simply waited to hear your voice. They will then go through a series of security questions "for data protection purposes". One of these questions may well include a request for you to confirm your bank card PIN number. Once this has been provided, they will arrange to send someone to your address to collect your bank card. They will state that the card has been cancelled by them and is no longer any use to you and will reassure you that you will be issued with a replacement card in due course. Once the 'courier' has taken possession of your card, the criminals can complete the fraudulent withdrawal of money from your account as they now know your PIN number and have possession of your bank card. Criminals have also started to request that you buy high-value jewellery, such as Rolex watches, which they will arrange to collect from you on the pretence that this will help with their fraud investigation. Please bear in mind that neither the bank nor the police will ever ask you to transfer money to another account in this way, ask you to withdraw cash for collection or ask you to reveal your PIN or other security details.

Computer repair fraud

I'm sure that a lot of people reading this will have received phone calls from people offering to fix your computer, I know I certainly have. Every single one of these calls is a 'scam' carried out by criminals. They may pretend to be from Microsoft, BT, Talk Talk or a number of other genuine organisations but the reality is that they are sitting in a call-centre, probably in another country, and are trying to rip you off. Quite a few people genuinely have the odd issue with their computer, so when you receive a call offering to help you or telling you that there is a problem with your internet connection, it may convince you that they are trying to help you. If you do talk to them, rather than politely declining and hanging up which would be my advice, they will ask you to log onto your computer and give you some instructions which will take you to a page which may convince you that there are issues. In actual fact, this particular page is simply a list of your computer performance which will show everything from when your computer runs slow or locks to when you are unable to access a particular website. All computers hold this information and it certainly doesn't mean that there is a problem with your computer, but if you don't use computers too often or have been worried by the nature of the call, I can perfectly understand how this may reinforce what is being claimed. The caller will then provide you with some more instructions which will enable them to remotely control your computer so that you are no longer in charge of the machine. They can then copy information and look to access areas such as your e-mail and online banking. Alternatively, they can place a virus into your computer which may lock it or prevent it from working properly. Microsoft and other companies will never cold-call you to offer to repair your computer so if the person on the other end of the phone is offering such a service, please remember it's a criminal scam. You could, of course, simply tell them that you don't have a computer (even if you do) or, as one person told me, keep them waiting on the line while they made a cup of tea and did some odd jobs. My advice would be to simply decline their offer and terminate the call.

Telephone Preference Service fraud
The Telephone Preference Service (TPS) is a free service which you can sign up to if you want to try to reduce the amount

of nuisance phone calls you receive. You can either phone or register online by providing a few basic details, including your phone number. There have been a significant number of phone calls made by criminals who pretend to be the TPS, although sometimes they may refer to themselves as the "telephone management service" or other similar name. They will try to obtain your banking details by claiming that you are entitled to a refund or that there has been a problem with your account which requires clarification. They may well already know your phone number, name, address and possibly other personal details when they ring you. The TPS will never cold-call anyone and will never ask for payment as they provide a free service. As with other scam telephone calls, the best advice I can give is to terminate the call and leave the phone for several minutes before using it again if you have to, as the scammers will sometimes stay on the line to see if anyone picks the phone back up.

As you can see, telephone scams can be varied and quite sophisticated in their methods. The criminals may even use 'number spoofing' (see **N**) to try to convince you that they are genuine. If you receive any unexpected or unsolicited phone calls on your landline or your mobile phone, you should exercise caution and never give out personal details. If you want to check with your bank or another organisation, you should use another phone, wait for at least 10 minutes before using the same phone or, if possible, go to the bank yourself.

CASE STUDIES – TELEPHONE SCAMS
1) Earlier this year (2018) an elderly man from North Wales lost nearly £300,000 of his life savings after being targeted by criminals. The fraudsters rang him, claiming that a dishonest bank employee was stealing money from his account and that he

needed to transfer his money into a "safe account". The victim received a series of phone calls over a period of weeks, during which he was persuaded to go to his bank and transfer £270,000 to another account which was fraudulent. The 'scammers' also succeeded in making a fraudulent application for a loan in the victim's name. At no point during contact with the fraudsters did the victim think that they were anything but genuine. A police spokesman estimated that "several million pounds" a year is lost by victims of fraud and cybercrime in North Wales alone. He commented "The most frequent cases involve phone calls where the scammers say they're from the police, the fraud department at the bank, mobile phone company, HMRC or even the National Crime Agency. They ask them to move money to "safe accounts" because people in the branches are involved in fraud. They'll probably keep them on the phone for several hours at a time, over several days or weeks. I would say we have several calls every day in relation to this type of fraud. It's not always the same amounts, but what they will do is contact them, and they will keep on contacting them over and over until they've got their end game which is to have the money transferred. They're very clever and very plausible. The victims are conned into believing that the people they are speaking to are police officers or a person working in the fraud department of the bank."

2) In October 2018, Cumbria Police warned the public about a scam which was operating in their area. The telephone scam, which has been used throughout the county, begins with a call from a person purporting to be a police officer investigating a fraud. The caller persuades the victim that their bank is involved in the fraud and that the victim can help their investigation by withdrawing a large sum of money. They are then advised

to meet a "police officer" who will give them a password, take possession of the money and leave the victim empty-handed. In one case, a victim handed over £7,000. Police have advised the public that, under no circumstances, would they ask anyone to withdraw money from the bank and take it from them.

3) Police in Wrexham have been warned about scam phone calls by people posing as police officers. Several victims have received phone calls alleging fraudulent activity on their bank accounts. The caller asks the victim to dial an extension number and they speak to another 'bogus officer' who asks them to go to their branch and withdraw money, claiming that they are investigating counterfeit currency offences within the branch. The victims are kept on the phone whilst in the bank and the withdrawn money is collected from their home address. This fraudulent activity has resulted in several victims withdrawing thousands of pounds from their accounts which they have subsequently handed over to criminals.

4) In November this year (2018) police issued a warning after an elderly Norfolk man was tricked out of hundreds of pounds by an iTunes voucher scam. The fraud involves a phone call informing the victim that they owe a significant amount in tax which can be paid off with the purchase of Google or iTunes gift cards. These cards are used by criminals as the codes are difficult to trace and they can be resold. Police have been visiting shops which sell gift cards to educate staff about the scam. A police spokesman commented "The shops have been really supportive. Basically, if someone comes into the shop and buys large quantities of gift cards, ask if they've been told to pay a debt off using the cards. If they say yes, call the police." Gift card scams are becoming increasingly popular with criminals.

TOOLS OF THE TRADE

Time to lighten things up a little, so let's talk about some things a detective will need every day and should never leave home without, the "tools of the trade" according to DCI Gene Hunt (*Life on Mars*).

Hip flask

"We all know there's only one way of clearing the head in the morning after an evening of quiet relaxation at the pub, and that's 'hair of the dog'. A quick shot of something warming sets you up for the day, especially if followed by a bacon butty. Single malt and pig grease, the oil that keeps the detection engine running."

Fags

"Keep the lungs clear of exhaust fumes and show you're a decent bloke when you offer them round. Nothing sets an informant at ease more than bunging him a Rothmans (even if you do knock it out of his gob the minute he tells a 'porkie' – all part of the game)."

Bottle of Brut

"Keeps the flies off and the birds on."

Radio

"You can't be out and about and cut off from home, can you? An essential piece of police equipment for picking the best jobs, calling back-up and keeping your ear on the football score."

Cash

"Last but not least, always keep a bit of cash on the hip. How else are you going to keep informants talking or stand your round if you've only a few pennies in your pocket."

TRAINING TO BECOME A DETECTIVE
(see also Recruitment and Training: Historical)

The journey from Police Constable (PC) to fully qualified Detective Constable (DC) is a challenging one and can take quite some time. During that journey you'll be referred to as a Trainee DC (T/DC) or a Trainee Investigator (TI) which indicates that you are in the process of training to become a detective. The national programme for detectives is known as the Initial Crime Investigators Development Programme or ICIDP (see **I**). The programme can last up to two years and consists of a number of different stages, all of which have to be successfully navigated before you can be confirmed as a Detective Constable. The three key stages of the programme consist of a written examination, attendance on a training course and then assessment in the workplace. During the final stage you will be required to gather evidence of your performance and complete a written portfolio of workplace competencies including arrest, search and interview. Once your portfolio has been satisfactorily completed and checked by your managers, you will then be eligible to become a DC. You may stay in your current role or be posted elsewhere, depending on the vacancies within the force. Police forces will normally have a selection process for anyone interested in a career in CID which will involve a written application form, which is shortlisted, followed by a formal interview. Successful applicants will then be eligible for the ICIDP at the next available date.

The current shortage of detectives has been described by some as a "national crisis" and undoubtedly requires urgent attention. Some forces are using 'direct entry' for investigators as a way of increasing the numbers. Applicants will carry out an investigative role as soon as they start in the police rather than having to carry out a probationary period in uniform first

276

(see **E – Experience**). However, the police decide to address the current situation, the initial training of a detective must provide our investigators of the future with the skills and knowledge to carry out their role effectively.

TWENTY-FIRST CENTURY CRIME

The changing face of crime is a real challenge for detectives as technology advances at a pace and criminals hone their tactics accordingly. We are now faced with cybercrime, scams and the unlawful use of drones, to name but a few. As I write, Gatwick airport is slowly trying to return to normal, having ground to a halt over the Christmas holiday period, following alleged intrusion by a drone(s). These devices have their legitimate uses but are also utilised by criminals (see **D**). Our everyday lives now look very different and the part played by the internet and social media cannot be overstated. Driverless cars and cashless banking are fast approaching and the future will be even more digital than it is now. The levels of violence often used to commit crime and the sophisticated methods adopted by some who commit it, present investigators with an unenviable task. Methods of detection are changing beyond recognition as the years pass but the future holds many challenges for the detective. The following are just two examples which reinforce my viewpoint.

Acid attacks

The UK has seen a disturbing rise in acid attacks in recent years with London being the worst hit. The total number of recorded attacks went up from 228 in 2012 to 601 in 2016. Last year (2017) was regarded as the worst to date, with more than 400 incidents reported up to April alone. The trend is very worrying and shows no sign of abating. These crimes are most common in South Asia but the UK has one of the highest rates per capita in the world. Unlike in other countries, where 80% of acid attacks are against women, most victims in the UK are men. Acid attacks go back to Victorian times when many considered the sentences given to those responsible to be unduly lenient. This may have been due to a judicial system at the time which valued property over people. In 1883, Mary Morrison was jailed for five years after she threw acid in the face of her estranged husband after he didn't give her a weekly allowance. The attack disfigured and blinded him. In the same year, another woman received a similar sentence for stealing a piece of bacon.

Many modern-day acid attacks appear to be gang-related, which helps to explain the rising number of cases in concentrated areas of major cities. Criminologists believe that gang members may be swapping guns and knives for acid as a weapon of choice as possession is hard to monitor, but its impact on victims can be devastating. There has been talk of new legislation to ban the sale of corrosive substances to under 18's to bring acid in line with the law on the possession of knives in a public place. In the meantime, shopkeepers have been advised not to sell bleach and corrosive substances to young people and the Metropolitan Police have been issued with 1,000 acid crime response kits.

CASE STUDY – AMMONIA ATTACK

Three men have been jailed after they sprayed ammonia and violently assaulted unsuspecting drivers in order to steal their cars. The three offenders described as "professional robbers" scoured the streets in a stolen vehicle looking for high value vehicles to steal. The group would approach their intended target from the rear, blocking them in or shunting them, before incapacitating the occupants by spraying a noxious substance in their face.

The first incident took place in the early hours of 4th February

2017 when a white Audi containing a 19 year old male driver and a 16 year old female passenger stopped on the forecourt of a petrol station in Essex. The Audi was quickly 'blocked in' by a white Mercedes which was stolen and bearing false number plates, containing the three offenders. Two of them got out and approached the Audi and a noxious substance was sprayed into the face of the driver, who suffered permanent damage to his eyes. The female passenger received burns to her legs as the liquid splashed onto her. The distressed victims fled the scene and the offenders made off in the Audi.

The second attack took place at about 4.50pm in East London when a VW Golf R was rammed from behind by the same stolen Mercedes used in the previous attack. One of the offenders attacked the driver, spraying ammonia in his face and forcing him to the ground, while another offender got into the Golf and sprayed the passenger, former professional boxer Michael Watson, in the face with ammonia. Mr. Watson tried to escape but became entangled in his seatbelt and was dragged along the road at speed, suffering burn injuries as a result.

The three offenders were identified by the police as a result of forensic evidence, mobile phone analysis, clothing and cloned number plates. Anselm Legemah was sentenced to 16 years for conspiracy to commit robbery and 10 years for applying a corrosive liquid with intent to burn, maim, disfigure, or disable, or to inflict grievous bodily harm. The sentences will be served concurrently (alongside each other), meaning a total of 16 years. Simon Luck and Paul Samuels were both sentenced to 10 years for two counts of applying a corrosive liquid with intent and conspiracy to commit robbery. They both received additional jail sentences for possession with intent to supply Class A drugs following the discovery of a quantity of drugs during police searches.

In a victim impact statement, the driver of the Audi commented "As soon as the acid hit me I was immediately terrified. A man approached my window asking for a lighter and, as I turned my head, acid was thrown in my face. My face and neck went numb and my vision blurred instantly. I was dragged from my car and left in the forecourt trying to find my way around while they drove off. My passenger had to jump from the moving car. The incident has had a negative impact on every aspect of my life and will continue to do so for the rest of my life." A senior detective added "The way the offences were undertaken by these males showed no regard for the victims and the consequences of their actions. I hope that the sentencing will give pause to those who might seek to use noxious substances to commit crime."

Digital pickpockets

Digital pickpockets are criminals who try to steal your bank card details by using technology. The bank cards which are susceptible to this type of crime are 'contactless' cards, either credit or debit cards, which you tap or hold close to the card reader to carry out the transaction. The card owner can use this method a number of times before they will be required to enter a PIN number into the machine. The use of contactless cards has risen as they are so much easier to use. There is a microchip in the card which sends a signal containing your card details to the machine, negating the need for you to insert the card into the machine. The technology in the card which allows the signal to be sent is known as radio frequency identification (RFID). Criminals have worked out that if they can get close enough to your contactless card, they can remove some of the card details without even having to touch the card itself. They would need to be around six inches or so away from the card, but if they were standing directly behind you in a queue or near to you when you had the card in your hand, this would be entirely possible. Even if the card was in your purse, bag or wallet it may not be safe. The activity is known as card 'skimming' and requires the criminal to be in possession of either an RFID card reader or a particular application on a mobile phone. Either of these could replicate a genuine card reader and transfer some of your card details into their possession. The scale of 'digital pickpocket' crime is a little unclear in the UK as it is difficult to identify and often people will discover that they have been the victim of a fraud, but be unaware how, where, or exactly when the fraud took place.

The method has been demonstrated by fraud experts on TV programmes such as *Rip off Britain* and *Watchdog*. On one occasion, the presenter, Angela Rippon, was given a credit card which she put into the front pocket of her cardigan. She was then introduced to a man who shook her hand and stood directly in front of her for a matter of seconds. Afterwards, the man, who was actually a security expert, opened his laptop and showed Ms. Rippon the details of the credit card which had been transferred onto his computer, with the use of an application on his mobile phone, which he was holding in his hand when they first met. In a different scenario, a man walked into a pub and put his wallet onto the bar next to him. Another man came in, chatted to him and placed his mobile phone on top of the wallet. When he left the bar, the phone was checked and found to contain details from a bank card inside the wallet. Although the three-digit security number on the rear of the card is unlikely to be copied, the long card number, name and expiry date probably will be. This is enough information for a criminal to order goods and spend money, particularly online.

If you are concerned about this type of activity, there are

a number of ways you can look to prevent it. You may have a bank card which is contactless but which you never use in that way. You can ask your bank to change it for a card which doesn't have the contactless facility. If your card is 'contactless' it will have the word printed on it or a symbol which is similar to)))) You can also buy card wallets or slips which are RFID protected as they have aluminium built into them, forming a protection against fraudulent card readers or applications. The card can be kept inside the wallet at all times when not in use and only removed to carry out a contactless transaction. These wallets are available at some shops, garden centres and online for a reasonable price and may give you some reassurance and protection against the unlawful actions of 'digital pickpockets'.

CASE STUDY – CONTACTLESS CARD FRAUD

Fraudsters are stealing money from contactless payment cards at the rate of almost £27 every minute, raising fears that the technology is becoming a 'magnet' for thieves. The security threat is increasing at an alarming rate as shoppers turn in droves to convenient 'tap and pay' cards and phone apps to ease the stress of waiting in queues. Spending in this way soared in 2017 to above £52 billion – double the amount from the previous year. Unlike conventional cards, contactless cards contain a special chip that emits radio waves that can be easily read by a payment terminal and cuts out the extra seconds it takes to enter a PIN. However, this flexibility has brought penalties, with crooks using stolen contactless cards to plunder a total of £14 million in 2017. Card providers offer reassurance to customers that any spending on stolen contactless cards is kept in check because each transaction is capped at £30, with a further safeguard that after a 'random' number of purchases, shoppers are asked to enter a PIN to prove the card is theirs.

Despite this, no bank will reveal after how many attempts such checks are made and a quirk in the technology has resulted in some cards being used months after being reported stolen and supposedly cancelled. A representative from a complaints service commented "The amount stolen may seem like a drop in the ocean compared to overall annual banking fraud of £609.8 million but given there are limits on the spending, there were still at least 867,000 incidents last year (2022). Probably a lot more if you allow for transactions less than £30."

A man from Notting Hill in West London is not impressed with the banks' empty promises over security after becoming a victim of contactless card theft nearing £600. He had his wallet stolen from his pocket whilst out drinking and informed his bank and John Lewis to cancel his three contactless cards as soon as he realised his wallet had been stolen. When he checked his accounts online the next day, he found that the thief had been on a rapid spending spree with his John Lewis credit card. It had been used to carry out 13 transactions in 75 minutes at various shopping outlets, many of them for the maximum spending limit of £30. He also discovered seven transactions totalling £180 had been carried out on his bank cards – appearing on his statement 36 hours after he cancelled the cards. The victim, who has now been refunded in full, commented "This technology is making our wallets a magnet for thieves. They know they can make off with your money easily. More should be done to prevent this crime happening, otherwise thieves are just laughing at us. These contactless cards make us 'honey pots' to them with greater values available to them than cash." He now plans to use only cards without the 'tap and go' feature, returning his contactless cards in exchange for cards without the facility. A spokesman for consumer magazine Which? Money commented "Obviously the banks have to balance convenience and security but it is the inconsistency of how many times a card can be used before the PIN is requested that concerns us. Some have high levels of security, including calling a customer if transactions look suspicious, while others seem to let the card be used ten times or more."

U

UNSOLVED MURDERS

Almost a quarter of all murders committed in the UK remain unsolved, many of them decades after the crime took place, despite rapid advances in forensic science, including DNA analysis. According to Home Office figures, around 17% of all murders over the last 20 years have failed to secure a conviction. These include the 1999 killing of TV presenter Jill Dando on the doorstep of her Fulham home. Sex offender Barry George was convicted of the murder and served eight years in prison, but his conviction was overturned. Other unsolved murders include the shooting of WPC Yvonne Fletcher in 1984 and the so-called "Torso in the Thames" boy in 2001.

There have been a number of murders which have been solved many years after they were committed, often with the use of advanced DNA methods. Christopher Hampton was convicted of the murder of 17-year-old Melanie Road more than 30 years after she was killed. Hampton's daughter (Clare) was arrested for damaging her boyfriend's necklace following a domestic row. As part of the routine arrest procedure, her DNA was taken and subsequently entered onto the national DNA database. Scientists were able to confirm that the sample taken from the daughter was a familial match to the crime scene sample belonging to the killer of Melanie Road. This meant that, although the sample wasn't identical, there were enough similarities to suggest that the killer could be a member of Clare's family. The police began to look at male family members which included her father. A voluntary DNA sample given by him to police outside his workplace was subsequently confirmed as identical to that of the killer of Melanie in 1984. In May 2016, Christopher Hampton pleaded 'guilty' to murder and was sentenced to life imprisonment with a minimum tariff of 22 years.

When other commitments allow, detectives will look at unsolved or 'cold case' murders to try to identify new evidence or leads which can be re-investigated. This will often be forensic evidence, which was secured at the time, but can now be subjected to further analysis using more advanced techniques which weren't available previously. Some police forces have their own 'cold case unit' to carry out these enquiries, whereas others will have to rely on a particularly quiet period when some resources from their current murder teams are able to be allocated some time to look at unsolved cases. It's right to say that these cases are never completely closed but also fair to say that they can only be re-examined if the resources are available to do this. Unfortunately, with the number of murder cases in some forces and the rise in violent crime, this isn't as often as everyone would like.

CASE STUDY – UNSOLVED MURDERS

Forensics expert Lorna Dawson won a Pride of Britain award for using cutting-edge technology to help convict a man who had got away with murder. In October 1977, she was studying geography at Edinburgh University when two young girls – Helen Scott and Christine Eadie – were brutally murdered after a night out at the city's World's End pub. The 17-year-olds had been beaten and sexually assaulted, their naked and battered bodies dumped in plain view. The murders shocked the city and had a profound effect on Lorna, who could so easily have been a victim herself, as she lived nearby and used to drink in the pub. Despite a huge police manhunt, the murder case was scaled down after a year with no-one charged.

In a curious twist of fate, Lorna, who by this stage was working as one of Britain's leading forensic scientists, found herself drawn back into the investigation decades later. In 2005 Scottish police charged a man called Angus Sinclair with the murder and rape of the two girls but a 2007 trial collapsed due to a lack of evidence. Then, in 2014, Lorna was approached by prosecutors to help solve this notorious cold case once and for all. Using revolutionary forensic techniques which she herself pioneered, Lorna examined tiny soil particles taken from the feet of Helen Scott and found vital incriminating evidence. The breakthrough played an important role in helping to convict Sinclair for the murders. He was later sentenced to life imprisonment with a minimum term of 37 years. Now considered to be Scotland's worst serial killer, Sinclair is also believed to have killed at least another six women.

The World's End case is just one of dozens of high-profile crimes that Lorna has investigated. The so-called "soil sleuth" has helped to solve more than 100 cases and put some of the UK's most notorious killers behind bars, as well as helping to clear many other defendants wrongly accused of crimes.

UNUSED MATERIAL
There has been quite a lot of adverse publicity concerning the disclosure (or lack of) unused material recently, some of which has led to the collapse of criminal cases. The process by which material is disclosed by the prosecution to the defence is known simply as 'disclosure' (see **D**). Unused material is anything which

is not going to be used as evidence by the prosecution but which may either undermine their case or assist the defence case. The investigating officer, or in a murder or other serious case, the disclosure officer, has to prepare a schedule of all items which fall into the unused material category. This schedule contains a description of the item and the reason(s) why it may undermine or assist. The schedule is included with the case papers which are sent to the Crown Prosecution Service (CPS) who have a duty to examine the schedule and carry out disclosure with the defence. Unused material items often include a copy of the crime report, a copy of the police incident report, CCTV footage which is not considered relevant to the prosecution case and witness statements from people who are not going to be called to give evidence by the prosecution. They could also include third-party material such as medical records or social service reports. There may be items or information relevant to the case which is considered to be confidential such as the use of CHIS (see **Informant**) or covert policing tactics. These should be included on a separate 'sensitive' unused material schedule and their existence should be brought to the attention of the CPS lawyer. They are unlikely to be disclosed to the defence unless on the orders of a Judge. Disclosure of unused material is a very important part of case file preparation and must be carried out thoroughly and correctly to ensure that our criminal justice system is fair and transparent.

V

VICTIMOLOGY
Victimology is a branch of criminology that scientifically studies the relationship between a victim and an offender by examining

the causes and the nature of the consequent suffering. Victimology focuses on whether the perpetrators were complete strangers, friends, or family, and why a particular person or place was targeted. Victimology first emerged in the 1940's and 50's when several criminologists examined victim-offender interactions, raising the possibility that certain individuals who suffered wounds and losses might share some degree of responsibility with the lawbreakers for their own misfortunes. For example, the carelessness of some motorists made it easier for thieves, reckless behaviour by intoxicated customers in a pub often attracted the attention of robbers, and provocation by some caused confrontations to escalate to the point that the instigator was injured or even killed. By systematically investigating the actions of victims, costly mistakes could be identified and risk-reduction strategies put into place.

Although the field originally focused on the varying degrees of victim blameworthiness, by the 1970's this preoccupation became overshadowed by studies intended to prevent victim-isation, to improve the way complainants are handled by the police and courts, and to speed recovery. Victimology is now enriched by other fields of study including psychology. Victimologists study the kind of help which injured parties need and the effectiveness of efforts intended to help them, both financially and emotionally. There is now much more focus on offences of domestic abuse, stalking and sexual assaults where the person responsible will often fit a specific risk profile.

Victimology is a key line of enquiry for detectives in criminal investigations, particularly murders. In the majority of murder cases, there has been some prior association between the victim and the offender and, for this reason, the answer to "Who did it?" may well lie within the victimology. There is a saying amongst senior detectives that if you "find out how the victim lived, you'll find out how they died" because the answer may well lie within the victim's background, lifestyle, relationships, routines and movements.

The sooner this information can be gathered the better as it could lead to the identification of the person(s) responsible. Interviews with close family members and those who knew the victim well may provide valuable information and, whilst it's so unfortunate that the police have to trawl through the victim's personal life at such a devastating time, the key to solving the case could be found in the victimology.

VIDOCQ

There are a few key characters in the history of crime whose names live on. Some achieved greatness in relation to their crimes, and others in their knowledge of crime and law. But a few select people, extraordinary in their achievements, stand out in this context, and one of these is the French detective, Vidocq.

Ironically, when the police force was being formed in England, the founding father of crime detection, Eugene Vidocq, was in England. He did visit the prisons of Pentonville, Newgate and Millbank, but he was really in London to organise an exhibition. He wanted to be a showman, not a professional adviser. As James Morton has commented in his biography of Vidocq: 'Not only was he on the premises during opening hours but he also put on a little production in which he appeared in various disguises, to the delight of the audience...' He had arrived in London three years after the detective force was formed, and had played no part in the detective policies; he had, however, been in London in 1835 to advise on prison discipline. He was a man who had known the worst prisons in France, as a prisoner as well as in his role as police officer. In 1845 he was thinking of starting up a detective agency, extending the one he had in France, but this was clearly not his real motive for being there.

Vidocq (1775–1857) is one of the most important figures in the history of detection. What defines his basic importance is the notion of setting a thief to catch a thief. He began life as a criminal, and as Sir Harold Scott once wrote, 'The only crimes of which Vidocq was ever convicted arose from youthful swashbuckling; the authorities' main complaint against him was that their prisons were not secure enough to hold him. He was never convicted of theft.' But he turned from criminal to detective during the Napoleonic years. He was given plenty of leeway to do things his way when a detective force was assembled, and he recruited men from the criminal underworld. What began as his group of picked men was later to become the 'Surete' – later called the *Police Judiciaire.*

France was thus in the forefront of detective history, leading the way well before Britain had its sleuths in 1842. Vidocq also became the first real private detective, as he worked as a freelance after leaving the French prefecture. He set up a number of agencies and tended to find himself annoying the police establishment. He is a considerably important figure in crime history, and it is generally agreed that the character of Vautrain in Balzac's novels is based on him. He also is found behind the figure of Jean Valjean in *Les Miserables*; the idea of a reformed villain siding with the law is irresistible, and Hugo saw the fictional value of having a character experience a revelatory vision- something that would inspire change, and thus, in real life criminal history in France, the first surge of change in the Surete came from a criminal.

W

WARRANT CARD

Every police officer is issued with a warrant card when they join up which they should carry with them at all times, whether on or off duty (except when travelling to a country which has security issues). The card will normally be credit-card size with a picture of the officer, their signature and the signature of the force Chief Constable (the Commissioner in the Metropolitan Police). The warrant card may be kept in a black leather-style wallet which will probably also include the force crest or badge. The card is designed to prove the identity of the holder and authorises them to carry out their duties as a police officer. Unfortunately, criminals will sometimes try to impersonate police officers and may be in possession of a fake warrant card (see **B – Bogus callers**). A person, whether in uniform or not, who calls at your address unexpectedly asking to come in should always be asked to produce their warrant card. A genuine officer will be happy to show you, allow you to examine it, and give you the opportunity to call their police station to verify them if you wish. Warrant cards are very important for detectives as they don't wear a uniform and they help to prove that they are who they say they are. They should always produce them when introducing themselves.

CASE STUDY – WARRANT CARD MISUSE

In 2015 it was revealed that dozens of Metropolitan Police officers and special constables were disciplined for using their warrant cards to obtain free train travel, trying to gain access to bars and clubs when drunk and attending football matches, claiming to be working undercover. A Freedom of Information

Act request revealed a total of 58 complaints of warrant card misuse between February 2013 and January 2015. Of these, 13 officers either retired or resigned from the force following investigations, four were dismissed without notice and four received written warnings. Of the remaining incidents, 25 were found to be either unsubstantiated or requiring no disciplinary action. Examples of the misuse include an officer who produced his warrant card to 'bouncers' stating that he would 'send his police friends after them' and an officer attempting to gain access to a social club by abusing their position.

WILD WEST BRITAIN

This is the term used by some media outlets as the UK has witnessed a shocking rise in violent crime during 2018. The number of murders in London alone overtook New York towards the end of the year as the Metropolitan Police launched more than 130 investigations. The beginning of 2019, to date, shows no sign of a reduction in this surge of violence.

Children as young as nine are being caught in possession of knives and the National Police Chiefs' Council (NPCC) lead for serious violence has claimed that, after more than 20 years in policing, the past year has felt "completely different". She commented "This level of violence, this constant torrent of every single day another stabbing, another violent incident that we can't seem to get ahead of. There are children as young as 12 involved in stabbings. It can be like the Wild West. These attacks are happening in broad daylight, in public spaces, that's what feels different. We have always had people shooting and stabbing each other but the increases and how sustained it is – it's not peaks and troughs anymore it's just constant." She told journalists that attackers appeared to be bolder and were prepared to commit gun and knife crime in full view of CCTV and passers-by. She quoted an incident where two teenagers were seen fighting with machetes in a Luton shopping centre while "people were pushing buggies past and toddlers were walking around."

Serious violence appears to be being driven by under 18's, with knife possession cautions for 10–17-year-olds rising particularly steeply. In the last five years the number of NHS admissions by 10–17-year-olds with stab wounds has increased by 67 per cent. There is no doubt that the Government, the police and partner agencies have a huge task to address this problem which is likely to need a combination of education, engagement and enforcement.

WOMEN IN DETECTIVE WORK

Because of television series such as *Cagney and Lacey* and its derivatives, we are now familiar with seeing women detectives on our screens. But it took a very long time for this to be the norm.

Women detectives, in the professional sense, began in the staff of the famous Pinkerton Detective Agency (see *Pinkerton*) in the USA in the nineteenth century. The Agency employed several women, and the first was Kate Warne. She was a widow, who was recruited in 1856, and in the plot against Lincoln's life which was hatched in 1861, before the successful assassination in Washington, Kate Warne played a major role. The Pinkertons infiltrated an anti-Union cell in Baltimore, and when Lincoln went through the city, Pinkerton himself, and Warne, accompanied him in the 'parlour car' and all was well.

When Kate was asked why she would be a successful detective, she gave the answer that dominated thinking about women detectives much later, in Scotland Yard. She said, as Graham Nown explained, '... that she could worm out secrets in many places to which it was impossible for male detectives to gain access.'

Kate Warne, and other women later employed by Pinkerton, had shown the world that women could have particular uses in detective work, but it was to be a very long time after the 1860s before Britain acknowledged that fact.

One particular aspect of crime always invited the participation of women in detective work: prostitution. In this context, they were always required as ancillary workers, and as the feminine element in such activities as dealing with suicides along the Thames, or working with lost children and strays; then, when the notion of 'white slavery' became a hot topic for the media, notably in the first three decades of the twentieth century, these women in the constabulary had a role.

In 1885, W T Stead, the writer and journalist, bought a young girl for £5 in order to show how easy it would be for a man to sexually exploit and abuse a female child. He went to prison for this, but the topic of child prostitution was the subject of a campaign at the time by the *Pall Mall Gazette*, on the theme of 'The Maiden Tribute of Modern Babylon' – using the image of the old myth of the minotaur, who grabbed and ate maidens who were sacrificed to him. As Christopher Howse wrote, 'White slavery was the banner for 1885 –more particularly under-age prostitution. It was something Parliament had been half-heartedly addressing since 1881.'

This led to the Criminal Law Amendment Act of 1885 which led to a result summarised neatly by H G Cocks in his history of the personal column: 'In other words, 'good girls' were protected by law, but 'bad girls' had to look after themselves.'

By the 1920s, there were prominent cases which highlighted the exploitation of young women, as in the Morriss Case of 1925, which sprang from an advert in *The Times* which read:

'Young girl of gentle birth required to look after large dogs in the country. Live in. Experience unnecessary. Common sense essential.' This case provides a template for the process involved: the wealthy man would use a female friend or relative to meet the young girls who applied, and then, after a seemingly innocent and normal introduction to the employment advertised, the man would make sexual advances to the young applicants. In other words, it was procurement, deception and often sexual attack or rape. Morriss was given a longish prison sentence. As this kind of crime was easily effected, it involved police work increasingly, and the women police officers were needed. It involved undercover work and also a high level of sensitivity and tact of course.

But as in the case of Lilian Wyles at the CID, who had a very successful and important career in the inter-war years, most work was, in normal circumstances, confined to work with women and children, and statement-taking. However, war was not part of normal circumstances.

There were several important advances in detective work during and soon after the second world war. In 1940, identikit was in its early phase of development, initiated by Hugh MacDonald; in 1941 the murder case of Rachel Dobkins was solved after work done on dental identification, and in 1953 television viewers saw the image of the first crime suspect on their screens. In the same year, the celebrated discovery of DNA by Crick and Watson provided the first step towards its application in forensics, although it was another forty years before it brought about a conviction. This was an exciting time to be a detective, so were women playing a part in the work at that time? The answer is, only to a very limited extent.

WOODENTOP

'Woodentop' was a derogatory term used by detectives to refer to their uniformed colleagues. It was a favourite of DCI Gene Hunt's and was often used in other police dramas, particularly those set in the 70's and 80's. The term is believed to have originated from the traditional cork construction of the police helmet. 'Woodentop' is also an episode of the Thames Television series *Storyboard* which was originally broadcast in 1983 and became the forerunner to *The Bill*, a hugely popular police series which ran for 26 years. The episode featured PC Jim Carver's first day at Sun Hill police station, where he was partnered with experienced WPC June Ackland. The term 'woodentop' is also an allusion to the children's TV series 'The Woodentops', a family of puppets first shown on BBC in 1955.

X

XAVIER

I've decided to explain the unusual case of Duarte Xavier who was convicted of sexual offences, to demonstrate the often varied and challenging work of a detective.

CASE STUDY – DUARTE XAVIER

A man who tricked four men into sexual activity with him, in the mistaken belief that he was a female has been jailed for 15 years. Duarte Xavier was convicted in October 2018 of six counts of causing a male aged 13 or over to engage in penetrative sexual activity.

The court heard that Xavier was a liar and fantasist who carried out his crimes over several years. He used online dating websites to masquerade as a woman called 'Ana', entering into conversations and sending provocative pictures to heterosexual men, who were fooled by his online persona into meeting for sex. When they agreed to meet for sex 'Ana' would set a series of conditions, including that the man must wear a blindfold for the duration of the encounter and were not allowed to touch 'Ana' in return.

The first incident occurred in February 2016 when a 45 year old man arranged to meet at 'Ana's' flat after communicating via a dating app. Rules had been agreed prior to the man's arrival making it clear that he would not see 'Ana' throughout their encounter. Upon arrival at an address in Wandsworth the man followed instructions and put a blindfold on. The pair began having sex, at which point the man realised that something was wrong and removed the blindfold to see Xavier. The man was enraged and immediately left the address. The man received a message from Xavier later saying "I got a mental health problem, sorry."

In October 2017, a 29-year-old male sent a message to 'Ana' via a dating app and received a response that 'she' was a recently single female "looking for a bit of fun." The pair talked on WhatsApp, exchanging pictures and even a video call with the victim having no reason to think that he was not speaking to a woman. They arranged to meet for sex and, as before, the man put a blindfold on as requested. He heard what he thought was a female voice saying "stay there, don't take off and don't move the mask." A person then approached from behind and tied the blindfold tighter. He was led blindfolded into another room where 'Ana' began to perform a sexual act. At some stage, he took off the blindfold, saw Xavier and immediately left the property in disgust. Once again messages were exchanged with Xavier apologising for any 'misunderstanding'. The man reported the incident to police and Xavier was arrested on suspicion of causing sexual activity with a person without consent. A number of mobile phones and masks were seized and Xavier was released under investigation.

A third incident took place in April 2018 when a 26-year-old man, looking for sexual relations with females on a website, received a message from 'Ana' claiming to be a 35 year old woman. The pair arranged a video call via WhatsApp, where 'Ana' stated that she had to conceal her identity because she was married. A meeting was arranged and he arrived at 'Ana's' address to find it in darkness. He was instructed to close the door and come upstairs. As he did so, he was grabbed, his trousers were pulled down and an item, believed to be a pillowcase was put over his head. He asked to see that the person he had been communicating with was actually female, to which 'Ana' said "no" and began performing a sexual act. The man used the light on his mobile phone and discovered it was Xavier. The man went outside and called police who again arrested Xavier. He was initially remanded in custody before being released on bail.

The fourth victim was identified by police after reviewing phone records from seized mobile phones. The victim, a 29-year-old man, had been too embarrassed to tell anyone. In December 2016 he began exchanging messages with 'Ana' on a dating website. 'Ana' explained that 'she' was looking for a role-play experience where he would be blindfolded. After exchanging pictures and videos, it was agreed that they would meet in a local park, due to the presence of the landlady at 'her' address. The man met 'Ana' at a secluded spot where 'Ana' performed a sexual act on him before they had sex. The victim was entirely unaware that he had been tricked into having sex with Xavier and, at no point, did Xavier reveal his true identity. The pair arranged to meet again a few days later, on the same terms and at the same place. This time the victim delayed putting on the blindfold as he was curious as to whom he was meeting. When Xavier approached, the pair saw each other and Xavier tried to hide. When the victim confronted him, Xavier claimed to have believed that the victim was bisexual and had approved of the arrangement. The victim was distraught by the revelation and told Xavier that he did not want any further contact from him.

A detective from the Southwest Command Unit commented "We are pleased to see that Xavier has received a significant sentence for what he did; all of the victims had no reason to believe that they were not engaging with a woman and all have stated unequivocally that they would never have given their consent to sexual relations with another man. Xavier demonstrated extreme manipulation and cunning in order to satisfy his own sexual gratification, setting bizarre conditions that the victims adhered, to in the belief that they were part of the experience. He is a sexual predator and I hope the victims, all of whom were traumatised by their experiences, will feel that justice has been done." Police also appealed for other potential victims to come forward and provided reassurance that they would be treated with the utmost sensitivity and in the strictest of confidence.

X-RAYS

Maybe the most obvious application of x-rays in detective work is in the area of snooping, or monitoring locations where information is needed on occupants. In the USA a large number of law enforcement agencies are employing a device known as Range-R, which consists of radio waves penetrating locations. It has been pointed out, however, that the use of this facility infringes the law. If a search warrant is not issued before use, then in the perspective on this from the angle of the very top of the justice system, the Supreme Court, the activity goes beyond permissible actions within the powers of the police.

The facility stems from its original use in warfare. But obviously, from the point of view of human rights, and of the ethical points raised by such matters, the activity is questionable.

Y

YOU'RE NICKED

This immortal phrase has been used throughout the decades, particularly in police series such as *The Sweeney* and *The Bill*. In one particular episode of the former, DI Jack Regan (John Thaw) bursts into a flat to confront a man in bed with his lady friend and, before he has a chance to grab the gun next to him on the bedside cabinet, Regan smashes his own gun onto his hand and growls "Get yer' trousers on, you're nicked!"

The phrase is used to explain to people that they are under arrest and is much easier to remember than the lengthy police caution (see **G – Giving Evidence**). I don't recall ever using it myself when arresting someone but I'm sure that it still makes an appearance from time to time. Phrases such as "he's been nicked" and "he's at the nick" (police station) are still quite common, particularly amongst more experienced officers.

Going back many years, criminals sometimes chose to deliberately repeat such well-worn expressions on arrest "You've got me bang to rights, guv', I'm well and truly nicked". When these comments were read out in court as a confession, it sounded so ridiculous that juries immediately jumped to the conclusion that it was a false documentation by police, thus causing them to side with the accused.

"You're nicked" is also a song (1982) by the UK reggae duo, Laurel & Hardy, about the "wicked police system" which also features phrases such as "Evening all" and "What have we here".

Z

Z-CARS

This police series, which ran on TV from1962 to 1978, played a major role in creating the now familiar character of the accessible, approachable detective: the figure who had a human side, a family, everyday worries, and a capacity for humour. In terms of the detective force, there was John Phillips, as D.C.S. Robins, and even more memorably, there was Stratford Johns as Inspector Barlow. The series was created by Troy Kennedy Martin, who developed the outline and themes after hearing radio police messages at the time he was ill in bed. There were 801 episodes, and later, stemming from this, we had *Softly, Softly*.

ZOMBIE KNIVES

"Zombie knives" are weapons which can have blades up to two feet long. They often have serrated edges and words etched onto them, glamorizing violence. They have been given the name as they mimic weapons frequently seen in horror films, particularly "zombie apocalypse" movies. They are regularly marketed as collector items and can be bought online for as little as £10. They are available in bright colours and emblazoned with names such as 'zombie killer' and 'slayer' with some being sold as machetes or swords rather than knives.

There are plans to crack down on the sale of "zombie knives" with the ultimate intention of the government to ban them completely.

Updated 2023

Owners of weapons such as zombie knives could be jailed under a new law. Possessing a knife or other offensive weapon in a public place was already illegal but the **Offensive Weapons Act 2019 (OWA)** makes it unlawful to have certain types of knives and weapons in private. This section of the Act came into force with effect from July 2021and also includes possession of other items such as knuckledusters and throwing stars. Other sections of the OWA which became law during 2021 include provision for the control of weapons sold online and the placing of responsibility onto delivery companies to conduct age verification at time of delivery. Police and Crime Commissioner for Devon, Cornwall and the Isles of Scilly commented 'Any incident involving a knife has the potential to be catastrophic. There is no excuse for possessing any of the weapons mentioned in this new legislation, such as knuckle dusters and zombie knives. These are vile implements which often advertise themselves as display pieces, but in reality, could be used to do a great deal of harm and potentially end someone's life.'

The Offensive Weapons Act 2019 has been well-received as another tool to assist in tackling knife crime but the legislation, particularly in relation to the sale of and possession of zombie knives in private, has attracted some criticism due to what is considered to be a legal loophole. For a weapon to be classed a so-called 'zombie knife' it must fit three criteria. It must have a cutting edge, a serrated edge and crucially, it must have 'images or words that suggest it is to be used for the purpose of violence.' In practice, this means that when police officers are raiding the homes of known criminals and discovering brutal blades that fit the characteristics of a zombie knife, but don't have violent imagery or writing on the blade, they are unable to confiscate the item or bring criminal charges for its possession. To demonstrate the point, a well-known London radio station legally bought a 21-inch knife via the internet as the 'machete-type' weapon had no visible writing on it. A solicitor and chair of the Law Society's criminal law committee commented 'You can have and buy quite openly an item that for all intents and purposes is exactly the same as the prohibited item, except it doesn't have writing on it that involves incitement to violence. The more you say it, the more difficult you may feel it is to understand, but that's what it says, and I can only interpret the law as I understand it from the statute.'

The vast majority of knives used to commit murders in London during 2019/20 were machetes and hunting knives, such as zombie knives, with no legitimate domestic purpose. This loophole, which relates to the sale of, or possession in private, of such a knife (possession in public is already a criminal offence) certainly needs to be addressed as knife crime continues to devastate our society and ruin the lives of so many people.

If you would like to know more about the Offensive Weapons Act 2019 you can view the whole Act via the following link: https://www.legislation.gov.uk/ukpga/2019/17/contents/enacted

CASE STUDY – ZOMBIE KNIFE

A teenager who was captured on dash-cam footage attacking a driver with a large 'zombie style knife' in rush hour traffic was convicted at the Old Bailey in November 2018. Joshua Gardner, from Croydon, had previously pleaded guilty to affray and possession of an offensive weapon before being found guilty of attempting to cause grievous bodily harm with intent.

The court heard that in May 2018 at around 4pm, a 19-year-old man was sat in his car in stationary traffic in London Road, Croydon, when Gardner, who was aged 17 at the time, pulled up alongside him on a bike. Upon seeing Gardner the man tried to pull away and attempted to overtake the stationary traffic in front of him and, as he did so, he almost made contact with Gardner's pedal cycle. In his panic to get away the driver crashed into oncoming vehicles. Gardner abandoned his cycle in the road and ran towards the man's car, producing a large 'zombie style' knife from his trouser waistband. He began hitting the windows of the car with the knife repeatedly and tried to get into the vehicle. The terrified driver remained in his locked vehicle for a short time before seizing his opportunity to get out and run off along the road, abandoning his vehicle in the process.

The incident was witnessed by several members of the public, with Gardner's outburst of violence caught on the dash-cam footage of a vehicle which had been travelling in the opposite direction. The images from the footage, which were widely circulated in the media, led to Gardner being identified by a police officer, who recognised him from a previous conviction for attempted robbery. Gardner was subsequently arrested, provided a 'no comment' interview, and was formally charged.

Gardner received a 2-year suspended prison sentence, was ordered to carry out 150 hours of unpaid work and will be subject to a curfew for nine months. The perceived leniency of the sentence, particularly considering the current issues with knife and violent crime, has been widely criticised. A senior police officer commented "My personal thoughts are that this sentence does not provide any form of deterrence. Nor does it lead front-line officers to feel that they are being fully supported by the rest of the judicial system. I'm not sure any reasonable person would see this as a deterrent." At time of writing the case had been referred to the Attorney General with a view to considering whether the sentence was appropriate in the circumstances.

In January 2019 the Court of Appeal overruled the original sentence as being "unduly lenient" and sentenced Gardner to three and a half years imprisonment. Solicitor General Robert Buckland QC said that Gardner "produced the knife and attacked the outside of the vehicle before smashing the passenger window and lunging into the car with the knife". He submitted that "what was intended was to strike the head or upper body of the victim". He added that the offence was aggravated by the fact that it was "committed during the supervision period" of a previous conviction for attempted robbery "involving the use of a knife to threaten a younger person". One of the Judges commented "one of the challenges facing society is the commonplace carrying and use of knives. In our judgement, taking into account all the circumstances, the original sentence on this offender should have been four years.

* * *

Timeline of Detective History

1750s   Henry and John Fielding active as London magistrates. Bow Street Runners formed: 'originally consisting of the only six of eighty Constables in Westminster not on the take; (Oliver Cyriax, *The Penguin Encyclopaedia of Crime*)

1796   Patrick Colquhoun's book, *A Treatise on the Police of the Metropolis* (throughout the Regency years, the Bow Street Runners undertook detective work)

1842   The detective department at Scotland Yard is created.

1877   'The Trial of the Detectives' – a corruption scandal involving several men in the detective branch. Three of them were given two-year prison sentences.

1883   The Special branch (SO12) was formed when Howard Vincent selected eight talented officers; they were to be the Special Irish Branch at first. Then in 1888, the word 'Irish' was no longer used and the Branch was born, being known at first as 'Section D'

1931   Lord Trenchard became Commissioner, and there followed an overhaul of detective training, along with innovations in other areas of police training.

1936   Major and influential reports issued on the training and recruitment of detectives. These two volumes itemise the curriculum favoured by Trenchard and his later advisers.

1950s   Revision of training philosophy, and a revision of Trenchard's measures.

1984   Police and Criminal Evidence Act (PACE)

Bibliography and Sources

Note: This is only a selected listing of resources. Obviously, there is a vast bibliography of crime and law today, relating to the detective, but this is a basis for further reading, at least. **Also,** this is only a selected listing of resources. Obviously, there is a vast bibliography of crime and law today, relating to the detective, but this is a basis for further reading, at least.

Regarding sources, it should be noted that in Stuart's entries, reference has been made to two volumes in particular: *The Rules of Modern Policing* (Bantam Press, 2007), a humorous volume linked to the TV personality Gene Hunt, and to *Blackstone's Senior Investigating Officer's Handbook* (OUP, 2016)

Books

Note: We have included here the books consulted as well as those cited.

Branston, Barry –*The Elements of Graphology* (Element Books, 1995)

Cobb, Belton – *Critical Years at the Yard* (Faber & Faber, 1956)

Cobb, Belton – *The First Detectives and the early career of Richard Mayne* (Faber & Faber, 1957)

Costello, Peter – *Conan Doyle, Detective* (Constable and Robinson, 2006)

Cox, David J – *A Certain Share of Low Cunning: a history of the Bow Street Runners 1792–1839* (Willan, 2010)

Critchley, T A – *A History of Police in England and Wales 900–1966* (Constable, 1967)

Donnelly, Daniel and Scott, Kenneth (Eds.) – *Policing Scotland* (Willan, 2005)

Emsley, Clive – *The English Police: a political and social history* (Pearson Education, 1991)

Farmery, J Peter – *Police Gallantry: the King's Police Medal, The King's Police And Fire Service Medal and the Queen's Police Medal,* (Periter, 1995)

Fido, Martin, and Skinner, Keith – *The Official Encyclopaedia of Scotland Yard* (Virgin Books, 1999)

Fitzgerald, Percy – *Chronicles of Bow Street Police Office* (Patterson Smith, 1972

Grosse, Alfred C – *The Master Book of Detection and Disguise* (Quaker Oats, 1936)

Harris, Andrew T – *Policing the City: crime and legal authority in London* (Ohio State University, 2000)

Herbert, Barry – *Ticket to the Gallows and other villainous tales from the Tracks* (Silver Link, 2002)

Holdaway, Simon (Ed.) – *The British Police* (Edward Arnold, 1979

Holman, Arthur – *Dog Versus Crime* (Pan Macmillan, 1957)

Jones, Steve – *The Illustrated Police News: Victorian court cases and sensational Stories* (Wicked Publications, 2002)

Kirby, Dick – *You're Nicked! Further memoirs from the real Sweeney on life in the serious crime squad* (Robinson, 2007)

Lock, Joan – *The British Policewoman, Her Story* (Robert Hale, 1979)

Lock, Joan – *Dreadful Deeds and Awful Murders: Scotland yard's first Detectives* (Barn Owl Books, 1990)

Lyle, D P – *Forensics: A guide for Writers* (Writers' Digest, 2006)

MacShane, Frank – *The Notebooks of Raymond Chandler (*Weidenfeld And Nicolson, 1977)

Moss, Alan and Skinner, Keith – *The Victorian Detective* (Shire, 2013)

Moylan, J F – *Scotland Yard and the Metropolitan Police* (Putnam's, 1929)

Nown, Graham – *Watching the Detectives* (Grafton Books, 1991)

O'Connor, Mary T – *On the Beat: a woman's life in the Garda Siochana* (Gill & Macmillan, 2005)

Palmer, Stanley H – *Police and Protest in England and Ireland 1780–1850* (Cambridge University Press, 1988)

Reith, C A – *Short History of the British Police* (OUP 1948)

Riggs, Ransom – *The Sherlock Holmes Handbook* (Quirk Books, 2009)

Sayers, Dorothy L (Ed.) – *Great Short Stories of Detection, Mystery and Horror* (Gollancz, 1929)

Scott, Sir Harold – *The Concise Encyclopaedia of Crime and Criminals* (Andre Deutsch, 1961)

Selwood, A V – *Police Strike 1919* (W H Allen, 1978)

Stead, Philip (Ed.) – *Pioneers in Policing* (McGraw Hill, 1977)

Stead, Philip – *The Police of Britain* (Macmillan, 1985)

St Johnston, Sir Eric – *One Policeman's Story* (Barry Rose, 1978)

Taylor, David – *Crime, Policing and Punishment in England 1750–1914* (Macmillan, 1998)

Wade, Stephen – *Plain Clothes and Sleuths: a history of the detective in England*

Williams, Sarah – *How to Write Crime Fiction* (Robinson, 2015)

Young, Hugh – *My Forty Years at the Yard* (W H Allen 1955)

Articles in Periodicals/ Online

The following refer to topics dealt with in the A–Z.

Corbyn, Zoe, 'How Taking a home genetics test could help catch a murderer.' www.theguardian.com/science/2018/dec/01

Draper, Robert, 'They are Watching You' *National Geographic magazine* Feb. 2018 pp. 32–65

Kaiser, Jocelyn, 'We will find you: DNA search used to nab Golden State killer Can home in on 60% of white Americans' www.sciencemag.org/news/2018/10

Official Publications

Home Office Report of the Departmental Committee on Detective Work and Procedure (HMSO, 1938)

Periodicals and Newspapers

The Illustrated Police News Available on the British Library and Gengage databases, and it may be accessed through libraries.

Also, the monthly true crime magazines from the True Crime Library are useful sources for tales of detective work through time. These are *True Detective, Murder Most Foul, True Crime* and *Master Detective*.

Internet Sources

http://c19.chadwyck.co.uk
This is part of the massive Chadwyck Healey reference resource network, and the topic here is in the nineteenth century. This contains a wide selection of printed works from the nineteenth century, and so subjects on crime and law are there.

http://www.oldbaileyonline.org/
The Old bailey records contain material accounts of over100,000 criminal trials at the Central criminal Court, covering the years from 1674 to 1834.

http://oralhistory.org.uk
This is the site run by the University of Essex on oral history.

http://www.rhs.ac.uk/bibl/
This is the site for the Royal Historical Society: the main attraction being the massive bibliography, parts of which cover every aspect of crime and law.

http://www.victoriantimes.org/
This has extensive material on the Victorian period.

Forensics:
www.exploreforensics.co.uk
www.forensicsciencesimplified.org
wwwforensicdocumentexaminer.co.uk/past_cases.html

Resources on Police History

In general, for broad accounts and listings of principal officers, check civic directories, *Whittakers Almanac* and general trade directories. The Police Almanac, as already discussed, has this information (senior officers) in most depth.

Carter, Paul and Thompson, Kate – *Sources for Local Historians* Phillimore, 2005
Cook, Chris – *The Routledge Companion to Britain in the Nineteenth Century* Routledge, 2005

Cyriax, Oliver – *The Penguin Encyclopedia of Crime* 1996

Dell, Simon – *The Victorian Policeman* Shire Publications, 2004

Fido, Martin and Skinner, Keith – T*he Official Encyclopedia of Scotland Yard* Virgin Publishing, 1999

Friar, Stephen – *The Sutton Companion to Local History* Sutton, 2001

Hickey, D J and Doherty, J E – *A New Dictionary of Irish History from 1800* Gill and Macmillan, 2005

Johnson, Charles – *The Public Record Office* SPCK/Macmillan 1948

Kuhlicke, F W and Emmison, F G – *English Local History Handlist* Historical Association, 1965

Pearsall, Mark – T*he National Archives Family History Companion* National Archives, 2007

Powell, W R – Local History from Blue Books *Historical Association Handlist*, 1948.

Scott, Sir Harold (Ed.) – *The Concise Encyclopedia of Crime and Criminals* Rainbird, McClean 1961

Stallion, Martin and Wall, David S – *The British Police: Police Forces and Chief Officers 1829–2000* Police History Society, 1999

Index

A
ABC Principle, 23
ABE, 24
Acid attacks, 277
Alibi, 28
Ammonia attacks, 278, 279
Automatic facial recognition, 93
Automatic Number Plate
    Recognition, 52

B
Bentley, Derek, 152
Bieber, David, 204
Big House, 30
Big Red Key, 30
Bite marks, 192
Body Language, 31, 32
Bogus Callers, 32
Bogus Police, 33
Bogus Water Board, 32, 35
30 Bow Street Runners, 36
Brief, 39
Briefings, 39, 40

C
Caminada, Jerome, 40
Carr, Maxine, 29
Cashpoint Robbery, 43
CCTV, 28, 35, 44, 45, 50
Chris Jeffries, 156
Computer repair fraud, 270
Conan Doyle, Sir Arthur, 49, 50

Confiscation Order, 215
Contactless Card Fraud, 280
County Lines, 82
Courier Fraud, 269
Covert Human Intelligence Source
    Act, 144, 146
Crimes Club, 47, 49
Criminal Investigations, 50
Criminal Procedure and
    Investigations Act 1996, 67, 68
Cyber Crime, 54

D
Detention Without Charge, 62
Dickens, Charles, 64
Digital Pickpockets, 280, 282
Disclosure, 67, 70
Discretionary Life Sentence, 169
DNA, 72, 192
DNA Tagging, 72, 73
Dogs in police work, 75
Drones, 79, 80
Drugs, 81

E
Early Morning Blues, 87
East Midlands Special Operations
    Unit (EMSOU) 18
Ethnicity Codes, 87–88
European Convention on Human
    Rights (ECHR), 134
Experience (in detective work), 90

F

Fabian of the Yard, 11
Facial Recognition, 93, 94
Familial DNA 97, 98
Fentanyl, 83
Fielding, Henry, 46
Fingerprints, 100
Firearms Act 1968, 124
Forensic evidence, 51
Forfeiture order, 215
Foxtrot 11, 110, 111
Flying Squad, 106
Footwear evidence, 108
Fox, Daniel, 177
Foxtrot 11, 101–102

G

Genealogy, 113, 114
Ghost Squad, 115
GIB Consultancy, 18
Giving Evidence, 118
Golden Hour, 120
Gun Crime, 122
Gun crime digital marker, 124
Graphology, 126
Grosse, Inspector Alfred, 17

H

Hannam, Chief Superintendent Herbert, 16
Hayward, Kayleigh, 60
History of detectives, 128
HOLMES, 132
Homicide, 134
Humble, John, 23
Hunt, Gene, 115

Huntley, Ian, 29, 172
Hypothesis, 138

I

Identification of Human remains, 191
Independent Office for Police Conduct, 151
Impersonation Fraud, 268
Informant, 143
Initial Crime Investigators Development Programme, 141
Inspector, 150
Interpol, 150
Interviews, 147
Intimidated witness, 25

J

JCB (cash points), 44
Jefferies, Christopher, 156, 157
Joint Enterprise, 152
Journalists, 152

K

Keyless Car Crime, 159
Key Witnesses, 157, 158
King's and Queen's Messengers, 162

L

Lansley, Cliff, 32
Lebanese Loop, 45, 46
Leonard 'Nipper' Read, 130
Life on Mars, 165
Life Sentence, 167
Locard's Exchange Principle, 170

M
Malware, 55
Mandatory Life Sentence, 167
Maxine Carr, 28
Mental Health Act (1983), 25
MG Forms, 174, 175
Modern Slavery, 175
Modern Slavery Act (2015), 175
Monkey Dust, 84, 85
Motive, 179
Murder Bag, 181
Murder Investigation Manual, 182

N
Newgate Calendar, 9
Newton Court Hearing, 183
Nitrous Oxide, 86
Novichok, 185
Number Spoofing, 187

O
Odontology, 190
Old Bailey, 193, 194
Online Grooming, 80
Operational Names, 197
Operation Canvas, 80
Operation Countryman, 197
Operation Pottery, 177
Operator initiated facial
    recognition, 94
Organised Crime Groups, 44, 45

P
Passive Data, 52, 199
Passive data detection, 77
PEACE Interview Model, 148
Peel, Sir Robert, 8

Perceval, Spencer, 131
Phishing, 59, 252
Phonetics, 202
Phonetic Alphabet, 200, 201
Phonetic science, 204
Pinkerton, Allan, 209
Plod, 210
Private Detectives, 211
Proceeds of Crime Act (2002) 214
Profiling, 219
Promotion, 222
Psychics, 224

Q
Q Car, 232
Qualities in a Detective, 226
Kings Counsel, 133

R
Rank Structure, 235
Recruitment (see also Training),
    236
Regional Detectives, 238, 239
Regulation of Investigatory
    Powers Act (2000), 144
Retirement, 242, 243
Retrospective Facial Recognition,
    94
Roberts, Harry, 112
Rogue Traders, 247, 248

S
Scam Mail, 251
Scams, 250
Scotland Yard, 255
Senior Investigating Officer, 258
Sexual Exploitation, 57, 58

Shoulder Surfing, 256
Significant Witnesses, 26
Smishing, 252, 253
Social media, 54
Special Branch, 260, 261
Specialist Dogs Unit, 75
Specialist Roles, 263, 264
Special Measures, 24
Spice, 85
Suicide notes, 205
Super Recogniser, 264
Sutcliffe, Peter, 24

T
Tactical Contact, 267, 268
Telephone Preference services
    (Fraud) 271
Telephone Scams, 268
Tools of the Trade, 275
Training (see also Recruiting) 276
Twenty-first Century Crime, 277

U
Unmanned Aerial Vehicle (see
    Drones), 79
Unsolved Murders, 284, 285
Unused Material, 286, 287

V
Victimology, 287, 288
Vidocq, Eugene, 10, 289
Vulnerable Witnesses, 25

W
Warrant Card, 291
Warrants, 291
Weapon Marks, 193
Wearside Jack, 23
Whole Life order, 169
Women in Detective Work, 293,
    294
Woodentops, 296

X
Xavier, 296
X-Rays, 299, 300

Y
You're Nicked, 287

Z
Z Cars, 301
Zombie Knife, 301, 302

CATCHING A KILLER

A Reference Guide to Murder Investigation Past and Present

Catching a killer is an essential research companion for crime writers and readers.

The book provides an in-depth guide to the investigation of murder from a historical and contemporary perspective. Relevant criminal and case law is included, with case studies for context. Includes unique insights from a former murder detective. The development and role of forensic evidence is discussed and explained. ISBN 978-1-80236-063-9 £10.99.

Reviews for Catching a Killer

Stephen Wade and Stuart Gibbon's 'Catching a Killer' is an incredibly inspiring and informative reference book. This essential reference tool for not only crime writers but all thriller writers who need to include a police procedural element, modern or historical, is packed with insider information on how the police, as a team, attempt to secure a conviction. If your detective is going to catch a killer, you must know how and who he might work with. Similarly, if your killer is going to try to get away with murder, you must know how that might be possible given the thoroughness of the investigative procedure. If he's caught, what might he be charged with? Catching a Killer looks at the many strands of a murder investigation: who people are and what they do, through to forensics experts. What evidence and samples would be collected? Which forensic or other expert might samples be sent to and why? What are they looking for? All of these questions are answered concisely. What brings this reference book to life, making it gripping reading, are the examples and case studies, which highlight how imperative it is that police procedural is followed and how important the roles of the people involved in an investigation are.

In short, Catching a Killer is easily digestible, gripping and essential reference reading for all crime and thriller writers.

Sheryl Browne – author of psychological thrillers

Another great guide from these authors, with a wealth of information to ensure that I can get things correct when I am writing my thrillers. An invaluable book on my bookshelf!

Philippa East – author of psychological thrillers

'Catching a Killer' is an essential resource for thriller/crime writers. As a thriller writer myself, I'm a big fan of Stuart Gibbon and Steven Wade's books. They're invaluable resources that help me finesse the details of scenes/plot lines in my novels. The case studies from past crime cases also spark ideas. Love these books!

Zoe Rosi – author of psychological thrillers

An invaluable and fascinating insight into all aspects of a murder investigation, this concise, easy-to-navigate reference guide is a must for every crime writer's bookshelf, providing a wealth of information in one place. Gibbon delves into contemporary procedure while Wade explores historical murder investigations (something I found particularly enthralling as a history graduate), both parts supported with interesting and relevant case law. Without a doubt this will be my go-to guide for my police/crime thrillers henceforth! Any crime/thriller lovers out there will also find it a gripping read. Highly recommended!

A.A. Chaudhuri – author of psychological thrillers

THE CRIME WRITERS' CASEBOOK
REVISED TO 2023

The companion guide to Being a Detective, A Straightforward Guide to **The Crime Writer's Casebook, Revised Edition,** is a reference work for all crime writers, and is an essential companion for research into modern police procedure as well as to crime investigations in history. **Updated to 2023.** ISBN 978-1-80236-148-3 £11.99

Reviews for the Crime Writer's Casebook

"A superb guide that I keep by my laptop at all times. I highly recommend you read it before putting pen to paper"

Carol E. Wyer – bestselling crime fiction author

"An excellent, up-to-date resource for anyone who writes crime fiction or has a keen interest in British police procedures and legal processes"

Jackie Kabler – TV presenter and crime writer

"I'm thrilled that Stuart Gibbon and Stephen Wade have written such a wonderful book – I think this is going to become a must-have for many authors. The Crime Writer's Casebook is an intriguing, fascinating, illuminating source of information. I love it!"

Ronnie Turner – Book blogger and author of psychological thriller 'Lies Between Us'

"The Crime Writer's Casebook is a brilliant easy-to-read guide to police procedure, whether you're writing crime fiction or just have an interest in the topic. It is a fascinating, well-written and well-planned book with so much packed into its 250 or so pages"

Victoria Goldman – Journalist, editor, proofreader and author

"A detailed and entertaining resource for writers of contemporary and historical fiction. I highly recommend it"

Tracey Emerson – author of psychological thrillers

"This is a comprehensive and well-written guide for anyone wanting to write a realistic crime novel or a non-fiction work involving police operations"

Police History Magazine

"That's me set up for my new writing project. Thank you for my invaluable crime reference writing tool ... I think it will be my writing bible."

Sheryl Browne – author of psychological thrillers

"A fantastic addition to any crime writer's bookshelf!"

Caroline Mitchell – author of psychological thrillers

"It's a must for all aspiring UK crime writers."

Stephen Booth – author of the Cooper and Fry crime fiction series

"What a massive compilation of facts this book is – a must for anyone writing crime. Everything that you need to know, expertly indexed for ease of reference. When I was writing my first book, which had a small part of it concerned with the abduction of a child, I would have loved to have had this book by my side".

Pam Fish – National Association of Writers' Groups

"A must buy for all crime authors..."

CL Taylor – author of psychological thrillers

CRIMINAL INVESTIGATION
AND POLICE PROCEDURE SERIES

A COMPREHENSIVE GUIDE TO ARREST AND DETENTION

A Comprehensive Guide to Arrest and Detention is an essential research companion for crime writers and readers. Crime historian Stephen Wade and former detective Stuart Gibbon examine the subjects of **Arrest and Detention** from a historical and modern-day perspective, with reference to criminal law and police procedure. ISBN 978-1-913342-51-7 £8.99

A COMPREHENSIVE GUIDE TO BURGLARY AND ROBBERY

A Comprehensive Guide to Burglary and Robbery is an essential research companion for crime writers and readers. Crime historian Stephen Wade and former detective Stuart Gibbon examine the subjects of **Burglary and Robbery** from a historical and modern-day perspective, with reference to criminal law and police procedure. ISBN 978-1-913342-50-0 £8.99

A COMPREHENSIVE GUIDE TO DRINK AND DISORDER

A Comprehensive Guide to Drink and Disorder is an essential research companion for crime writers and readers. Crime historian Stephen Wade and former detective Stuart Gibbon examine the subjects of **Drink and Disorder** from a historical and modern-day perspective, with reference to criminal law and police procedure. ISBN 978-1-913342-52-7 £9.99